Introduction to American Corrections

Consulting Editors for the
Holbrook Press Criminal Justice Series

VERN L. FOLLEY
Director
Police Training Institute
University of Illinois

DONALD T. SHANAHAN
Associate Director
Southern Police Institute & University of Louisville

WILLIAM J. BOPP
Director
Criminal Justice Program
Florida Atlantic University

Introduction to American Corrections

PAUL K. CLARE
State University of New York / Plattsburgh

JOHN H. KRAMER
The Pennsylvania State University

HOLBROOK PRESS, INC.   BOSTON

Photo Credits

From the New York State Department of Correctional Services: pp. 43, 52, 54, 56, 82, 85, 86, 122, 159, 164, 168, 169, 171, 186, 203, 296, and 311. *From Raney Ellis:* pp. 102 and 233.

© Copyright 1976 by Holbrook Press, Inc., 470 Atlantic Avenue, Boston

All rights reserved. No part of the material protected by this copyright notice may be reproduced or utilized in any form or by any means, electronic or mechanical, including photocopying, recording, or by any informational storage and retrieval system, without written permission of the copyright owner.

Printed in the United States of America

Library of Congress Cataloging in Publication Data

Clare, Paul K   1939–
   Introduction to American corrections.

   Includes bibliographical references and index.
   1. Corrections—United States   I. Kramer, John H., 1943–   joint author. II. Title.
HV9304.C57   364.6'0973   75-37605
ISBN 0-205-05465-X

To
SUE and MARCIA

Contents

PREFACE   xi

1   THE CRIMINAL JUSTICE SYSTEM   1

   The System Nature of Criminal Justice   3
   The Criminal Justice System   7
   Intake: The Decision to Prosecute in Court   15
   Court   18
   Summary   20

2   THE HISTORY OF PUNISHMENT AND CORRECTION   25

   Inherited Penal Methods   27
   Social Problems in Colonial America   30
   The Rationale for Punishment   35
   The Early Use of Imprisonment   36
   The Growth of a New Philosophy: 1790–1830   38
   The Birth of the State Prison   40
   18th Century Prison Reforms   42
   The Individual Criminal   44
   The Penitentiary Movement   46
   The Competition between Systems   54
   Summary   58

3 THE DEVELOPMENT OF MODERN CORRECTIONS   63

Captain Alexander Maconochie   65
Sir Walter Crofton   69
Theoretical Advancements in the Pre-Civil War Period   70
Practical Concerns   71
Some Evidence of Progress   72
The First National Prison Congress   74
Progress in the Early 20th Century   79
The Predominance of Convict Labor Programs   81
Years of Abuse: 1900–1940   83
The Creation of the Federal Bureau of Prisons   87
The Rise and Decline of Inmate Self-Government   88
The Modern Goal of Rehabilitation   90
Summary   93

4 THE SOCIAL ORGANIZATION OF THE PRISON   97

The Functional Analysis of the Social Organization of the Prison   100
The Diffusionist Perspective   116
Male Sexual Behavior within the Prison Setting   126
The Social Organization of the Women's Prison   132
Summary   139

5 CORRECTIONAL INSTITUTIONS IN TRANSITION   147

The Emergence of a Treatment Emphasis   150
Official and Operative Goals   152
The Possibility of Change   155
Internal Conflict: An Increasing Problem   158
Differing Value Orientations   161
The Breakdown of Organizational Effectiveness   162
Disorder in a Changing Prison World   165
"Brutal" Riots   166

The Dynamics of the Collective Riot   176
The New Militancy   182
Summary   187

6   JUVENILES IN TROUBLE   193

   The Background of Juvenile Justice   196
   Juvenile Corrections: Its Foibles and Failures   200
   Types of Facilities   202
   The Return to a Pre-*Gault* Philosophy   213
   Summary   214

7   CORRECTIONAL LAW   219

   Sentencing   221
   Legal Safeguards and Controls in Probation   225
   The Incarcerated Offender   230
   Internal Discipline   240
   Legal Rights and Parole Practices   242
   Summary   247

8   PROBATION AND OTHER COMMUNITY BASED CORRECTIONS PROGRAMS   255

   Protection of the Public and Community Based Corrections   258
   Probation   259
   Other Community Based Programs   275
   Post Institutional Community Programs   279
   The Communities' Responsibility in Community Based Corrections   281
   Summary   282

9   PAROLE   285

   Conceptions of Parole   288
   The Historical Perspective   305

Recent Developments and a Perspective
on the Future   309
Summary   312

10 THE FUTURE OF CORRECTIONS   315

The Impetus for Change   318
Diversion   319
Reform in Corrections—Will It Occur?   323
Alternative Subsidy Programs   328
Administrative and Democratic Reform   331
Credibility of Reform   333
Summary   336

INDEX   341

Preface

In the past, few people other than the employees of the criminal justice system and the criminals themselves knew about or were interested in the organization, objectives, or effectiveness of American penal/correctional systems. However, in recent years the mass media coverage of appellate court decisions, the activities of ex-inmate organizations, and prison riots have led to greater interest in and concern for convicted offenders. Some groups regard the American prison population as a discriminated-against, brutalized minority—victims of a corrupt capitalistic society. In response to such claims, correctional officials adamantly defend their actions and their professionalism although they do not "get the press" that their critics do.

As a result of criticisms, however, correctional administrators have re-evaluated their policies and priorities. They have realized the necessity of upgrading the educational level of employees. This emphasis has been furthered by the allocation of state and federal funds for the education of in-service and pre-service correctional employees. This book is intended to meet the needs not only of those presently working in criminal justice agencies, but also of students of criminal justice.

Until recently, the literature on criminology and corrections has been theory and research oriented, with a few notable exceptions. Here, the emphasis is on factual material, theory, and research findings that can be meaningful to those who are or will be employed in corrections or law enforcement. We hope that the reader will gain an appreciation of both the theory and research which served as the foundations for the practical corrections programs that have been implemented. In addition, we are of the opinion that by analyzing corrections from the perspectives of more than one academic discipline the student will gain a more realistic picture of what will be encountered in the field. Therefore, we have drawn on the insights of scholars in many disciplines including history, psychology, sociology, public administration, political science, education, and social welfare. Our primary purpose is to assist the reader in developing a broad and balanced understanding of the total criminal justice process and to specifically focus on the development, organization, and effectiveness of corrections within that process.

The information and ideas presented here also provide the necessary knowledge for coordinating the efforts of correctional personnel and other human service professionals. The student-citizen can find the information needed to evaluate intelligently criminal justice legislation and the creditability of various correctional reform proposals and movements.

It is impossible to mention all of the professors, students, correctional employees, and clients who have provided us with valuable insights into corrections. We do, however, wish to express our gratitude to Professor Robert G. Caldwell, formerly of the University of Iowa, and Mr. Richard Ericson, executive director of Correctional Services of Minnesota. Professor Caldwell's kind assistance and encouragement did much to enrich our educations and further our careers. Mr. Ericson has graciously allowed us to share his viewpoints regarding the creditability of the reform movement with our readers. We feel that our presentation of his ideas significantly enhances our final chapter.

A special thanks also goes to Professor Fred Hussey of The Pennsylvania State University for authoring chapter nine. His innovative analysis of the parole process should serve to enlighten both the experienced worker and the introductory student.

We are also grateful to Robert Price for reading and commenting on chapter seven and to Gail Johnson, Brenda Gennari, and Robynn Abrams for providing us with a student's perspective on the material. The assistance, patience, and understanding of Becky Boyter and John DeRemigis of Holbrook Press are also greatly appreciated. The photographs taken for this volume by Professor Raney Ellis of the State University of New York as well as those generously loaned to us by Lt. George Myers of Clinton Correctional Facility were significant contributions to the final product. Our thanks also go to Mark Corrigan of the New York Department of Correctional Services for giving us permission to print these pictures.

Lastly, we would like to thank our wives, to whom the text is dedicated, for their continued support and for their assistance in typing and editing the manuscript.

P. K. CLARE

J. H. KRAMER

1

The Criminal Justice System

It is the intent of this book to introduce the reader to the basic concepts, programs, and trends in corrections. Corrections is defined (for purposes of this book) as those parts of the criminal justice system responsible for treatment and/or control of adults and juveniles who have been convicted of an offense. But corrections is only one aspect of the criminal justice system; it also embodies the system that creates the laws and the processes through which an offender passes from arrest "through charging, adjudication, sentencing, imprisonment, and release on parole."[1]

THE SYSTEM NATURE OF CRIMINAL JUSTICE

A system is a set of interrelated elements. When the criminal justice system is referred to in this book it is in direct reference to the interconnections and interdependence of criminal justice agencies. It is possible to view criminal justice as a sequence of decision-making stages. Through this system offenders are either passed on to the next stage or diverted out of the system. This diversion may be due to any number of reasons such as lack of evidence or a desire to reduce the load on the system. Each subsequent stage of the process is dependent upon the previous stage for its clients; it is this dependence that best exemplifies the "system" nature of criminal justice.

The basic stages involved in the criminal justice system are identification and apprehension, prosecution, adjudication and sentencing, and corrections. A brief discussion of these preliminary stages is necessary in the development of an understanding of the final stage—corrections.

IDENTIFICATION—APPREHENSION THROUGH DISPOSITION

Recent studies into the public's reporting of crimes to the police indicate that there is extensive non-reporting of criminal offenses.[2] In a national survey in 1965, only one burglary victim out of three reported the offense to the police.[3] Taken from this study, the data in Table 1.1 indicates that only one out of two of the offenses listed were reported to the police. Therefore, the victims of criminal offenses have a significant role in the filtering process of criminal justice. If a victim decides not to report an offense to the police, the likelihood of the offender being caught is almost nil. Since most criminal offenses come to the attention of the police only through citizen complaints, the public really controls the gateway to the criminal justice system.[4]

There are various reasons why crimes are not reported. The victims in the 1965 survey who did not report their experiences were asked why they failed to notify the police. The majority of responses indicated that they thought the police would not be able to do anything about it anyway or would not want to be bothered. Therefore, the implication is that people, in part because of their attitudes toward the police, often exercise their discretion in invoking the legal process.

Most criminal offenses come to the attention of the authorities only if the victims or witnesses choose to notify the police. In-

Table 1.1 Offenses Known, Cleared, Persons Arrested, Charged, and Disposed of in 1973
[2,342 cities; 1973 estimated population 50,299,000]

Type	Crime Index Total	Violent crime[1]	Property crime[2]	Murder and non-negligent manslaughter	Forcible rape	Robbery	Aggravated assault	Burglary—breaking or entering	Larceny—theft	Auto theft
Offenses known	2,362,863	204,654	2,158,209	4,586	12,181	93,932	93,955	632,893	1,265,817	259,499
Offenses cleared	495,512	99,881	395,631	3,715	6,751	27,518	61,897	117,739	235,812	42,080
Percent cleared	21.0	48.8	18.3	81.0	55.4	29.3	65.9	18.6	18.6	16.2
TOTAL ARRESTS	452,058	82,501	369,557	4,590	5,555	28,784	43,572	96,732	236,039	36,786
Per 100 offenses	19.1	40.3	17.1	100.1	45.6	30.6	46.4	15.3	18.6	14.2
Arrests under 18	214,667	19,180	195,487	479	1,144	9,370	8,187	53,961	118,811	22,715
Per 100 offenses	9.1	9.4	9.1	10.4	9.4	10.0	8.7	8.5	9.4	8.8
Persons charged	442,214	84,669	357,545	4,360	5,606	28,377	46,326	93,555	228,390	35,600
Per 100 offenses	18.7	41.4	16.6	95.1	46.0	30.2	49.3	14.8	18.0	13.7
Persons guilty as charged	123,003	20,067	102,936	1,209	1,216	6,343	11,299	17,256	80,701	4,979
Per 100 offenses	5.2	9.8	4.8	26.4	10.0	6.8	12.0	2.7	6.4	1.9
Persons guilty of lesser offenses	23,477	8,248	15,229	620	568	2,163	4,897	6,167	7,317	1,745
Per 100 offenses	1.0	4.0	.7	13.5	4.7	2.3	5.2	1.0	.6	.7
Persons acquitted or dismissed	65,784	20,755	45,029	887	1,557	5,419	12,892	11,540	28,673	4,816
Per 100 offenses	2.8	10.1	2.1	19.3	12.8	5.8	13.7	1.8	2.3	1.9
Juveniles referred to juvenile court	151,135	14,900	136,235	349	960	7,537	6,054	42,950	74,693	18,592
Per 100 offenses	6.4	7.3	6.3	7.6	7.9	8.0	6.4	6.8	5.9	7.2

[1] Violent crime is offenses of murder, forcible rape, robbery, and aggravated assault.
[2] Property crime is offenses of burglary, larceny-theft, and auto theft.

vestigation and arrest are major functions of the police although most police time is spent in directing traffic, providing general and emergency services, settling family squabbles, and numerous other non-legal activities. The chances of the police apprehending an offender, especially one who commits an act of stealth such as burglary, are relatively small because the public frequently fails to preserve the crime scene and often delays in reporting the offense.

The best data available on the apprehension rates of particular offenses comes from the Federal Bureau of Investigation's (F.B.I.) *Uniform Crime Reports*.[5] For several reasons the *Uniform Crime Reports* represent only a small fraction of the actual crimes committed. Many crimes are not detected, the public fails to report offenses, and often the local police department lacks interest and/or ability in accurately compiling the data. The *Uniform Crime Reports* do, however, provide pertinent information on the responses of law enforcement to those crimes of which they are aware. Table 1.1 provides data from these reports concerning the seven index offenses (murder, forcible rape, robbery, aggravated assault, burglary, larceny, and auto theft) and the disposition of those cases which came to the attention of the police.

The information in Table 1.1 also illustrates what happens when a specific crime is committed. For example, look at the column entitled "Burglary—breaking or entering." (The F.B.I. defines burglary as "the unlawful entry of a structure to commit a felony or theft."[6]) Looking down the column, it will be noted that 18.6 percent of the burglaries are cleared by an arrest. Also, for every 100 offenses, 15.3 persons are arrested, 14.8 persons are charged, but only 2.7 persons are found guilty as charged and 6.8 are referred to juvenile court.

Although the quality of this particular set of data is questionable due to potential reporting errors, it does indicate that even an offense as serious as burglary is not very likely to result in the apprehension of a suspect. Of those few that are apprehended, only a small percentage are found guilty in adult court and a large percentage are referred to juvenile court.

Based on these statistics, the chances of being apprehended for burglary are minimal, and the certainty of punishment if apprehended is also relatively small. However, if an offender commits a large number of offenses the risk increases. Risk of apprehension also increases with the seriousness of the burglary, e.g. the Brink's Robbery. The addage "crime does not pay" may be a slight exaggeration. Thus, the risk of being pulled into the justice system is slight and those few who end up being sentenced are only a small, not very representative, sample of those committing criminal offenses.

THE CRIMINAL JUSTICE SYSTEM

JUVENILE JUSTICE PHILOSOPHY

In almost all states the legal definition of a juvenile is anyone below the age of eighteen. The juvenile court has traditionally operated on the basic premise that a majority of the children who violate the law have done so, in part, because they were unable to completely discern right from wrong. Thus, they are not, in a legal sense, totally responsible for their behavior. Furthermore, such youngsters have not developed career patterns of criminality from which they are irredeemable. The juvenile justice system approaches youngsters with greater hope for their redemption than is the case for adults.[7] A juvenile who violates the law should not, according to this philosophy, be punished for his misbehavior; rather he should be "treated." The juvenile is not considered to be as responsible, and consequently not as accountable, for an offense; therefore, he should not be punished as an adult would be for the same offense. Also, the juvenile is seen as being more open to reformation because he is not yet at the advanced stage of criminality. Both of these reasons emphasize the need for treatment, not punishment.

Because the juvenile justice system does not punish the offender, but rather "treats" him, it has often failed to provide the traditional safeguards of due process such as the right to cross-examine witnesses, the right to be represented by counsel, and other such legal protections found in a formal court hearing. The court in handling juveniles was to view the child as a parent viewing a misbehaving son or daughter, frequently referred to as the *parens patriae* orientation of juvenile justice.

As an outgrowth of this philosophy, laws defining juvenile delinquency have been very broad. For example, Minnesota's statute states:

> 260.015 Definitions. Subd. 5. "Delinquent Child" means a child:
> a. who has violated any state or local law or ordinance;
> b. who has violated a federal law or a law of another state and whose case has been referred to the juvenile court; or
> c. who is habitually truant from school; or
> d. who is uncontrolled by his parent, guardian, or other custodian by reason of being wayward or habitually disobedient; or
> e. who habitually deports himself in a manner that is injurious or dangerous to himself or others.

In effect, the Minnesota statute encompasses a wide range of offenses within the potential jurisdiction of the juvenile court. The two types of behaviors included in the statute are: 1) those offenses which are also offenses for adults; and 2) those special behaviors which are only offenses for juveniles but not for adults. This latter type of clause, examples of which are c., d., and e. above are "catch-all" clauses, which vaguely define offenses specifically for juveniles, not adults. Such offenses are generally referred to as status offenses because of their specific application to juveniles.

There is another feature of this law which is typical of most states—the protective nature of clauses d. and e. These imply that the juvenile is not the offender, but the victim; and the courts frequently refer to them as "deprived" or "neglected."

The Extensiveness of Delinquent Behavior   A sizable majority of juveniles violate the delinquency laws. With such vague definitions as those contained in the Minnesota statute, this should not be surprising. According to studies asking juveniles to indicate whether or not they have committed offenses, more than 80 percent, and in some cases as high as 95 percent, report that they have violated the law.[8] Most of these offenders do not become "official" delinquents, meaning that although they are in fact delinquent they never become officially labelled as such. It is generally found that there is a 10 to 20 percent chance of a youth appearing in juvenile court before the age of 18,[9] although in particular neighborhoods the chances are much greater.[10] Since the chances are slim that a juvenile will turn himself in to the authorities, the important factors in whether a particular offender will come to the attention of the authorities appears to be the risk involved in the offense and the risk of being observed, and, if observed, the chance that the offender will be reported to the police. Among the factors affecting the likelihood that an offense will be observed are a) the frequency with which it is committed, and b) the seriousness of the offense.[11] Further, if the offender commits an offense on the street corner instead of in his own recreation room, the probability of someone (especially the police) seeing him is greatly increased.

Juveniles and the Police   Just as committing a delinquent act does not generally lead to official attention, being observed by the public or an official agency like the police, the school, welfare department or other such agency does not usually lead to referral to the juvenile court. In fact, of all the juvenile offenders and offenses known to the police, about 50 percent are referred to court.[12] One of the leading textbooks in police administration recommends that only 50 percent of juveniles taken into custody *should* be referred to court.[13] Within this context, it is important to consider what factors influence the decision to refer a juvenile to court, to his parents, or to some other agency.

Generally speaking, very little is known about most decisions made in regard to handling juveniles who are alleged to be delinquent, but there is some information available concerning police decisions. The police decision can be viewed as a two-stage process. An officer, either as a result of his own observation of the violation, or more commonly in response to a complaint by a citizen,[14] must first decide whether or not to take the youth into custody (arrest would be the term used for adults). If the juvenile is taken into custody, then an officer (frequently called a juvenile officer becauses he specializes in work with juveniles) must decide whether or not the juvenile should be referred to court, sent home to his parents, or perhaps referred to another agency.

Police decisions to take a juvenile into custody seem to reflect the officer's assessment of the seriousness of the offense, the youth's prior record, and the youth's attitude towards the officer and his offense more than any other variables.[15] This is not to suggest that race and social class are not at all important—they are—in that a department usually concentrates its officers in lower class and especially lower class black areas where official crime rates are highest.

After a juvenile has been taken into custody, the second stage of the decision-making process takes place. Many departments have created a special bureau to make decisions about juveniles. These officers usually do not make the initial contact with the juveniles, but receive juveniles on referral from other officers. One noted officer in the field suggests the following criteria be used in deciding whether or not to refer a juvenile to the juvenile court:[16]

1. The particular offense committed by the child is of a *serious nature*.
2. The child is *known* or has in the past been known to the *juvenile court*.
3. The child has a record of *repeated delinquency* extending over a period of time.
4. The child and his parents have shown themselves *unable* or *unwilling* to cooperate with agencies of nonauthoritative character.
5. Casework with the child by *nonauthoritative agency* has *failed* in the past.
6. Treatment services needed by the child can be *obtained only* through the court and the probation department.
7. The child *denies* the offense and the officer believes judicial determination is called for, and there is *sufficient evidence*

to warrant referral, or the officer believes the child is in need of aid.

Research into police referrals to juvenile court have found a number of factors which are important. For example, in a study of the youth bureau in Racine, Wisconsin, Robert Terry found that of the 9,023 known offenses between 1958 to 1962, only 755 were referred to the probation department (court).[17] He found that the factors which most affected the decision to refer to court were the seriousness and frequency of the offenses. Nathan Goldman, in a study of four communities in Allegheny County, Pennsylvania, found that seriousness of the offense was most important in officers' decisions; however, for minor offenses blacks were more likely to be referred to court than whites, while for serious offenses there was basically no difference between the racial groups.[18] Goldman went one step further than Terry by asking the officers what criteria they used in handling juveniles. The officers' responses indicated that in addition to seriousness of the offense, they were influenced by the nature of the juvenile court. If the officers felt that the court had a negative impact on the juvenile, then they tried to avoid making referrals there. The officers also indicated that the attitude of the youth was frequently a significant factor in their decision.[19]

ADULT JUSTICE PHILOSOPHY

In contrast to the juvenile justice system, the adult system focuses more upon punishment of the offender. Because of this punitive focus the system is more accountable for its decisions than was true of the juvenile justice system; due process is of more concern. By looking at Figure 1.1 this difference becomes somewhat apparent in that the adult system has many formal procedures prior to court which are not a part of the juvenile system.

The Extensiveness of Adult Offenses   As it is with juvenile violations, relatively little is known about offenses committed by adults. One study, which asked adults if they had committed

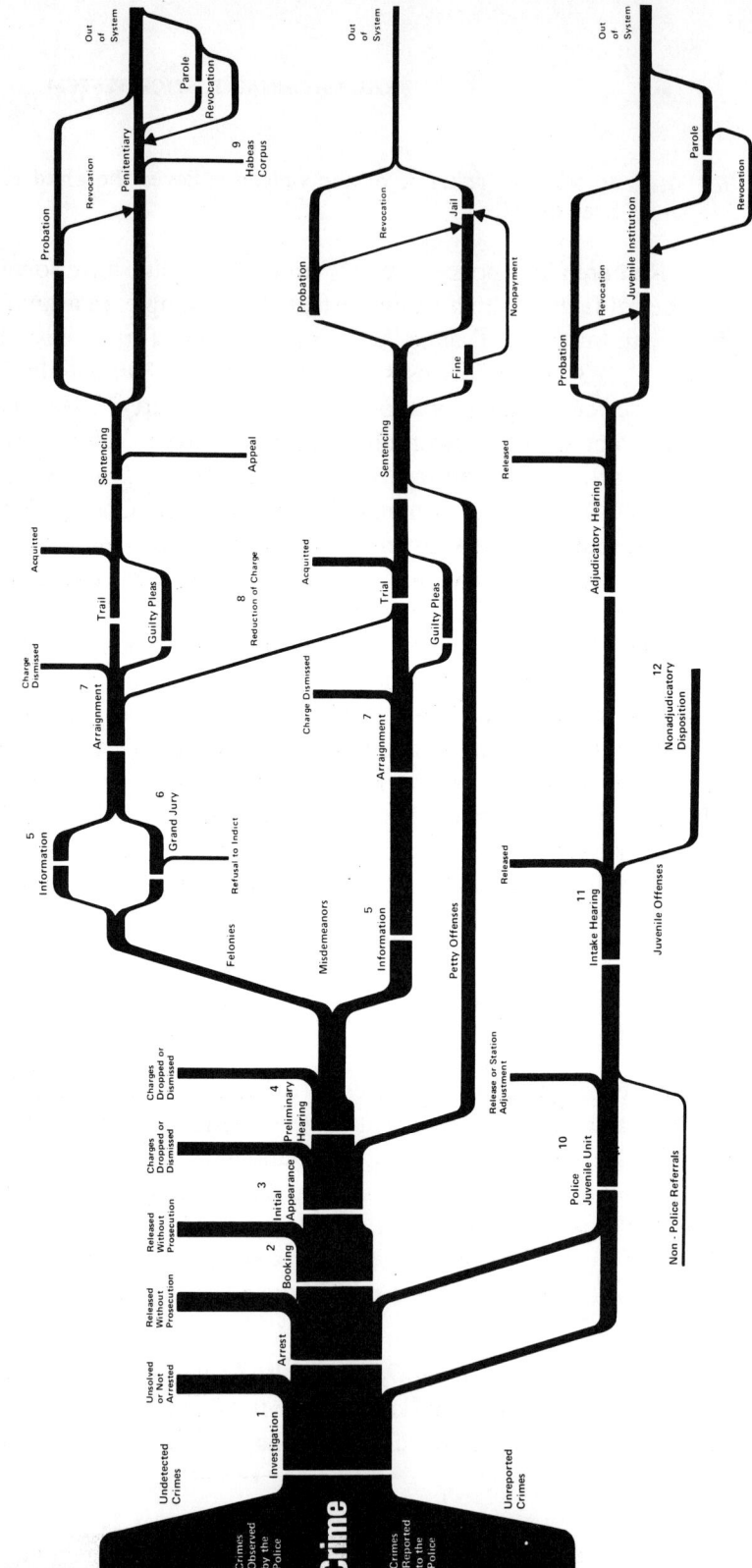

FIGURE 1.1 A general view of The Criminal Justice System. This chart seeks to present a simple yet comprehensive view of the movement of cases through the criminal justice system. Procedures in individual jurisdictions may vary from the pattern shown here. The differing weights of line indicate the relative volumes of cases disposed of at various points in the system, but this is only suggestive since no nationwide data of this sort exists.

1. May continue until trial.
2. Administrative record of arrest. First step at which temporary release on bail may be available.
3. Before magistrate, commissioner, or justice of peace. Formal notice of charge, advice of rights. Bail set. Summary trials for petty offenses usually conducted here without further processing.
4. Preliminary testing of evidence against defendant. Charge may be reduced. No separate preliminary hearing for misdemeanors in some systems.
5. Charge filed by prosecutor on basis of information submitted by police or citizens. Alternative to grand jury indictment; often used in felonies, almost always in misdemeanors.
6. Reviews whether Government evidence sufficient to justify trial. Some states have no grand jury system; others seldom use it.
7. Appearance for plea; defendant elects trial by judge or jury (if available); counsel for indigent usually appointed here in felonies. Often not at all in other cases.
8. Charge may be reduced at any time prior to trial in return for plea of guilty or for other reasons.
9. Challenge on constitutional grounds to legality of detention. May be sought at any point in process.
10. Police often hold informal hearings, dismiss or adjust many cases without further processing.
11. Probation officer decides desirability of further court action.
12. Welfare agency, social services, counselling, medical care, etc., for cases where adjudicatory handling not needed.

Source: From *The Challenge of Crime in a Free Society,* (Washington, D.C.: U.S. Government Printing Office, 1967), pp. 8–9.

offenses, indicated that most of the respondents admitted to one or more criminal offenses (many of which were relatively harmless).[20] This study implies that most adults have committed an offense that could lead to their arrest. But since most people are not arrested, the basic conclusion is that the risk of any particular offender's coming to the attention of the police is relatively slim for both juveniles and adults.

Adults and the Police Article V of the Constitution states that "an individual cannot be deprived of life, liberty, or property, without due process of law." In this context, due process refers to the procedural guidelines that the police must follow in gathering evidence, whether it be in interrogating an accused or searching for evidence. It also refers to the system of checks that is designed to review criminal cases and tests whether or not they warrant passage further into the criminal justice system. This is illustrated in Figure 1.1. If a judicial officer finds that the police have violated the rights of the accused by coercing a confession from him, or by obtaining evidence by illegally entering his home, then the evidence obtained through these illegal procedures cannot be used against the accused in a court of law.

In general, the justice system accepts the premise that an adult is totally responsible for his behavior. As a consequence of the greater responsibility of adults as compared to juveniles, and the admission that the sentences they receive are "punishments," the justice system reviews much more closely the due process safeguards for adults. Therefore, police have less discretion in handling adults, in part, because of these greater due process concerns. This is not to imply that they do not utilize discretion in handling adults, for they certainly do. However, officers are usually less concerned about the possible negative effects of the court experience on the adult than they are about such harmful effects on juveniles. This is so because the adult is not thought to be as malleable as a juvenile, and because the adult system focuses much more strongly upon protection of society than is the case for the juvenile system. That police departments have created juvenile specialists, reinforces the special treatment afforded juveniles.

IDENTIFICATION AND REFERRAL: SUMMARY

Juveniles are "taken into custody;" adults are "arrested." The previous discussion has focused on the decision-making process that culminates in the juvenile offender being taken into custody and referred to court, and the adult being arrested and charged. While relatively little is known about how these decisions are made, it is known that a great number of those committing offenses are diverted, either by not being caught or, if caught, by being released.

INTAKE: THE DECISION TO PROSECUTE IN COURT

JUVENILES

Referral to the juvenile court does not necessarily lead to a hearing before the court. Although procedures vary somewhat from jurisdiction to jurisdiction, referrals to the juvenile court usually first pass through an intake officer (frequently a probation officer) whose responsibility it is to carry out an investigation of the case and decide whether or not it is necessary for the juvenile to actually appear in court. If the intake officer decides that the youth does not warrant appearing before the judge, then the officer frequently sends the youth home with no further restrictions; or he may require that the juvenile report to him periodically for several months. The officer's decision to "divert" the juvenile from court may be based on such factors as the offense being a minor one, the first offense, or the juvenile's parents providing an alternative (e.g., private psychiatric counseling). These or any of several other factors may affect the officer's decision for "informal adjustment" or "informal disposition," or to refer the juvenile to court for formal disposition.

Thus, once the juvenile is referred to an intake officer, there is still a large amount of discretion for the officer in terms of deciding the fate of the juvenile. How this discretion is used can have a significant effect on the perception the juvenile develops of the court. The fact that criteria other than the seriousness of the offense are often used may make the probation officer's decision incomprehensible to the juvenile. For example, three youths were picked up for joyriding in a stolen car. One youth was released directly to his parents, one was put on informal probation for six months, and the other was asked to appear in court with the chance of being sent to a correctional institution. The discrepancy in handling this case was not easily explainable to the third youth, and conseqently he felt that the system had treated him unjustly. Thus, while the probation officer operates on the basis of the best interest of the youth, the youth usually sees their decision in terms of "getting off" with the least amount of constraints. What is treatment for one is punishment for another.

ADULTS

The intake and decision to prosecute stage in the criminal justice system is considerably different for adults than for juveniles. After an accused offender is apprehended by the police, he is taken before a magistrate. If the offense is minor (a misdemeanor), then the complaint is usually made by the arresting officer or by a private citizen. These petty offenses usually result in the defendant pleading guilty and being punished immediately. The defendant may, however, plead not guilty or ask for a continuance so that he can consult with an attorney and decide his plea.

For felony cases (those punishable by more than one year imprisonment) the process is usually more involved. When an accused felon is brought before the magistrate, it is for the purpose of setting bail and making arrangements for a preliminary hearing. The preliminary hearing is a testing of the prosecution's evidence by the court to decide whether there is sufficient cause, referred to as "probable cause," to hold the accused for prosecution. If the court finds "probable cause," then the case is either presented to a grand jury of citizens who decide whether the evidence is sufficient for an indictment (a formal charge against the accused), or the prosecutor simply files the indictment, called an *information*.[21]

While adult prosecution is much more formalistic and legalistic in orientation than that for juveniles, there is still a wide range of latitude in the decision-making process. For example, from an examination of prosecution in one Wisconsin county, Donald Newman concluded:

> . . . the majority of the felony convictions in the district studied were not the result of the formal, combative theory of criminal law involving in effect a legal battle between prosecution and defense, but were compromise convictions, the result of bargaining between defense and prosecution. Such informal conviction processes were observed in over half of the cases studied.[22]

Newman found that these "compromise" convictions were the result of four types of negotiations. In one negotiation the accused pleaded guilty in exchange for a reduction of the charge to a lesser offense than the original allegation.[23] A second type of negotiation observed by Newman involved the entering of a plea of guilty in return for a lesser sentence than the maximum possible sentence for the offense. For example, an offender may agree to a guilty plea in return for a sentence of probation instead of a prison sentence. Because the accused was frequently charged with several offenses, another type of agreement struck between the prosecution and the defendant was a plea of guilty in exchange for receiving concurrent sentences as opposed to consecutive sentences. The final type of negotiation was a bargain for the dropping of charges. This usually involved the prosecution agreeing "not to press formally one or more charges against the offender if he (defendant) in turn pleaded guilty to (usually) the major offense."[24]

In summary, in adult justice, the prosecution (intake) has the option of dismissing the case or, more likely, determining the kind of disposition that the offender will receive. Thus, "making it" to court involves prosecutorial discretion, but the sentence one receives in court is frequently an outgrowth of negotiation with the prosecutor.

COURT

The Juvenile Court

The juvenile court has several legal functions to perform. First, the court has the responsibility of reviewing the case to insure that the youth has been accorded the appropriate due process procedures. This particular role for the court usually receives only minor emphasis because the needs of the youth are considered more important. A second due process concern of the court is to make a determination of guilt or innocence; and a third aspect of the court's role (if the youth is guilty) is the disposition of the case. The alternatives for the judge are "outright dismissal, probation entailing loose and infrequent supervision, or commitment to a state reform school."[25]

While the *parens patriae* orientation has not been abandoned, there have been some significant changes in the direction of greater emphasis on due process. This change in orientation is best exemplified by the *Kent v. United States*[26] decision of 1966 which stated:

> There is much evidence that some juvenile courts, including that of the District of Columbia, lack the personnel, facilities and techniques to perform adequately as representatives of the State in a *parens patriae* capacity, at least with respect to children charged with law violation. There is evidence, in fact, that there may be grounds for concern that the child receives the worst of both worlds: that he gets neither the protections afforded adults nor the solicitous care and regenerative treatment postulated for children.

Following closely upon the philosophy expressed in *Kent,* the Supreme Court ruled on a case in which 15 year old Gerald Gault was found to be delinquent as a result of an accusation that he had made an obscene phone call.[27] Gerald and his parents were never given notice of the specific charges against him nor were they advised of their having a right to counsel. The woman who made the accusation was not at the court hearing so her testimony was not cross-examined. These court proceedings, or the lack of them, were not previously deemed necessary for juveniles since the outcome was most contingent upon the needs, and consequently, the most appropriate treatment for the juvenile. But, in view of the Supreme Court's statement in the *Kent* decision, it was obvious that the Supreme Court of Arizona's belief that ". . . the parent and probation officer may be relied upon to protect the infant's interests"[28] was not shared by the Supreme Court of the United States. Consequently, the Supreme Court of the United States held in the *Gault* decision that juveniles must be accorded the right to written notice of charges, the right to counsel in court, the right to cross-examine witnesses, and to be protected against self-incrimination. The *Gault* case and its relevance to juvenile corrections will be analyzed in greater detail in chapter six. It should be emphasized here, however, that (changes in philosophy and operation notwithstanding) the juvenile justice system still basically operates on the conception that juveniles are to be "treated," not "punished."

Adult Court

The adult court serves as a check upon the procedures of the police and prosecutor, as the arena for the adversarial confrontation between defense and prosecution, and as the determiner of guilt and innocence. For the purposes of this book, the most important aspect of the court is its ability to choose a method of disposition from a number of alternatives. How the court uses these alternatives has a great impact on the effectiveness of the correctional system. Although there has been increasing concern about correctional alternatives, the basic options available to the court if the defendant is found guilty are: 1) suspended sentence, 2) fine, 3) probation, and 4) incarceration. The court has some discretion in sentencing; however, this discretion is subject to legislative restriction. In some jurisdictions the judge not only decides the disposition, but he can also place restrictions on the length of the probationary period or set minimums and maximums for the length of incarceration. In other cases, the length of incarceration is set by statute. Thus, in many cases the court not only sets the type of sentence (perhaps carrying out prosecutorial negotiation), but may also set limits upon the length of the sentence.

Both the juvenile and adult courts have a great amount of formal decision-making power, but the court process is often an acting-out of inputs from prosecutors, defense attorneys, and probation officers. Part of the court's power is its ability to veto these recommendations and negotiations. While the court usually would not formally reverse these recommendations and negotiations, the judge may specify what types of bargains he is willing to accept. It is through the combination of both the formal power and informal influence that the judge can affect both findings of guilt and innocence, and the sentences for those found or pleading guilty.

SUMMARY

The criminal justice system has been described as a filtering process. While many people violate the law, few are actually funneled all the way into the correctional system. Thus, corrections applies not to those who violate the law, but to those who violate the law, are apprehended, prosecuted, found guilty, and placed into the correctional system. While considering this filtering process, it has also been pointed out that there are, in effect, two systems—one for adults and one for juveniles. Thus, the youths who are involved in corrections are considerably different from the adults involved in corrections.

It should also be noted that the movement of individuals through the criminal justice process is *not* similar to the operation of a well-oiled, coordinated machine; in fact, at times the relationships between the police, prosecution, courts, and corrections seem best described as conflictual rather than cooperative. Thus, we frequently hear the police decrying the leniency of courts and corrections; the courts decrying the inability of corrections to correct, and police to operate according to due process; and we hear correctional officials decrying the reluctance of the police, prosecution, and the courts to accept their innovations, and to understand the problems of attempting simultaneous reform and control.

This chapter has attempted to provide only a cursory view of the justice system. Any such view is necessarily oversimplified because laws vary from state to state, and within states. Furthermore, the working relations between the different representatives of the justice system such as police, judges, probation officers, and prison officials vary considerably from jurisdiction to jurisdiction. Each of these can have tremendous implications for the total operation of the system.

ENDNOTES

1. Donald J. Newman, *Introduction to Criminal Justice* (Philadelphia: J. B. Lippincott Company, 1975), p. 2.
2. See for example Philip H. Ennis, "Criminal Victimization in the United States: A Report of a National Survey," *Field Surveys* II, President's Commission on Law Enforcement and Administration of Justice (Washington, D.C.: U.S. Government Printing Office, 1967).
3. Ibid.
4. Donald J. Black and Albert J. Reiss, Jr., "Production of Crime Rates," *American Sociological Review* (August, 1970), pp. 733–748.
5. *Uniform Crime Reports for the United States—1973* (Washington, D.C.: U.S. Government Printing Office, 1972).
6. Ibid., p. 118.
7. For a good discussion of this see F. Wines, *Punishment and Reformation* (New York: T. Y. Crowell and Co., 1895), p. 302.
8. See for example: Martin Gold, "Undetected Delinquency Behavior," *Journal of Research in Crime and Delinquency* 3(1966): 27–46, and Larimar M. Empey and Maynard L. Erickson, "Hid-

den Delinquency and Social Status," *Social Forces* 44(1966): pp. 546–54.
9. President's Commission on Law Enforcement and Administration of Justice, *Juvenile Delinquency and Youth Crime* (Washington, D.C.: U.S. Government Printing Office, 1967).
10. See, for example, Michael Lalli and Leonard Sawitz, *Interim Report: A Study of Delinquency and Criminal Careers*, U.S. Department of Justice.
11. Maynard L. Erickson and Lamar T. Empey, "Court Records, Undetected Delinquency and Decision-making," *Journal of Criminal Law, Criminology and Police Science* (December, 1963), pp. 456–469.
12. *Uniform Crime Reports*, op. cit.
13. In George D. Eastman, ed., *Municipal Police Administration* (Washington, D.C.: International City Management Association, 1969), p. 48.
14. Donald J. Black and Albert J. Reiss, Jr., "Police Control of Juveniles," *American Sociological Review* (February, 1970), pp. 63–77.
15. Irving Piliavin and Scott Briar, "Police Encounters with Juveniles," *American Journal of Sociology* (September, 1964), pp. 206–214; and Black and Reiss, op. cit.
16. Edward Eldefonso, *Law Enforcement and the Youthful Offender* (New York: John Wiley and Sons, Inc., 1967), pp. 291–292. Copyright © 1967 by John Wiley & Sons, Inc. Reprinted by permission of John Wiley & Sons, Inc.
17. Robert M. Terry, "Discrimination in the Handling of Juvenile Offenders by Social Control Agencies," *Journal of Research in Crime and Delinquency* 4 (1967), pp. 218–230.
18. Nathan Goldman, *The Differential Selection of Juvenile Offenders for Court Appearance* National Council on Crime and Delinquency, (1963).
19. Ibid., pp. 93–124.
20. J. S. Wallerstein and C. L. Wyle, "Our Lawabiding Lawbreakers," *National Probation* (March–April, 1947), pp. 107–112.
21. Donald Gibbons, *Society, Crime, and Criminal Careers* (Englewood Cliffs, N.J.: Prentice-Hall, Inc., 1968).
22. Donald J. Newman, "Pleading Guilty for Considerations: A Study of Bargain Justice," *Journal of Criminal Law, Criminology, and Police Science* (March–April, 1956), p. 780.
23. Ibid., p. 788.

24. Ibid., p. 789.
25. Sanford J. Fox, *Juvenile Courts in a Nutshell* (St. Paul, Minn.: West Publishing Co., 1971), p. 203.
26. *Kent* v. *United States,* 383 U.S. 541, 86 S Ct. 1045, 16 L.Ed.2d 84 (1966).
27. In Re Gault, 387 U.S. 1 (1967).
28. *Kent* v. *United States,* 383 U.S. 541, 86 S Ct. 1045, 16 L.Ed.2d 84 (1966).

2

The History of Punishment and Correction

For centuries the methods chosen for punishing or correcting social deviants were brutal and inhuman. Boiling people alive, castration, stretching the body "until the bones and joints were almost plucked asunder," having people drawn and quartered, pulling out of tongues, and other atrocities were legal forms of punishment in England during various stages in history.[1] Such extreme practices were seldom used in America, however, primarily because England itself had eliminated most of them by the time the colonies were established. The penal measures adopted by the colonists were not so cruel as England's at least in part because of the influence of humanitarian groups (especially the Quakers). Also, some of the more perceptive settlers who came to America to escape from a corrupt criminal system were understandably opposed to establishing an identical system within their new communities.

INHERITED PENAL METHODS

Although the colonists never did accept all of the English legal and penal traditions, it is important to understand that most colonial laws were technically enacted in the mother country, and were enforced to a large degree by its representatives. As far back as 1664, penal codes that originated in England were transported to the colonies.[2] Thus, while the criminal justice systems that were established in colonial America were somewhat more humane than their English counterparts, they amounted to little more than modified versions of the same.

From an historical perspective, the American methods of punishment and correction that were patterned after English penal methods can be divided into the following three categories: capital punishment, corporal punishment (and its related public humiliation), and institutionalization.

Capital Punishment

In the 17th century the death penalty was used quite extensively in the colonies, not only for dangerous offenders, but also for those guilty of "moral" transgressions, including "idolatry, blasphemy, and adultery." If an individual was found by the authorities to be an habitual offender, in all probability he would be executed regardless of the seriousness of his crime. Even those who committed relatively minor offenses were put to death if convicted more than once in the same community.

The statutes that legally sanctioned capital punishment and the methods of execution were similar to those in England. Hanging was the most popular, but burning at the stake and slowly pressing an offender to death under weights (usually by piling rocks on the individual's chest) were also used. There is evidence that New York and Virginia officials sometimes used the notorious "wheel." However, with the exception of the pressing method and the occasional use of the wheel, the colonists rejected those traditionally English techniques that were designed to elicit the most excruciating forms of pain prior to death.[3]

Corporal Punishment

The corporal punishments of the day were designed, as they had been in England, not only to cause the offender physical discomfort, but also to humiliate him in front of the community. Public whipping, for example, could accomplish both of these goals and was therefore the most frequently used method of corporal punishment in colonial times.

The stocks and pillory, whose origins date back to the feudal period in English history, were also used by the colonists to inflict pain and publically shame minor criminals. In the pillory "offenders stood on public display . . . their head and arms inserted through openings in a wooden brace."[4] In its cruelest application the victim's ears were nailed to the head board so that he would be unable to duck his head when members of the community jeered and threw garbage at him.[5] When secured in the stocks, the offender's ankles and sometimes his hands, but not his head, were held in a brace.[6]

The "ducking stool" was a method of punishment that was usually reserved for women who were judged to be guilty of nagging their husbands or of engaging in "immoral" activity. The culprit was strapped into a chair-like structure and submerged periodically into a pond. While the victim usually was hoisted out of the water before drowning, there were times when this procedure proved fatal.

Branding was another accepted form of punishment in the colonies. If an offender was convicted, a letter signifying the crime that he had committed was burned into his "forehead, cheek, or hand" with a branding iron. For example, a person found guilty of drunkenness might have the letter D branded on his forehead. As the colonial penal codes became more humane, the actual branding was replaced with having the offender wear a badge signifying his crime.[7]

Even in the latter part of the 17th century, it was not uncommon for English officials to torture the accused either for the purpose of eliciting a confession or to force him to enter a plea of some sort. Such practices were not as prevalent in the colonies, but were not unheard of. Pre-conviction tortures, when used, were patterned after some of England's relatively milder techniques such as twisting an individual's thumbs with a "whipcord." However, in 1692 at the infamous Salem witch trials, at least one person was pressed to death in an effort to make him confess.[8]

INSTITUTIONALIZATION

In the colonies, as in England, institutions were designed for different purposes. The "houses of correction" were constructed for the purpose of incarcerating and punishing "immoral" deviants; they were designed to confine "those who would not work unless compelled to do so: the shiftless beggars, tramps, and prostitutes."[9] Thus, houses of correction were penal institutions and should not be confused with the more charitable almshouses and workhouses which were built for the "deserving poor."

The almshouse was founded for the purpose of tending to the needs of the impotent poor, while the workhouse was established so that the able-bodied poor could be gainfully employed. The almshouse and the workhouse were segments of the "poor relief system," and as such were not penal institutions. Nevertheless, as Professor Robert G. Caldwell points out, the distinction between the workhouse and the house of correction was lost with the passage of time and the terms were used interchangeably throughout most of history.[10]

SOCIAL PROBLEMS IN COLONIAL AMERICA

From an historical perspective, the attitudes of the 18th century colonists regarding deviant behavior and some of the methods that they devised to control such behavior were unique. The early settlers did not consider poverty or crime to be pressing social problems. While they had no illusions about eradicating either crime or poverty, they felt perfectly capable of keeping such conditions under control.

POVERTY

The "poor," by colonial standards, included widows, orphans, the elderly, and even the insane. In fact, almost anyone who needed physical or financial assistance was considered to be poor. In the early communities the less fortunate were treated surprisingly well because those who were self sufficient felt that it was their duty to assist them in times of need. This sense of obligation was largely due to the prevailing religious beliefs of the day. Giving aid to the poor was considered to be something more than a mere religious obligation. Being charitable was viewed as a prerequisite to salvation. Ministers instructed their congregations that poverty existed so that men would have the opportunity to serve as God's "stewards." In such a capacity a man would have the responsibility of distributing his wealth, and if he did so selflessly he would be assured of heavenly rewards.[11]

The religious and secular philosophies of the day were often mutually supportive. Church congregations were also told that it was not sinful to maintain social class differences. According to heaven's law a hierarchial social order must exist and one need not apologize for his worldly possessions as long as he was charitable to his needy (but socially inferior) townsmen. This position coincided with the prevailing secular veiwpoint regarding poverty. Colonists attached great importance to the maintenance of an ordered society; they felt secure within a rigid social structure that was relatively free of nonconformity and social chaos. Therefore, as long as the local poor knew "their place" and did not attempt to disrupt the established social order, they could expect charity from the upper classes. Because it was generally believed that change within the social order would bring about chaos, the poor were rewarded for their complacency. Even most of those who were instrumental in bringing about the American Revolution adhered to this philosophy.[12]

The religious and secular demands for an ordered society were also bolstered by English tradition. Elizabethan laws had confirmed each parish's responsibility for attending to the needs of its poor. In accordance with these laws, relief for the poor was usually administered by elected overseers.[13]

The "Outside" Poor Whether based on their religious, philosophical, or practical convictions, colonial Americans did not consider local poverty to be a threat to the social order, and in a sense they even welcomed it as a necessary condition in an ordered society. But their charity rarely extended beyond the bounds of their local communities. They did not consider the outsider to be their responsibility under any circumstances.

The colonists felt that allegiance to their individual communities was absolutely necessary for economic reasons, for their own protection, and in many cases for their survival. They were more than willing to take care of their own, but they also expected other communities to do the same.[14]

THE VAGABOND AND THE ROGUE

Within the social order that was established by the colonists, there were two types of deviants that were avoided or punished because they were considered to be either non-productive nuisances or dangerous. The needy outsider was one of the type usually referred to as "vagabond" and was treated with suspicion.

"Settlement" laws, one of the earliest means of controlling crime and poverty, detailed the requirements that an individual had to fulfill before he could be considered a resident of the community. Because the vagabond did not satisfy the conditions of settlement, he was usually "warned out" of the community. This meant that local officials would escort him to the town or village limits, and inform him that if he returned he would face a more severe punishment.

Houses of correction or workhouses, as they were sometimes referred to during the latter years of the colonial period, were few in number and located only in some of the more populated areas. The occupants of these early institutions (despite the original benign intentions of the founders of the workhouse) received harsh treatment that was purposely designed to deter vagabonds from entering or returning to certain geographic areas. However, historian David J. Rothman convincingly argues that because such institutions were so scarce during colonial days their importance as a means of social control was negligible.[15]

The second type of person the colonists considered undesirable was commonly referred to as a "rogue." Individuals in this category ranged from the dangerous criminal to the ordinary rowdy, who roamed from town to town supporting himself by petty thievery. Unlike vagabonds, who were merely nuisances, rogues were "real" criminals who were either threats to public safety or habitual offenders. When apprehended and convicted, rogues were usually punished severely.

Late 17th century and early 18th century penal sanctions could be brutal, and they were designed to intimidate both the actual offender who was being punished and the potential offender witnessing the punishment. The whip was commonly used to punish the first time offender; however, magistrates were granted a great deal of discretion in choosing from a wide range of other penalties. The less serious offender was usually fined, but if he did not have the necessary funds to pay the fine, he was often forced to spend time in the stocks. The stocks and pillory were also used to discipline the drunk and disorderly members of the community. Thus, the punishments of the day were not only designed for disciplining the intruder, but also for controlling the members of the community.

While the fine, the whip, and the stocks were used most often to control the minor offenders, other penal practices were common. To terrorize and thereby (theoretically) deter the offender from engaging in further criminal activity, he was sometimes forced to stand on the gallows with a noose around his neck for several hours before being released. Others were put on public display in cages and then whipped. Punishments such as branding emphasized the community's contempt for the wrong-doer.

Therefore, public opinion, or more specifically, the scorn of one's neighbors was regarded as a primary method of social control.[16]

Banishment or "warning out," which was usually preceded by other types of punishments such as whipping, was also used as a means of protecting the community from those suspected of being rogues. Incarceration was seldom regarded as a method of securing such protection. Jails were used only to detain individuals awaiting their trials or punishment. Large scale prisons were non-existent, and as previously mentioned only a few communities constructed houses of correction or workhouses. Thus, the 17th and early 18th century emphasis on corporal punishment and banishment as methods of combating crime did not serve to remove offenders from society, but contributed to the number of wandering deviants.

The frequent use of the death penalty perhaps represented a desperate attempt on the part of the colonists to control the criminal population after all other methods had proven to be inadequate. Reliance on the hangman made evident some glaring weaknesses in the criminal justice system of the day. David J. Rothman, in his book *The Discovery of the Asylum,* demonstrated that the perceived necessity of applying such stern measures usually resulted in "a vacillation between lenient and harsh punishment." As Rothman indicates, many criminals would roam from one community to the next engaging in pickpocketing and other forms of petty thievery. Even when they were apprehended by local authorities, these rogues usually did not receive severe punishments. While magistrates could legally impose the death penalty for relatively minor crimes, in many jurisdictions they were hesitant to do so if they thought that there was any possibility that a culprit was a first time offender. Therefore, the roving petty criminal usually had to endure only a few strokes of the lash, public ridicule, and banishment. However, if his reputation preceded him in the community and he was caught engaging in further criminal activity, he most likely would have been labeled as an habitual offender and put to death. Known recidivists, even though their crimes may have been minor ones, were usually executed along with the more dangerous criminals. Primarily because colonial authorities did not usually make use of "middle range" punishments such as imprisonment, there was little consistency in the administration of justice. Frequently, only chance would determine whether or not an individual would face the gallows or some relatively mild form of punishment.[17]

THE RATIONALE FOR PUNISHMENT

Why would a religiously oriented society that took great pride in its emphasis on Christian charity rely almost exclusively on public ostracism, corporal punishment, and the death penalty as methods of social control? Perhaps an answer to this question can be found by examining the religious doctrine of the day more closely. To a large extent sin and crime were equated in the minds of the colonists. Various offenses against religion such as idolatry, blasphemy, and witchcraft were punishable under the law, and even crimes that were seemingly unrelated to religion such as those against person or property were often proclaimed to be "offenses against God."[18]

The colonists regarded crime as the devil's work and as evidence of man's depraved state. Great importance was attached to preventing the basic evil that was believed to exist in all men from surfacing and creating social chaos. Crime prevention was primarily regarded as a family responsibility. Parents were held legally responsible for training and disciplining their children and for protecting them from the temptations of the devil.

As shocking as it may seem today, there were some colonial statutes which stated that children who were incorrigible and disrespectful to their parents, could legally be put to death. Both religious and lay leaders in colonial society were convinced, however, that if one adopted an evil life style he should pay the supreme penalty. Not only should society be protected from him personally, but his untimely demise should also serve as a reminder to others of the consequences of performing the devil's work. To serve as an example to all prospective sinners, the condemned criminal was often forced to stand by his coffin on the morning of his execution and listen to a minister preach a sermon admonishing the congregation not to be tempted, as the offender before them had been, by the evil that existed in all of them.

Colonists were taught that the wickedest of men differed from themselves only in degree, and all people were capable of committing the vilest deeds if they did not abide by the teachings of their family, church, and community. By associating the common sinner with the most serious of criminals, they perhaps blurred the distinction between major and minor offenses. A first time offender might not be completely under the influence of Satan and therefore was not regarded as being beyond redemption. Because there was hope for the reformation of such an individual, he was usually treated quite leniently. However, the habitual criminal, even if his offenses were minor ones, had proven by adhering to a deviant life style that the evil within him had won out and there was no chance of reform.[19]

THE EARLY USE OF IMPRISONMENT

The Pennsylvania Quakers, under the guidance of William Penn, were the first to seriously attempt to establish imprisonment as an intermediate or middle range punishment. They were probably influenced by the Bridewell, a house of correction that was built near London in 1555.[20]

Authority to substitute incarceration at hard labor for corporal and capital punishment came from a penal code, "Penn's Great Law," that was formulated in England and adopted by the new colony in 1682. West Jersey, which was also founded by Quakers, developed a similar body of laws. For a time in both Pennsylvania and West Jersey, imprisonment was used as punishment for all serious crimes except first degree murder.

By 1692, when William Penn was removed from power and the Anglican Code had replaced his Great Law, the humanitarian innovations created by Penn and his enlightened associates had all but come to an end. Pennsylvania then, as did West Jersey, gradually incorporated harsher penal sanctions similar to those of other colonies and England.[21]

Because the colonists were in obvious need of intermediate penal sanctions, on the surface it seems surprising that only West Jersey and Pennsylvania used imprisonment as means of punishment and social defense. However, closer examination of how the colonists viewed their existing institutions makes it clear why they were hesitant to propose the use of such establishments for confining criminals. For example, the early almshouses were constructed on a type of family model which would have made them inappropriate for housing dangerous offenders. The proprietor of the almshouse and his family slept, ate, and went about their daily affairs with the poor who lived in the institution. Almshouses were little more than large households that could hardly be distinguished, even by their physical appearances, from ordinary dwellings. The poor were well treated as a rule and since officials were determined to keep the undeserving poor out of the institutions, it was a privilege to be accepted into one of these households.

As previously indicated, houses of correction and workhouses were few in number and the colonial jails were not designed for punishment or correction. Most of the jails, as well as many of the workhouses, were administered in the same family type of arrangement that characterized the almshouse.

Those who were physically incapacitated or mentally disturbed to the extent that they could not remain in their own homes or in almshouses were often placed in other institutions that were designed as substitute households. The first hospital for the insane or "lunatic asylum," was established at Williamsburg, Virginia in 1769. While this structure differed from the typical institution of the day, it was used only as a last resort to house those individuals who were too dangerous or uncontrollable to be taken care of by any other means. Nevertheless, institutional officials did attempt to establish a family type atmosphere within this and subsequent institutions. The "lunatic asylum" then provided living arrangements that were superior to those previously used, e.g., confining the insane in the attics of almshouses or in small individual shacks that were constructed on town commons. Hospitals such as the Pennsylvania Hospital, which was established in Philadelphia in 1751, and some almshouses that were converted into refuges for the physically and mentally ill were also regarded as places of last resort and therefore were inhabited only by those unfortunates who could not be cared for by their friends and relatives.

Because late 17th century and early 18th century Americans were accustomed to these kinds of charitable institutions, they gave little thought to incarceration as a possible solution to the crime problem. To confine criminals in institutions similar to the ones that they were familiar with would be, from the colonists' perspective, a means of rewarding the offender with a better existence than he was accustomed to, and certainly would not provide a deterrent influence on potential offenders.[22]

The colonists adhered to a demonistic explanation of crime causation. All men were believed to be basically depraved; and confirmed criminals, because they were completely under the influence of the devil, definitely could not be salvaged. Certainly such rogues could not be reformed in an institution or even frightened by the threat of incarceration. Those who cast their lots with Satan simply had to be eliminated. From the colonists' viewpoint, the gallows represented the only remedy to the problems created by the habitual criminal, while the minor or first time offender could be driven out of the community. The colonists believed these sanctions to be satisfactory means of ridding the community of undesirables and they assumed them to be economically superior to incarceration.[23]

THE GROWTH OF A NEW PHILOSOPHY: 1790–1830

From 1790 through 1830 there was a substantial increase in population accompanied by a remarkable growth in urban industrialized society. As the cities increased in size and the population became more mobile, the assumption that the community should police its own affairs, primarily through the use of corporal punishment and banishment, became less credible. Unlike the inhabitants of colonial towns and villages, citizens in an urbanized and mobile society could not be expected to know all of the other residents of their home cities or towns, nor were they well informed about the internal affairs of the community. Therefore, because individuals were no longer as concerned about gaining the approval of their neighbors, the deterrent potential of the public humiliation associated with corporal punishment was decidedly weakened.

Likewise, the growing allegiance to larger political units such as state governments helped to bring about the realization that banishment was an inadequate method of social defense. To "warn" an offender out of a town or city was, at best, a temporary means of crime control. He most likely would either journey on and menace a neighboring community or, within a short time, return to the original one and become lost in the urban environment. Also, because traveling for business and pleasure was becoming increasingly popular in America, citizens became more insistent in their demands for protection from roaming criminals.[24]

Along with American independence came the acceptance of an Enlightenment philosophy that also gradually altered traditional colonial thinking with regard to crime causation and control. Both America and Europe were greatly influenced by the Italian mathematician and legal scholar, Cesare Beccaria. His essay *On Crimes and Punishments* inspired many Americans to re-examine both the philosophical basis of the "barbaric" colonial penal codes and the traditional demonistic explanation of criminality.

Beccaria contended that the potential offender would refrain from engaging in criminal activity if he thought that there was a good chance of being caught. Therefore, he considered the certainty of punishment to be a most important factor in crime prevention. However, he believed that severe punishment only embittered and brutalized the individual, causing him to become even more involved in criminal behavior. Beccaria asserted that those governments which utilize the cruelest penal sanctions are the ones that encounter the most serious crime problems.[25]

During the Enlightenment there were others, like Beccaria, who placed primary emphasis on the reform of the criminal law. Their pleas for moderation in punishment fell on receptive ears. From the time the first colonists arrived, harsh penal sanctions had been prescribed for serious violations of the law. By 1790, however, Americans had begun to realize that the effects of brutal punishment had not reduced the crime rate and that judges and juries were often hesitant to find an accused criminal guilty if it meant that he would receive the death penalty. Therefore, to both those who favored the humane treatment of offenders and those who were primarily concerned with societal protection, the colonial criminal justice had proven to be less than adequate.

THE BIRTH OF THE STATE PRISON

The new attitudes regarding crime and criminals were instrumental in causing the states to revise their penal codes during the latter years of the 18th century and the first part of the 19th century. States either abolished the death penalty (except as punishment for first degree murder) or drastically limited its use. Imprisonment was eventually to replace most of the colonial forms of punishment.

It was brought out previously that the jails, workhouses, and even the houses of correction that existed in colonial society did not provide adequate societal protection, nor did they serve as proper instruments of punishment or reform. However, Americans were beginning to realize that some type of intermediate penal sanction was needed. Likewise, because the humanitarianism of the Enlightenment philosophers had left its impact, the crude colonial punishments were viewed by many as being entirely inappropriate.

By 1790, European prison reform had been widely publicized, largely because of the work of John Howard, an Englishman. At that time most of England's penal institutions were corrupt, unsanitary, and generally deplorable. However, Howard's written reports on his investigations of both the best and the worst institutions in Europe contained many constructive suggestions for improving prison conditions. He and other reformers did much to bring about the acceptance of prisons, not only as adequate means of protecting society, but also as more humane alternatives to capital punishment.[26]

Being aware of the emphasis that was placed on incarceration by European authorities, and feeling a need for the establishment of an intermediate type of punishment, officials in most of the states finally committed themselves to the extensive use of legal imprisonment.

In 1790 the state of Pennsylvania converted Philadelphia's Walnut Street Jail into a state prison. New York and New Jersey soon followed Pennsylvania's example and by 1800, Virginia, Kentucky, and Massachusetts had also established state controlled penal institutions. After the turn of the century the growth of state prisons continued to increase. As David J. Rothman indicates, "Within twenty years of Washington's inaugural, the states had taken the first steps to alter the traditional system of punishment."[27]

During this period in history, however, some states continued to rely on county jails and corporal punishment as means of controlling the criminal population. Such methods were frequently used in southern states where local officials were granted a great deal of discretion in handling penal affairs.[28]

While incarceration was indirectly associated with reform in the minds of the early 19th century legislators and legal authorities, they expressed little interest in the administrative affairs of the jails and prisons. What was important to them was not the actual institutions, but the laws that sanctioned imprisonment.

Lawmakers accepted the predominant utilitarian explanation of criminality and its control. They believed that if punishment was going to deter the criminal from engaging in further deviant activity, it would have to cause him enough pain, preferably of a psychological nature, to out-weigh the pleasure that he received from such activity. They also assumed that the more serious crimes required correspondingly severe penalties. However, as Beccaria cautioned, any punishment that is in excess of that needed to prevent future criminal behavior is "tyrannical."

Prisons provided an opportunity to carefully and humanely punish (incarcerate) the criminal in accordance with the seriousness of his offense. Therefore, understanding the personality and social background of the individual was not usually considered relevant to his rehabilitation. What was important was the selection of the appropriate penalty for the particular offense. Prisons were considered important to legal reformers because they were thought to be humane substitutes for corporal and capital punishments. While a few prison administrators were attempting to develop rehabilitation programs within their institutions, the reformers at that time were more concerned about other matters.[29]

18TH CENTURY PRISON REFORMS

National interest in the internal affairs of prisons did not really gain impetus until the 19th century. However, in a limited way, some prison reforms were instigated in the late 18th century. As far back as 1776 a group of concerned Pennsylvanians established the Philadelphia Society for Alleviating the Miseries of Public Prisons. This organization was devoted to improving what its members regarded as the revolting conditions that existed in some institutions. They particularly objected to the manner in which miserable fettered inmates who were confined in the Walnut Street Jail during the night were often placed on public display during the day and forced to clean the city streets. The public disturbances that often resulted from such practices were also viewed with alarm. Within a year after the Philadelphia organization was established, it was instrumental in abolishing the public labor of prison inmates.[30]

During the last decade of the 18th century some crude attempts to rehabilitate offenders took place in the Walnut Street Jail. Felons were kept in solitary confinement, but they did engage

HISTORY OF PUNISHMENT AND CORRECTION 43

The "Douche." This 18th century "rehabilitation" device released large quantities of cold water upon recalcitrant prisoners.

in productive labor and were given religious counseling. Also, as a result of the same 1790 legislative act that made the Walnut Street Jail a state prison, prisoners could legally be released prior to the expiration of their sentences if in the opinion of the sentencing court they were rehabilitated. By the early 1800s, however, the institution was so overcrowded that it became administratively unmanageable.

During this time period a few other attempts to reform prisons were made, but as Blake McKelvey indicates, "Serious overcrowding and the consequent disruption of industry and discipline rapidly converted all these prisons into riotous dens of iniquity and roused a wave of popular indignation that in turn prepared the way for a new era of prison reform."[31]

THE INDIVIDUAL CRIMINAL

By the 1820s a more widespread public interest had begun to focus on the internal affairs of the prison. It had become evident by then that the enactment of more humane laws had done nothing to lower the crime rate. Likewise, because riots and escapes were common occurrences, the existence of prisons did not substantially alleviate the concern about societal protection.

As the failures of the prisons became more obvious, the pre-Civil War era witnessed the first concentrated attempts by legislators, scholars, and interested laymen to devise a system that would actually reform the criminal. The new emphasis on reform began with a re-assessment of some of the traditional beliefs regarding the causes of criminality. If prison officials were to rehabilitate offenders, the new reformers assumed that they would have to have a better understanding of the factors that made them turn to crime in the first place.

Philanthropic organizations, legislatures, and judges, among others, enthusiastically ventured forth to solve the mystery of crime causation. However, it was the prison officials themselves who did the most to advance a semi-theoretical position that would soon be accepted by almost all of the "experts" of the day. Rothman quoted from numerous "biographical sketches" of prisoners written by officials and attached to the annual reports to their state legislatures. These un-scientifically selected case studies purposely drew attention to one recurring theme: criminals were invariably victims of circumstances that were beyond their control. In these narratives, which represented only the prisoners' unsubstantiated assertions, officials went to great lengths to describe the offenders' early developmental years and the failures of both their families and the community in molding their moral behavior. With few exceptions the roots of crime could be found in the lack of or faulty training and guidance in childhood. Alcohol and the morally corrupting temptations that the soldier and the railroad worker encountered were also cited as factors contributing to criminality.[32]

As the idea of the criminal as a victim of society became widely accepted, legal reform was no longer regarded as the primary solution to the crime problem. Relying principally on unsubstantiated evidence, such as the biographical sketches, reformers began to focus their attention on the individual offender instead of on the law. They no longer accepted the older colonial view of man as being inherently evil. What emerged in the 19th century was a more secular notion of the individual as a victim of a disordered society.[33]

However, Americans during the pre-Civil War years still believed in the necessity of maintaining an ordered society and were therefore disturbed by the social and geographic mobility that they witnessed. How could a corrupt society repair itself and provide a socially stable environment in which its young could mature into morally sound adults? Reformers were quick to offer practical but simplistic solutions such as constantly reminding parents to closely supervise their children's activities and moral educations so as to avoid the risk of their coming under the corruptive influence of their more criminalistic peers or deviant adults. Taverns and houses of prostitution were considered breeding grounds for crime and action was taken to shut them down.

Campaigns designed to arouse public indignation over unhealthy social conditions or to remove all "immoral" establishments from the community were slow in evolving into workable programs. Many reformers of the day, however, believed that there was a more appropriate solution to the problem. They maintained that the offender should be separated from societal temptations and be retrained in a morally pure atmosphere. He should not be herded into a prison with other deviants where his future would be left to chance. He should be incarcerated in an institution where he would be provided with the Christian education and discipline that he did not have in his youth.[34]

THE PENITENTIARY MOVEMENT

Beginning in the 1820s, the new penal philosophy lead to a greater emphasis on institutional reform. Newly erected institutions and remodeled older ones were designed to rehabilitate the offender and they became a great source of pride to reformers who were confident that such a goal could be realized through their use. As Rothman indicates, "Rather than stand as places of last resort, hidden and ignored, these institutions became the pride of the nation. A structure designed to join practicality to humanitarianism, reform of the criminal, stabilize American society, and demonstrate how to improve the condition of mankind, deserved full publicity and close study."[35]

New York and Pennsylvania were in the forefront of the penitentiary movement and the differences between the types of institutions that were advocated by authorities in each of these states became a source of world-wide attention as well as intense and often bitter debate. Both systems were products of the "penitentiary movement" and were, therefore, philosophically and structurally similar. As the name indicates the penitentiary was an institution designed for the purpose of making men penitent. Authorities reasoned that if they were to accomplish such a goal, they would have to provide a setting in which the criminal could be encouraged to contemplate his sins and seek societal and divine forgiveness. To both Pennsylvania and New York officials, creating such an ideal atmosphere in which rehabilitation could take place, necessarily involved separating offenders from each other, thereby preventing any corrupting communication between them and keeping the contact between staff and inmates to a minimum.

Historians have credited American reformers with developing the penitentiary philosophy and making it operational. European visitors examined both Pennsylvania and New York institutions and took back plans to construct similar establishments, especially the Pennsylvania type, in their own countries. Despite this distinct American influence on European penology, the maintenance of separate confinement, which is basic to the penitentiary philosophy, can be traced back to European sources. John Howard maintained that when offenders were housed in close proximity to each other, physical as well as social contamination usually occurred. Traveling in Europe, Howard (who coined the word penitentiary) was impressed by several institutions that he visited, particularly the house of correction in Rome that was established by Pope Clement XI in 1704, and the "maison de force" at Ghent that was constructed in 1773. Both institutions segregated different types of offenders, required inmates to engage in productive labor, and confined each prisoner in his own private cell.[36]

On the basis of Howard's findings, Sir William Blackstone supported a bill that made possible the establishment of national penitentiaries in England. This bill became law in 1779. Blackstone's faith in the correctional potential of separate confinement was evident in his charge to a grand jury.

> Imagination cannot figure to itself a species of punishment in which terror, benevolence and reformation are more happily blended together. What can be more dreadful to the riotous, the libertine, the voluptuous, the idle delinquent, than solitude, confinement, sobriety and constant labour? Yet, what can be more truly beneficial? Solitude will awaken reflection; confinement will banish temptation; sobriety will restore vigour; and labour will beget a habit of honest industry: while the aid of a religious instructor may implant new prin-

ciples in his heart; and when the date of his punishment is expired will conduce to both his temporal and eternal welfare. Such a prospect as this is surely well worth the trouble of an experiment.[37]

Those who were active in the American penitentiary movement held views that were quite similar to the ones voiced by Blackstone, and Americans were undoubtedly influenced by such English reformers. They maintained that if an individual were to contemplate his sins, seek divine inspiration and forgiveness, and thus be able to re-construct his immoral life style, he would have to be isolated from his fellow criminals. It was assumed that by removing worldly temptations from the prisoner and maximizing the control over his activities he would be afforded the supposedly necessary regimentation and discipline that both the community and his parents had failed to provide for him in his youth. The failures of previous prisons were thought to be attributable to the practice of confining inmates in close proximity to each other and not providing them with adequate supervision.

To the early reformers the penitentiary could serve to accomplish more than the immediate goal of rehabilitating the individual offender. They were convinced that the well ordered and disciplined social environment that was to be found in such an institution would provide a model upon which the outside community could rebuild itself along traditional lines. The solution to the crime problem, as they saw it, involved the development and maintenance of a stable non-chaotic social structure. In the words of Rothman, "The penitentiary, by its example, by its discovery and verification of proper principles of social organization, would serve as a model for the entire society. Reformers fully anticipated that their work behind prison walls would have a critical significance beyond them. Since crime was symptomatic of a breakdown in traditional community practices, the penitentiary solution would point the way to a reconstitution of the social structure."[38]

The controversy concerning the superiority of one type of institutional system over another, particularly the architectural style, was of immense public concern. In the minds of many, the penitentiary represented the last hope for society to avoid being engulfed in corruption and chaos. Therefore, the debate between the supporters of the Pennsylvania system and the advocates of the New York system (more popularly referred to as the Auburn system) became extremely important to both the layman and the "expert."

The Pennsylvania System

Legislation in 1821 called for the erection of a penitentiary in Philadelphia. The institution, which was not completed until fourteen years later, was officially known as the Eastern State Penitentiary, but was more commonly referred to as the Cherry Hill Prison. Penologists as well as art critics praised the efforts of John Haviland, whose design and directing of the construction of the institution established him as one of the world's foremost architects.

Haviland, who was also under contract to design and build the Western Penitentiary in Pittsburgh, was influenced to some degree by previous architects and penologists. A section of the old Walnut Street Jail referred to as the "penitentiary house" served as a crude model for the much more elaborate Cherry Hill Prison. The "penitentiary house" was designed as an experimental program in which prisoners were confined to separate cells and required to engage in individual work projects.[39]

Three outstanding features characterized the Pennsylvania system:

1. *Prisoners were completely isolated from each other.* Housed in individual cells, each prisoner was unable to communicate with or even see other offenders. When a new prisoner was taken to his quarters, or when one was being moved within the institution, a hood was placed over his head so as to prevent the prisoners from seeing each other. The cells were

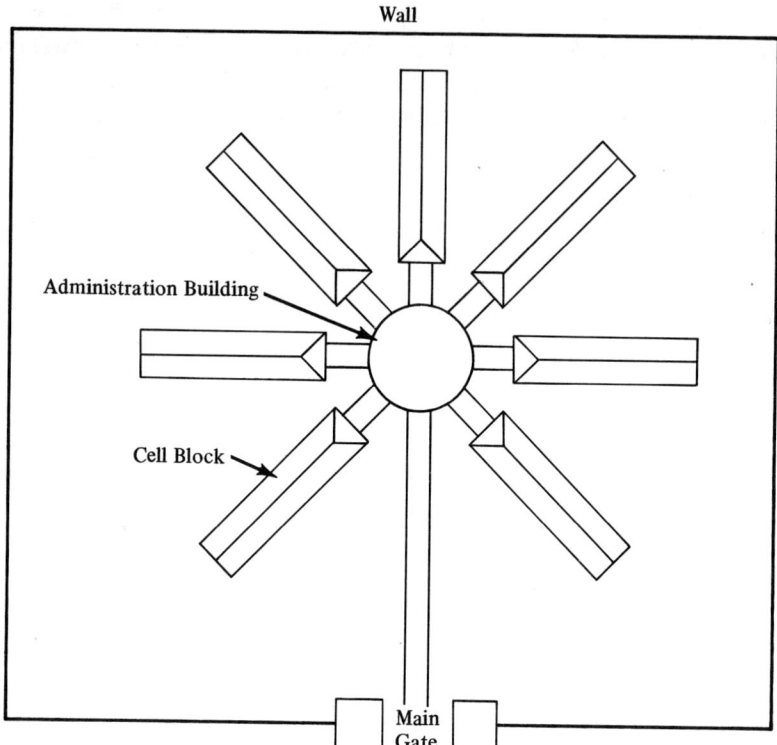

Figure 2.1 The Pennsylvania Plan

relatively large (8 by 15 feet) and had adjacent exercise yards in which they were sometimes allowed to walk about.[40]

2. *Prisoners engaged in solitary labor under the supervision of officials.* The first stage in the reform plan called for isolating the offender without access to reading materials, visitors, or the opportunity to engage in work activities. After he was left for a time to reflect on his own depravity, a work program consisting of individual projects such as shoe making or spinning and weaving was introduced. The Pennsylvania reformers were convinced that such labor would provide welcome

relief from the boredom that was assumed to be associated with the previous state of idleness. Therefore, while the prisoner was forced to comply with the work demands of officials, it was believed that he would regard such demands as being non-oppressive. In addition, the regimentation and discipline that he was subjected to would supposedly instill self discipline and healthy work habits in the offender. The desired result was to release a productive citizen.

3. *On a regular basis respected members of the community visited with and counseled prisoners.* Many of the Pennsylvania wardens, who were usually Quakers, along with some other prison officials, counseled prisoners and were genuinely interested in their welfare. However, it was perhaps the visitors from the outside who played the major role in the rehabilitation plan. In particular the Quakers who made up the Philadelphia Prison Society called upon incarcerated offenders regularly. While their advice to the prisoners consisted primarily of instruction on religion and morality, the devotion to and sympathy with the offenders that these "friendly visitors" evidenced will probably never be surpassed by any other group.

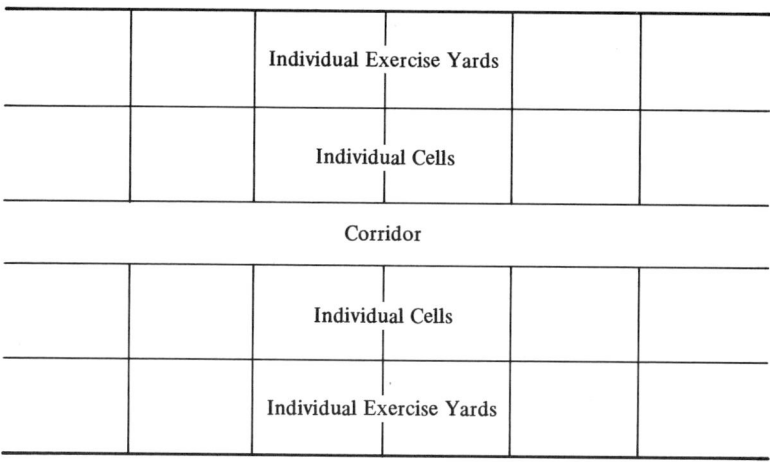

Figure 2.2 The Pennsylvania Type Cell Block

The Early Auburn Type Cell. After returning from the congregate workshop and dining hall, the prisoner was confined in a cell that measured 3½ by 7 feet.

The Auburn System

The Auburn type prison consisted principally of a large stone shell in which rows of back-to-back cells were built in tiers. The original cells were built of heavy stone and therefore the prisoners could not see or communicate with each other.[42]

The Auburn plan called for the housing of each prisoner in a solitary 3½ by 7 foot cell. Unlike the Pennsylvania system, the Auburn system allowed the prisoners to work and eat their meals together, but whether they were in the congregate work shops or in the dining hall, prisoners were still forbidden to communicate with each other in any way or even to glance in another's direction.

Auburn inmates were marched to and from work and meals in a "lock step" fashion. Barnes and Teeters describe the "lock step" as follows: "Each man placed one hand on the shoulder of the person in front of him and, with downcast eyes, or all facing the officer, and in strict silence, proceeded to shop or cell block. Conversation or even simulated communication between inmates was regarded as the most heinous of offenses."[43]

Regardless of his mental condition, the recalcitrant inmate in the Auburn type prison was either threatened with or received corporal punishment. Elan Lynds, the notorious warden of Au-

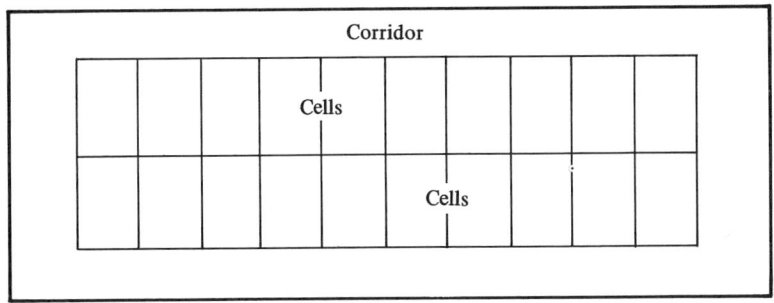

Figure 2.3 The Auburn Type Cell Block

The Lock Step. Inmates were marched to and from work and meals in this fashion.

burn, and later of Sing Sing Prison, regarded all offenders as cowards who could not be reformed unless their spirits were broken. Floggings, usually administered by Lynds himself, were common occurrences in such institutions.

THE COMPETITION BETWEEN SYSTEMS

While the Pennsylvania system had many critics, including Charles Dickens and the Reverend Louis Dwight, they were far outnumbered by those who praised it. After visiting the Cherry Hill Prison, the Swedish novelist Fredrika Bremer felt "more edified than on leaving a church." The well-known humanitarian and reformer, Dorthea Lynds Dix, exclaimed that "Pennsylvania has the high praise of establishing a model prison."[44] Perhaps surprisingly, testimony from both men and women inmates frequently confirmed the visitors' positive impressions of the institution.[45]

Defenders of the Pennsylvania system, led by spokesmen for the Philadelphia Society for Alleviating the Miseries of Public Prisons, were extremely vocal in their criticism of the Auburn model. They insisted that it was extremely difficult for the administrators of Auburn type prisons to prevent communication between prisoners. It was claimed that by requiring inmates to eat and work in such close proximity and by forcing them to observe strict rules against communicating with each other, the Auburn officials were tempting them unmercifully. Thus, the officials all too frequently had to resort to the use of the lash or other forms of severe corporal punishment in order to maintain control over those who could not resist such temptation.

Opponents of the Auburn system also claimed that Pennsylvania guards, unlike Auburn guards, would not have to be as highly trained or skilled because they were not required to supervise dining halls and congregate workshops, but only had to look after the prisoners' needs while they were confined in their individual cells. Other claims in favor of the Pennsylvania system were that there would be little need for corporal punishment because there would be no opportunity for inmates to violate communication rules, and collaboration on escape plans or other security problems would be non-existent.

Reverend Louis Dwight and the Boston Prison Discipline Society lead the attack against the Pennsylvania system. Some criticism revolved around the belief that the actual administration of the Cherry Hill Prison did not coincide with the original plan. For example, it was asserted that the walls of the institution were not thick enough to prevent communication and the prisoners could also signal each other by striking the sewer pipes.[46]

These were minor criticisms, however, and the Auburn advocates focused their attack on the following three issues:

1. *The Pennsylvania type of prison was thought to be both excessively expensive to build and to operate.* Pennsylvania prisons may very well have been more expensive to construct and administer than were Auburn type institutions. It is possible that the attention that was paid to the individual needs of prisoners in the Pennsylvania system created additional expenses. However, such allegations were never proven.

Auburn Type Cell Blocks. These interior cell blocks were constructed prior to the Civil War.

Nevertheless, the claims made by Auburn supporters that their system was less expensive to build and to operate brought many taxpayers into their camp.

2. *Within the congregate workshops of Auburn styled institutions, inmates could use power machinery and could therefore manufacture more and better goods than could the prisoners working in their individual cells at Cherry Hill.* The Auburn type of prison represented an attractive source of cheap labor, and therefore many industrialists made contracts with prison officials enabling them to establish factories within the walls of the institutions. Such arrangements proved to be economically beneficial to both the industrialists and the officials.[47] Of course, the profits that accrued from inmate labor reduced the operational costs of the prisons and made the Auburn system all the more attractive to the taxpaying public.

3. *Critics also maintained that the Pennsylvania type of solitary confinement caused many prisoners to become insane.* This was the first major criticism that was unrelated to the alleged economic superiority of the Auburn system. Some attempts were made to compare the mental health of Auburn prisoners with that of the Cherry Hill prisoners. The results of such studies were generally meaningless, since both sides in the controversy persisted in offering subjective judgments as factual information.[48] It should also be noted that because so little was known about mental illness during the middle of the 19th century, the diagnoses of insanity by the experts of the day were not necessarily reliable by today's standards.[49] However, because such criticism appeared to be logical, at least on the surface, many more citizens were persuaded that the Auburn system was the superior one.

The Pennsylvania plan became the model for a number of penal institutions in other countries, and therefore was regarded as being an international success. However, primarily because of economic considerations, it was not received as enthusiastically in most of the states. Maine, Maryland, Massachusetts, and New Jersey all experimented with Cherry Hill type facilities for a time, but soon abandoned them in favor of the Auburn plan.[50]

Remnants of the Pennsylvania system survived in its home state until 1913. However, the practice of separate confinement, which was basic to the Pennsylvania philosophy, was discontinued by the 1860s. As the prison population increased, officials, who were perhaps disheartened by the realization that the system had not developed into what its original advocates had hoped, terminated separate confinement by refusing to build the new cell blocks that would be necessary if such a practice were to continue. The system's longevity in Pennsylvania was probably a result of the insistence by Quakers that reformation should be the primary goal of penitentiary programs and that economic considerations should be secondary.[51]

SUMMARY

While America did not inherit some of the more brutal legal punishments that were employed in England during the 17th century, many colonial statutes and methods of punishment had distinct English origins. Our methods of capital and corporal punishment and institutionalization were patterned after those that were developed in England. The death penalty was used for the dangerous felon as well as the habitual petty offender. Because the latter was believed to be under the control of the devil, all efforts to reform him were thought to be futile. Lesser, non-habitual criminals were usually corporally punished and subjected to various forms of public humiliation.

Because they assumed that they were serving as God's "stewards," most of the early colonists were quite charitable to the deserving poor, as long as they did not attempt to rise above "their place" within the social order. Respectable citizens, however, felt no obligation to assist wandering vagabonds or rogues or even needy outsiders.

With the exception of a ten year period in which "Penn's Great Law" was in effect in two colonies, the colonists did not use imprisonment as a means of punishment or correction. While institutions may have provided a satisfactory type of intermediate punishment, they were not used, primarily, because most of the existing institutions failed to serve as appropriate models. They were not designed to house criminals, but to provide food and shelter for the deserving poor. In the minds of the colonists, confining criminals to such institutions would be tantamount to rewarding them. In addition it was believed that institutionalization would have no positive effect on those who were possessed by the devil.

Changing social and political conditions and the emergence of the Enlightenment philosophy eventually made colonial methods of punishment and correction obsolete. In an increasingly urbanized and industrialized society, such methods, which relied extensively on the deterrent effects of public humiliation, could no longer protect communities from a more mobile class of criminals. Also the development of a greater allegiance to larger political units created a concern for the safety, not only of the local community, but also of citizens of the state and nation as well. Cesare Beccaria and other Enlightenment thinkers advocated exact but humane laws and protested against the brutal punishments of the day. The colonists, being aware of the ineffectiveness of the old methods, were receptive to these new ideas.

Reformers such as John Howard did much to convince the public that prisons, if they were humanely administered, could provide the needed intermediate type of punitive measure. By 1800 numerous state prisons were established. In accordance with the Enlightenment philosophy, however, legislators were primarily concerned with matching the appropriate punishments to the various crimes, and were not concerned enough about developing superior methods of prison administration and treatment.

Again the public became disillusioned with ineffective methods of coping with the crime problem. New reformers began to focus their attention on what they discerned to be the causative factors of crime. A new picture of the offender emerged. He was viewed by the experts of the day as a victim of circumstances, who was improperly socialized and unprotected from worldly temptations by the family or the community. While the Enlightenment thinkers attached prime importance to the development of proper legal standards, the new reformers switched their attention to the individual criminal. Coupled with this concern for the individual was the desire, on the part of the new reformers, to establish a more ordered society reminiscent of non-chaotic colonial times. The new experts concluded, therefore, that the offender should be separated from the society that corrupted him and re-socialized in a morally pure environment.

During the first half of the 19th century the rivalry between the Pennsylvania and the Auburn penitentiary systems attracted world-wide attention. While both systems were based on a philosophy of separate confinement, the advocates of each maintained that their system came closer to creating the ordered environment that would reform the criminal and provide a model upon which the outside community could re-structure itself.

ENDNOTES

1. Christopher Hibbert, *The Roots of Evil: A Social History of Crime and Punishment* (Minerva Press, 1963), p. 24.
2. For a detailed analysis of these laws see Robert G. Caldwell, *Criminology* (New York: The Ronald Press Co., 1965) pp. 500–2; Harry Elmer Barnes and Negley K. Teeters, *New Horizons in Criminology* (Englewood Cliffs, N.J.: Prentice-Hall, Inc., 1959) pp. 325–27.
3. Ibid., p. 32.
4. David J. Rothman, *The Discovery of the Asylum: Social Order and Disorder in the New Republic* (Boston: Little, Brown and Co., 1971) p. 49.
5. Hibbert, *The Roots of Evil* p. 28.
6. Ibid., also see Caldwell, *Criminology* p. 450.
7. Ibid., p. 449.
8. Hibbert, *The Roots of Evil* pp. 32–36.
9. Staff Report on the Joint Commission on Correctional Manpower and Training, *Perspectives on Correctional Manpower and Training* (Washington, D.C.: 1970) p. 10.
10. Caldwell, *Criminology* p. 493.
11. Rothman, *The Discovery of the Asylum* pp. 7–8.
12. Ibid.
13. Ibid., pp. 11–12. For an excellent analysis of the historical development of the Elizabethan Pan Laws see Karl de Schweinitz,

England's Road to Social Security (New York: A. S. Barnes and Co., 1961).
14. Rothman, *The Discovery of the Asylum* pp. 12–14.
15. Ibid., p. 25.
16. Ibid., pp. 48–51.
17. Rothman, *The Discovery of the Asylum* pp. 51–53.
18. Ibid., p. 13.
19. Ibid., pp. 14–16.
20. Blake McKelvey, *American Prisons: A Study in American Social History Prior to 1915* (Montclair, N.J.: Paterson Smith Publishing Co., reprinted 1968) p. 3.
21. Barnes and Teeters, *New Horizons in Criminology* pp. 325–27.
22. Rothman, *The Discovery of the Asylum* pp. 30–78.
23. Ibid.
24. Ibid., pp. 57–58.
25. Ibid., pp. 59–61. See Henry Paolucci's translation of *On Crime and Punishments* (Indianapolis: The Bobbs-Merrill Co. Inc., 1963) and Hermann Mannheim, ed., *Pioneers in Criminology* (Chicago: Quadrangle Books, Inc., 1960) pp. 36–50.
26. See D. L. Howard, *John Howard: Prison Reformer* (London: Christopher Johnson, Pub., 1958).
27. Rothman, *The Discovery of the Asylum* pp. 7–8.
28. McKelvey, *American Prisons* pp. 7–8.
29. Rothman, *The Discovery of the Asylum* pp. 61–62.
30. Thorsten Sellin, "The Origin of the 'Pennsylvania System of Prison Discipline,' " *The Prison Journal* Vol. L, No. 1, Spring–Summer, 1970, p. 13.
31. McKelvey, *American Prisons* pp. 6–7.
32. Rothman, *The Discovery of the Asylum* pp. 61–62.
33. Ibid., pp. 72–73.
34. Ibid., p. 71.
35. Ibid., p. 79.
36. McKelvey, *American Prisons* p. 4.
37. Blackstone's charge to a grand jury was quoted in *The Prison Journal* Vol. L, pp. 18–19.
38. Rothman, *The Discovery of the Asylum* p. 84.
39. *The Prison Journal* Vol. L, p. 14.
40. McKelvey, *American Prisons* p. 8.
41. Rothman, *The Discovery of the Asylum* p. 86.
42. Fred E. Haynes, *The American Prison System* (New York: McGraw-Hill Co., 1939) pp. 29–30.

43. Barnes and Teeters, *New Horizons in Criminology* pp. 325–27.
44. Negley K. Teeters, "The Passing of Cherry Hill: Most Famous Prison in the World," *The Prison Journal* Vol. L, Spring–Summer, 1970, p. 8.
45. For a remarkable account of a woman prisoner who credited the institution, her keepers, and her friendly visitor for her salvation, see "An Account of Julia Moore, a Penitent Female, Who Died In the Eastern Penitentiary of Pennsylvania, in the Year 1843," *The Prison Journal* Vol. L, No. 1, Spring–Summer, 1970, pp. 33–41.
46. Rothman, *The Discovery of the Asylum* pp. 87–88.
47. McKelvey, *American Prisons* p. 13.
49. Barnes and Teeters, *New Horizons in Criminology* pp. 343–44.
50. Ibid.
51. *The Prison Journal* Vol. L, p. 10.

# 3

The Development of Modern Corrections

Correctional practices did not develop evenly; some 19th century attempts at rehabilitating offenders had closer philosophical and organizational relationships to the current programs that are considered innovative than they do to the correctional practices of the 1930s. When were the philosophical foundations and techniques of "progressive" modern corrections first established? While there is no specific answer to such a question, several pre-Civil War reformers should be recognized for their contributions to modern corrections. An examination of the ideas and activities of the 19th century pioneers will help to form an understanding of modern probation, parole, and institutional treatment services.

CAPTAIN ALEXANDER MACONOCHIE

Several outstanding correctional experiments that were conducted outside of the United States during the first half of the 19th century had a great impact on American penology. The innovative programs that were established by Captain Alexander Maconochie and Sir Walter Crofton never received the recognition they deserved, however.[1] The contributions made by these two men, and their insights and services to humanity were not realized until long after their programs had been initiated.

From 1837 to 1860 Maconochie, while under constant criticism by governmental officials and others, dedicated himself to reforming the English penal system. At the age of 49, with distinguished naval and academic careers behind him, he happened to have the opportunity to observe the brutal methods of control and punishment used by officials to control felons in their custody in an English penal colony in Tasmania. Maconochie was so appalled by what he saw that he began to devote most of his time to publicizing these injustices. In 1839, as a reward for his advocacy of penal reform, Maconochie was appointed superintendent of the previously mismanaged penal colony on Norfolk Island. This was the island to which the presumably incorrigible offenders were sent and were subjected to the most cruel and inhumane treatment.

It was on Norfolk Island that Maconochie devised a program that was the forerunner of modern behavioral modification programs. Under his "mark" system, instead of serving "time sentences," prisoners were required to earn a certain number of marks. Depending upon the seriousness of their offenses, they had to earn marks in order to obtain various privileges and eventually their freedom. Marks were earned and retained by maintaining a good behavior record and by being industrious. Likewise the prisoners' access to decent food, clothing, housing, and other privileges was dependent upon their conduct and productivity.

Prisoners were required to progress through several stages before they were eligible for release. In the initial stage, or the "penal" stage, the offender was placed under close supervision and put to hard labor. If he performed satisfactorily and was not a disciplinary problem, he was then allowed to enter the second, or "social" stage. In the social stage, inmates lived and worked in groups of six. The inmates were rewarded and punished as a group; marks were taken away from the whole group if individuals misbehaved or otherwise failed to live up to expectations. In the final "individualized" stage, the group was disbanded and individuals were permitted to maintain their own living quarters, gardens, and livestock.

The available statistics indicate that Maconochie was quite successful in rehabilitating offenders by the use of these methods. However, it is more important to emphasize that he, for a time, humanized at least one segment of a brutalizing and decadent system, and in doing so laid the ground work upon which future reformers built their progressive programs. When he arrived on Norfolk Island, Maconochie was confronted with "a turbulent, brutal hell, and left it a peaceful, well-ordered community."[2]

Like many reformers before and after him, Maconochie's innovative ideas and practices were too revolutionary for most of his contemporaries. His kindness and respect for all human beings were regarded by many as weaknesses, and because he allegedly coddled criminals he was dismissed not only from his position at Norfolk Island, but also later from a similar position as the Governor of Birmingham Borough Prison. The great reformer did, however, continue to be a leading advocate of enlightened penology until his death in 1860.

The Philosophical and Practical Significance of Maconochie's Contributions

In order to fully appreciate the relevance of Maconochie's contributions to modern corrections, we must first develop a basic understanding of the penal philosophies that were accepted by his contemporaries. Societal protection was to be accomplished through the pursuit of the two traditional objectives of penal confinement: retribution and deterrence. Retribution, which is closely akin to revenge, is when pain (psychological or physical) is inflicted upon an individual because he is thought to deserve it in return for the harm that he caused another. To many, a society is justified in punishing its wrongdoers without offering any additional rationalization or explanation. Others, however, defend retribution for more practical reasons. One of the most common defenses involves the contention that a government must punish law violators, sometimes harshly, because if it fails to do so, irate citizens will take it upon themselves to seek retribution by inflicting punishments which are even more brutal than those which are legally administered. Thus, to avoid the societal chaos that would be created by vigilante groups and enraged friends and relatives of the victims of crime, some contend that the citizens' need for their "ounce of blood" must be acknowledged and carried out in an orderly and perhaps more humane way.

Deterrence was, and probably still is, a second major objective of penal confinement. Individual deterrence is accomplished when the offender, after being punished, refrains from engaging in further criminal activity because he fears being punished and wants to avoid being punished again. General deterrence is accomplished through using the punished offender as an example to others of what might happen to them if they commit criminal acts similar to those committed by the offender. For example, it is a commonly accepted belief that when a criminal is sent to prison, many noncriminals will remain law-abiding only because they do not want to be subjected to similar punishment.

Maconochie's historical importance can be attributed primarily to his enlightened advocacy of rehabilitation as a third objective of penal incarceration. While Maconochie was not the first to champion this objective, his rehabilitation philosophy became the basis for nearly all of the progressive reforms that were developed by those who came after him. Maconochie's primary goal was the restructuring of human lives, not through the fear of punishment, but by teaching responsibility, industriousness, and most importantly self-respect. Today the rehabilitation objective is the principal concern of many reformers and correctional authorities. However, viewed in their proper historical context, Maconochie's ideas and programs were, indeed, revolutionary, and the revolution that he initiated was eventually to result in the general acceptance of rehabilitation as an important objective of prisons.

Captain Maconochie's practical proposals for penal reform were very much ahead of his time. He suggested many innovations, such as the segregation of offenders in accordance with the seriousness of their crimes, the decreased use of fortress-like prisons, and even conjugal visiting, which still are not universally accepted today. However, it was his actual rehabilitation techniques that had the most significant effect on future reforms. Most of the individuals, organizations, and movements that are discussed in this chapter (including Sir Walter Crofton, Zebulon Brockway, The New York Prison Association, The First Prison Congress of 1870, and the Reformatory Movement) reflect Maconochie's belief in the necessity of training prisoners to re-enter free society through the progressive rewarding of good behavior and industriousness. Writing in 1960, Maconochie's foremost biographer asserted that "the principles established by Maconochie now flourish vigorously in the Borstal system in England and the California Institution for Men at Chino and the Federal Institution at Seagoville, Texas, and in all penal institutions which apply the concepts of modern penology."

While some legislation, programs, and policies (such as indeterminate sentence legislation) which were patterned to some degree after Maconochie's innovations will be severely criticized in this text, penology and/or corrections has never known a more insightful or progressive pioneer.

SIR WALTER CROFTON

Sir Walter Crofton, Chairman of the Board of Directors of the Irish Prisons, was probably the best known of all of the penal administrators who were directly influenced by Maconochie. Crofton also initiated many progressive programs that would serve as models for later reformers. He developed a system of positive reinforcements in which a prisoner, as he became increasingly industrious and socially conscious, could progress through a stage of regimented confinement, to the relative freedom of an intermediate prison, to a period of official supervision in the community under what was known as a "ticket of leave," and finally to complete freedom. It is easy to understand why Sir Walter Crofton is acclaimed by many to be the father of modern parole. As will become evident in chapter nine, there are many different and sometimes conflicting definitions and conceptions of parole.

Parole, however, can be generally defined here as a trial period during which the offender (whose sentence has not expired) is allowed to reside in the free world while under the supervision and control of correctional officials. The third stage of the Crofton system or, as it is better known, Irish system was the first parole type arrangement to gain wide recognition.

THEORETICAL ADVANCEMENTS IN THE PRE-CIVIL WAR PERIOD

At least in theory, if not in practice, some Americans were attempting to make significant advancements in penology during the pre-Civil War period. Edward Livingston, for example, proposed a well planned correctional system for the state of Louisiana. His blueprint for reform called for the establishment of reform schools for juveniles, specialized treatment programs for minor offenders, and the constructing of two different grades of prisons. As a reward for good behavior the offender would be able to progress from an initial stage of solitary confinement into subsequent stages in which his living conditions would become increasingly more comfortable.

The total rejection of Livingston's proposal perhaps typified the times. During the pre-Civil War period, significant philosophical and theoretical advancements were made in penology, but the majority of those who advocated progressive reforms did not have the societal or political support that would be required if their plans were to be implemented.

The New York Prison Association, established in 1844, became the leading voice of reform during this period. In addition to championing the superiority of reformation over retribution, spokesmen for the Association advocated a graded correctional system that was similar to the one proposed by Edward Livingston. The prisoner, according to these early reformers, should be given the opportunity to associate with a select group of his prisonmates only after he had endured a trial period of separate confinement.

The Quakers, as always, were leading proponents of progressive penal administration. When Friend Isaac Hopper "was appointed special agent to help prisoners find jobs and homes at the time of their release," he not only became a forerunner of the modern parole agent, but he also became one of the few, at that time, to succeed in putting some sound correctional theory into practice.[3]

PRACTICAL CONCERNS

While visionaries proposed humanitarian reforms, most prison administrators were more concerned about the development of prison industries. First established in 1825, the lease system rapidly gained in popularity. Under the lease system, private contractors paid the various states for the use of convict labor. Thus, outside industrialists were provided with a source of cheap labor and in return the expense to the states of administering the prisons was reduced considerably.[4]

Southern and Western penal officials, during the first half of the 19th century, were even less likely than their counterparts in other sections of the country to be influenced by the theoretical and humanitarian concerns that were so important to the Eastern reformers. Their thoughts were more often occupied with the hardships of Southern and Western life and everyday practical affairs. Therefore, they were usually anxious to cooperate with private industry in hopes that their institutions could become self-supporting.

As is the case today, local jails were designed to house less serious offenders or misdemeanants. Also, as is the case today, jails were often administered by corrupt officials and were characteristically in deplorable condition. The fate of some misdemeanants was made more bearable by the establishment, especially in the East, of a number of separately administered and more progressive local penitentiaries and/or houses of correction.

Such institutions, however, were not widespread until after the Civil War.

SOME EVIDENCE OF PROGRESS

By the 1850s little progressive change had taken place and American penal administrators still seemed oblivious to the contributions of Crofton and other European innovators. In all but a very few prisons, such as the Cherry Hill institution, the focal concerns of the administrators were the maintenance of industry and the lease system. By the advent of the Civil War the majority of the states were employing a somewhat distorted type of the Auburn system. While the practice of separate and silent confinement was for the most part discontinued, the majority of the prisons were still architecturally patterned on the Auburn plan. Unfortunately such institutions were neither designed nor administered in a manner that was conducive to the advancement of penology. The states tended to ignore the lessons of history, and once again they herded various types of inmates together, where they were often morally corrupted and psychologically and physically harmed by each other.

While progress was meager and in some instances retrogressive during the first half of the 19th century, the following improvements did occur and should be recognized for their significance:

1. *The public became increasingly aware of the need to upgrade welfare and correctional services for children.* Beginning in the 1820s, the recognition of this need resulted in the development of numerous state and local reform schools for young offenders. The administrators of these schools, which were commonly referred to as Sabbath schools, placed a great deal of emphasis on education, constructive employment, and reformation. Reformation, however, was primarily thought of in terms of religious conversion and enlightenment. While the

public should be credited for recognizing the need to develop special programs for children, the institutional administrators of the day created a regimented and, by today's standards, harsh atmosphere that was hardly conducive to accomplishing positive change in the young offender. During this period in history several European countries had developed juvenile institutional programs that were superior to ours, both in terms of their rehabilitation efforts and the physical construction of their facilities. Their programs were primarily based on a system that closely resembled our modern "cottage plan" in which considerable effort is made to respect the youngster's privacy and to allow him to reside in relative comfort.

2. *The welfare of the ex-prisoner and his adjustment to the free community became the concerns of a number of progressive individuals and organizations.* Along with adopting the practice of "commuting sentences for good behavior," many states during this time period provided the new releasee from prison with a small amount of cash and other necessities. Private organizations such as the New York Prison Association and the Prisoners' Friend Association of Boston also began to devote a great deal of effort to assisting the released offender.[5]

Parole, as it is strictly defined, did not come into formal existence until after the Civil War. However, many prior innovations certainly furthered its development. As early as 1817, New York state passed a commutation or "good time" law which authorized prison wardens to release exemplary inmates before the expiration of their sentences, but neither New York nor any of the other states that enacted similar legislation during this period provided for the supervision of the offender in the community by a correctional official or state agent.[6]

3. *Probation services were formally established.* A Boston industrialist by the name of John Augustus is said to be the "father of probation." It can be rather convincingly argued that Matthew Davenport Hill, who was initiating probation-like services in England at almost exactly the same time, was equally deserving of such recognition. Nevertheless, there can be little doubt that John Augustus' contributions to humanity and the development of modern corrections were of great significance.

In 1841 he secured bail for a drunkard and convinced the presiding judge that the offender should have his sentence suspended and be placed under Augustus' supervision. One of the foremost authorities on probation and parole defined probation as "a treatment program in which final action in an adjudicated offender's case is suspended, so that he remains at liberty, subject to conditions imposed by or for a court, under the supervision and guidance of a probation worker."[7] The action taken by John Augustus in 1841 came close to creating a probation service that included all of the elements that are present in this modern definition of probation. The only major consideration that differentiates the role that was played by Augustus from that of today's probation officer was the fact that he was not an officially designated agent of the court.

John Augustus continued his volunteer service to the courts and by the time of his death in 1859 he had served as an unofficial probation officer for thousands of unfortunates. The first state law authorizing the use of a paid probation officer to serve the courts was not enacted, however, until 1878 in Massachusetts.[8]

THE FIRST NATIONAL PRISON CONGRESS

The end of the Civil War brought many new reform movements and, likewise, created a social and political environment that was conducive to a renewed interest in the implementation of a number of pre-war theoretical solutions to social problems. Citizens, no longer preoccupied with the hostilities between the states, could now afford the luxury of listening to and, at least occasionally, lending their support to the growing number of zealous reformers who were proclaiming the necessity of providing more enlightened educational, social work, and mental health services. Several of these dynamic reformers joined with interested laymen and prison administrators in efforts to improve existing penal conditions.

What Joseph W. Eaton referred to as the "pivotal event in the history of correctional reform" took place in Cincinnati in 1870. It was in Cincinnati that numerous reformers and penal administrators gathered from all sections of the United States and Canada to discuss common problems and to plan a cooperative, concerted effort to scientifically and humanely improve correctional services. This first "prison congress," under the leadership of the then Secretary of the Prison Association of New York, Enoch Cobb Wines, produced two major contributions. The delegates to the congress founded the National Prison Association and also set forth a "Declaration of Principles" that was intended to guide all future reform efforts.[9]

The principles called for the implementation of many now familiar "solutions" to the crime problem such as treatment programs as opposed to punitive incarceration, probation-type services, a positive reward or incentive system for inmates, and the professional upgrading of prison staffs. While the formulation of the Principles did represent correctional progress, as the years passed more and more observers began to regard them as only superficial remedies to an enormously complex social problem. Such growing skepticism was to be expected, for it eventually became obvious that most of the lofty ideals that were represented in the Principles did not profoundly affect the actual administration of penal facilities and programs. The 1870 Principles were reaffirmed by the National Prison Association in 1930, again in 1950, and once again in 1960 (after the organization changed its name to the American Correctional Association) with only a few alterations made in the original document. The picture should be quite clear. Since 1870 reformers have been professing to know how to best rehabilitate the offender and otherwise improve the correctional system, but few of the suggested reforms were ever satisfactorily implemented and, indicating our *lack* of progress, the reformers of the 1970s are emphasizing the need for many of the same correctional improvements that were regarded as being necessary in 1870.[10]

When one considers the backwardness of the correctional programs of the day, it does seem astonishing that Wines and his associates could persuade many of the delegates who were traditional penal administrators to agree to such far-reaching reforms. Even more surprising, a few such delegates actually attempted to put some of their newly learned theories into action. In explaining why most of the delegates supported the proposed reforms, Eaton indicates that the "punitively oriented prison administrators had no equally effective spokesmen" as Wines, and the social climate within the country was ripe for change. He continues:

> The correctional movement emerged in an era when humanist sentiment and an interest in a scientific approach to man were in ascendancy. The idea that man could plan his own future shaped human endeavors in education, in public welfare and child care, in work with the mentally ill and the mentally retarded, in movements affecting working conditions, and in governmental affairs.[11]

We have already noted that the participants in the 1870 congress did not succeed in bringing about the anticipated massive change in the penal system. However, it is important to understand that some of these individuals, encouraged by an era that was characterized by a faith in social engineering, did produce legislation and programs that changed the future of corrections.

The Indeterminate Sentence

The delegates to the prison congress of 1870 believed, as evidenced in the Declaration of Principles, that rehabilitation could be achieved more readily if prison officials were allowed to treat offenders within the framework of the indeterminate sentence. They, like many of today's reformers, were firmly convinced that the courts should not sentence criminals to serve fixed amounts of time in correctional institutions. Instead, they believed that experts, correctional administrators, after having studied and treated the offender, should determine if he has been rehabilitated and when he should be returned to free society.

Most so-called indeterminate sentence legislation, past and present, has required some minimum and maximum limits on how long the offender can be deprived of his freedom, usually depending on the type of crime that was committed. While a completely indeterminate sentence has been a rarity in America, various states have experimented, since the late 1900s, with allowing correctional officials a great deal of discretion in determining how long an offender should remain under their control.[12] Allowing such discretion appears, on the surface, to be quite logical and humane. Correctional officials and not judges are usually more familiar with the offender's psychological condition and his progress towards being rehabilitated. Therefore, according to some, the correctional officials should be the ones to decide when the individual should be released. However, history has shown that correctional officials—whether they be psychiatrists, psychologists, social workers, or officers who came up through the ranks—like individuals in any other field of endeavor, have not always been wise or humane. To run the risk of taking an individual out of the public eye and placing him under the almost complete control of correctional officials would be to subject the prisoner to the prejudices of the individual official. Others, protected by indeterminate sentence legislation, might be tempted to unjustifiably keep certain inmates who they simply do not like or with whom they have political differences in prison for excessive lengths of time. Conversely some misguided officials might release an offender who still represents an extreme danger to the community. Having had limited opportunity to learn from the mistakes of others, the 1870 reformers who advocated completely indeterminate sentences can be forgiven. Modern reformers who continue to extoll the imagined virtues of such legislation have no such excuse.

The Elmira Experiment

One of the most influential of the delegates to the 1870 congress and a leading proponent of both the indeterminate sentence and parole was a penal administrator from Detroit by the name of Zebulon R. Brockway. In 1876 Brockway was appointed as the first superintendent of the Elmira Reformatory in New York. He developed a program that was to serve as a model for reformatories soon to be built in twelve other states, and for the Borstal system, the English method of reforming younger offenders.[13]

While the physical structure of the Elmira Reformatory was

of the Auburn type, the institutional program was specifically designed for first offenders, ages 16 to 30, who presumably needed to be segregated from hardened adult criminals. These less serious offenders, usually younger criminals, were to be provided with the academic, vocational, and religious training that would enable them to lead normal law-abiding lives when released.

Firm but fair discipline, mandatory participation in military drills, and an emphasis on proper dress characterized life at Elmira. The institution became best known, however, for its mark system, which was directly influenced by the Irish System. It was also recognized for the introduction of a relatively sophisticated parole program. Each new inmate was placed in grade two and accordingly received two marks which were represented by stripes on his uniform. After being in the institution for at least six months, if he had been industrious, cooperative, and had progressed satisfactorily in his trade training, he was promoted to grade one. If he misbehaved or otherwise failed to live up to his obligations, he was demoted to grade three and could not be reestablished in grade two until he completed another month of satisfactory behavior. After completing six months in grade one, the prisoner could become eligible for parole. For the first time in the history of the United States, institutional officials were authorized to maintain control and supervision over an offender for at least six months after his release.[14]

New York state also pioneered the development of reformatory type programs for women offenders. By 1893 New York had initiated the indeterminate sentence, the mark system, and vocational and academic training in two of their facilities for women. The women had the added advantage of residing in cottages rather than in Auburn type cell blocks as their male counterparts did. While the first institution that was designed exclusively for women was established in Indiana in 1873 and the Massachusetts Reformatory Prison for Women was opened in 1877, New York was the first state to actively follow the Elmira example and provide female inmates with more than custodial services.[15]

Because research evidence has been so contradictory, it is next to impossible to determine the effectiveness of the reformatory methods. Whether statistically successful or not, however, the reformatory movement had declined in popularity by 1900 and by 1910 it remained in name only. Elmira became overpopulated and some critics protested the lenient treatment inmates received when under Brockway's care. Others were unjustifiably accusing him of being cruelly abusive to his prisoners. In 1900 he resigned his position and, like most of the other reformatory superintendents of the time, was succeeded by less capable administrators.[16]

Robert G. Caldwell attributes the failure of the reformatory movement primarily to an over emphasis on "custody and security, which stifled all ingenuity and enterprise and dominated the construction and operation of the great majority of reformatories." He continues:

> Elmira itself was established in a structure that originally had been built as a maximum security prison for hardened adult criminals. Inadequate appropriations, incompetent personnel, politics, overcrowding, and repressive discipline helped to complete the picture of bitter disillusionment and failure. The reformatories soon became junior prisons in which education and trade training were largely nominal and the grading system degenerated into a mechanical routine.[17]

PROGRESS IN THE EARLY 20TH CENTURY

With the decline of the reformatory movement, there was also a tremendous increase in the population of prisons and a growing emphasis on prison industries which proved to be formidable obstacles to reform in the early 20th century. These and other factors led to the deterioration of correctional programs during this period.

By 1910 the federal government had established its own correctional facilities in Fort Leavenworth, Kansas and Atlanta,

Georgia and a small jail on Puget Sound.[18] A rather crude federal parole system was also established in 1910. It should be noted here that, while the creation of federal parole was in itself a progressive step, the system was poorly administered and generally ineffectual. While the federal government did not, as in the past, have to rely on the states to take care of federal criminals, it was not yet in a position of leadership whereby it could provide the country with much direction in correctional reform. Some of the individual states and a number of private philanthropic organizations were, however, becoming quite imaginative in their attempts to further the implementation of correctional services.

There was, during this time period, considerable emphasis being placed on coordinating correctional activities and on developing relatively sophisticated state-wide systems. Numerous centralized organizations, the majority of which were referred to as state boards of charities, were being designated as the controlling heads of state prison systems. While some of these agencies were controlled by political partisanship, they usually functioned effectively as the administrators of state prison systems. If one were to study all of these state agencies, he would probably discover ample evidence of inefficiency and incompetence in every one. Nevertheless, they did represent a beginning attempt to avoid duplication of services and to make prison officials accountable for their actions.[19]

The most impressive of the specialized institutions in operation in the early years of the 20th century were some designed for the female offender. Two of the most accomplished correctional leaders of the day were Dr. Katherine B. Davis and Mrs. Jessie D. Hodder. Dr. Davis was the superintendent of New York's reformatory for women at Bedford Hills, and Mrs. Hodder was the first of several extraordinary women who became the administrative head of the Massachusetts Reformatory for Women at Sherborn (now Framingham). They continued to attempt to carry out the reformatory ideals and methods and, at the same time, adapt their programs to the changing culture.[20]

Located mostly in the North and in the Mid-West, private prisoner aid societies were dedicated to improving the welfare of prisoners and to assisting ex-convicts in adjusting to the free community. Some organizations, such as the Brighter Day Leagues, provided friendly visitor services for the prisons, while others attempted to make food, shelter, and employment available to ex-offenders. However, as Blake McKelvey indicates, "One survey listed thirty-nine aid societies active in 1911, but they hardly scratched the surface of the problem, and their services did not begin to compare with the more efficient work in this field in several European countries."[21]

THE PREDOMINANCE OF CONVICT LABOR PROGRAMS

While a significant amount of progressive legislation was operative at the turn of the century, it was not always put to good use. For example, many judges regarded the use of indeterminate sentences as being a threat to their power, and therefore, they failed to make use of the laws that authorized them to employ such practices. Also, because of similar judicial interference, under-staffing, and poor selection procedures, parole was far from being effective or widely used.[22] A pronounced lack of adequate financial appropriations and consequent staff shortages at least partially accounted for the growing neglect of treatment and vocational training programs in the over-crowded institutions. Reformatories were still in operation but there was little to differentiate most of them from adult prisons. As Caldwell observes, "almost every prison during this period was custodial, punitive, and industrial."[23]

For the first 35 years of the 20th century most penal administrators, attempting to make their institutions economically self-sufficient and to keep the increasing mass of convicts occupied, concentrated on developing and maintaining prison industries and convict labor. Laws and policies which determined what types of manufactured goods could be produced by convict labor and to whom they could be sold were not uniform throughout the states. However, even as early as 1900, nearly half of the states had adopted the "state-use system." States, under this system, were prohibited from selling goods that were manufactured by convicts on the open market. Because of the limited number of outlets for prison-made goods, such as public schools and other state owned institutions, administrators were not allowed to manufacture as much as they would have liked to. Consequently, there were not enough jobs for all of the country's inmates and most of them were idle. Eventually, as a result of the influence of competition-fearing industries and unions and some concern about the exploitation of convicts, the state-use system was all but made mandatory by federal legislation. The Hawes-Cooper Act, passed in 1929, prohibited the shipment of prison-made products in interstate commerce.[24]

As is the case today, those who were confined behind prison walls were not the only convicts who were required to work for the state. Numerous Alabama convicts, for example, spent long hours working in mines while immense farm labor programs flourished in Texas and Oklahoma. The majority of the convicts who

Inmate road gang before the turn of the century.

worked outside of the large institutions, however, were engaged in the construction and repair of state or county owned roads and buildings.

Inhumanely administered road gangs, particularly the chain gangs in the South, were used extensively in the 1940s. While road gangs still exist today, the kind that was used during the early part of the century was particularly brutal. Convicts usually spent their nights in filthy shacks or in caged wagons, and during the day they worked under the threat of being beaten, or of being shot if they attempted to escape. Nothing was offered in the way of rehabilitative or educational services, and as late as 1940 it was still a common practice to lease prisoners to local officials and to some private contractors.[25]

While the history of American road gangs is, for the most part, a sad one, it should be understood that the use of prisoners to work on road construction or other outdoor projects is not always inappropriate. Shortly after the turn of the century, for example, several prison administrators in both eastern and western states successfully reduced the incidence of convict idleness and related discontent by developing road labor programs. Perhaps the most enlightened of these programs was located in Colorado. Officials there, like many who administer today's outside labor projects, allowed only a select group of inmates to participate in the program. To qualify, each individual had to be eligible for parole within a short period of time and be willing to demonstrate that he could accept responsibility. The inmates worked hard, but during this transitional period their living conditions were considerably more relaxed and pleasant.[26]

YEARS OF ABUSE: 1900–1940

We have already discussed some of the changes in correctional programs that were made during the early years of the 20th century, but in general the first 40 years of the 20th century witnessed shamefully little progress. In fact, the conditions in prisons and reformatories deteriorated considerably during that time span.

Some institutions, of course, were better administered than others, but only a few administrators placed as much emphasis on rehabilitation as they did on custody. Most of the institutions were architecturally obsolete and, as late as 1933, 21 percent of all of the penal facilities in the country had either inadequate plumbing or none at all. Inmates were often required to keep buckets in their cells for toilet purposes and they filed out in the morning to empty them.[27]

A few wardens resorted to extreme forms of cruelty and harassment when attempting to control their prisoners. Others allowed aggressive inmate leaders, some of whom were notorious hoodlums on the outside, to organize illicit rackets within the institutions and otherwise do as they pleased. In return for receiving such indulgences, these powerful leaders would keep the rest of the inmates from being noticeably disruptive, either by permitting them to participate in the rackets or by force. A third type of administration, fearing that staff members would be adversely manipulated, prohibited all but essential communication between guards and inmates. In hopes of preventing inmates from exploiting and corrupting each other, strict rules of silence were enforced in the mess halls and other gathering places, and prisoners were required to spend the majority of their time locked in their cells.[28]

As is the case today, the kind of treatment that an inmate had to endure depended greatly on the state and the institution in which he or she was incarcerated. However, an offender in the 1930s would be considered fortunate if he were sent to one of the few institutions where he could serve his time and not be physically or psychologically damaged in the process (even if there were no educational or rehabilitative opportunities available to him).

In some of the institutions, administrators would rely on the cruelest measures when attempting to control their charges. Beatings, extended stays in "holes," (solitary cells used for disciplinary purposes) and a life of terror and despair awaited many who were

Prison Dining Halls. The dining hall of the 1940s (which is similar to many still used today) offers little more comfort than the one used in the early 1900s.

Only the addition of electrical appliances distinguishes this typical cell of the 1940s from the way it appeared when it was built during the latter part of the 19th century.

sent to some of those unsanitary, disease ridden hells that were the country's prisons. In other facilities prisoners were not openly harrassed by officials. Their fates, however, were determined by inmate leaders who assigned jobs and cells, granted favors of all kinds to their followers, and punished those who refused to abide by their wishes. The wardens, many of whom were politically appointed and correctionally incompetent, regarded these conditions as ideal because most of their administrative duties were handled by the inmate leaders.[29]

Generally speaking, those institutions that were designed for misdemeanants (individuals convicted of minor offenses) and people awaiting trial were the most neglected and poorly administered facilities in the correctional system. This seems to be particularly unfortunate when we realize that there were (and still are) many more people in local jails than in prisons and reformatories. The jails of the 1930s and 40s were particularly abhorrent, yet approximately three million individuals were committed to them each year.[30] Their populations consisted of juveniles, old men, first time offenders, "hardened" criminals, mental defectives, sexual perverts, alcoholics, physically aggressive criminals, and those presumably innocent individuals who were awaiting trial. Some of these institutions were so overcrowded that inmates did not have room enough to lie down at night, and in most, vice, extortion, assaultive behavior, and sexual perversity were prevalent.[31]

The jails were administered by sheriffs who were paid on a "fee" basis. This method of remuneration authorized them to collect a certain amount of money from their home counties for the care and feeding of each prisoner. Many of the sheriffs used most of the fees for themselves and provided the inmates with only the essentials.[32]

THE CREATION OF THE FEDERAL BUREAU OF PRISONS

Some authors have said that "the year 1930 may well mark the beginning of the modern era of prison progress," even though most of the country's prisons were still in severely neglected condition in 1930. In fact, the prison reform movement did receive its "greatest impetus . . . from the complete reorganization and reform of the federal prison system, begun in 1929–1930."[33] While there were several correctional institutions under the administrative control of the federal government prior to 1930, there was little to distinguish these facilities from the typical state-run facilities of the day. However, after Congress established the Federal Bureau of Prisons in 1930 and appointed Sanford Bates as its director, the federal system rose to a position of national leadership.

Bates developed, implemented, and coordinated numerous innovative educational and treatment programs that were to serve as positive models for the state systems. A brilliant administrator, he recruited extremely competent associates and placed them in key positions where their expertise could best be employed. Under Bates' directorship, federal corrections was freed from political favoritism, and his system became the most nonpunitive of all of the major penal organizations in the country. As great as Bates' contributions were, however, he and his associates could do little before the close of the 1930s to lift the majority of America's penal systems out of their states of backwardness.[34]

THE RISE AND DECLINE OF INMATE SELF-GOVERNMENT

There is a renewed interest today in developing correctional programs which give inmates (especially in institutions for juveniles) more responsibility in deciding how they will be governed. The ideas of allowing prisoners to decide what rules and regulations will guide their behavior, what the disciplinary procedures will be, and who will administer them, and even when an individual should be released on parole are based on the philosophies of such men as William Reuben George, Thomas Mott Osborne, Mordecai Plummer, and Howard B. Gill.

William Reuben George was the founder and director of a New York institution for delinquent boys. Within the confines of the George Junior Republic, as the institution was known, "citizen" inmates participated in a kind of democratic community that was governed by inmate representatives elected by the Republic's population.³⁵ Encouraged by George, Thomas Mott Osborne initiated similar programs for adults at Auburn Prison in 1914 and later at Sing Sing Prison. Osborne's program was referred to as the Mutual Welfare League and was governed by elected inmate representatives. A judicial board, whose members were appointed by the representatives, administered disciplinary proceedings. While technically the board's decisions could be appealed to the warden, its power was nearly absolute. A token economy was developed whereby inmates, using simulated money, were allowed to purchase goods and otherwise manage their own financial affairs. Graduates of the League (former inmates), who had successfully adjusted to the free community, were encouraged to assist staff members as they attempted to provide opportunities for similar adjustment on the part of newly released convicts. This method of continuing the program after the offender was back in the community was the most innovative facet of the total Mutual Welfare League program. Despite his significant contributions to progressive penology, Osborne was regarded by many as a pamperer of criminals. While under severe public criticism, he resigned his position, even though he still had much more to offer society.³⁶

Mordecai Plummer, who was directly influenced by Osborne, established his own inmate self-government program at the New Castle County Workhouse which, at the time, served as the only state prison in Delaware. He developed an inmate guard system (using prisoners as guards and shop foremen) and an "honor" court, which was made up of inmates. The decisions of the honor court became the rules which everyone was obligated to obey. The program emphasized the importance of respecting the rights of others and a concern for the dignity of man. Therefore, it should not be equated with some of the brutal latter-day employment of inmate guards. Under the dynamic leadership of Warden Plummer, the New Castle County Workhouse was a stable, well run facility. After his death, however, despite the efforts of his successors, the inmate self-government program deteriorated.³⁷

In 1927 Howard B. Gill, who is still active in correctional reform movements, initiated a type of inmate self-government program at the State Prison Colony at Norfolk, Massachusetts.

While guards were instructed to refrain, as much as possible, from communicating with inmates, other staff members participated equally with inmates in running the internal affairs of the institution. Numerous committees, which were formed to meet various occurring needs, were the institution's chief administrative bodies. Gill, another victim of unfair public criticism, was relieved of his position at Norfolk in 1934.[38]

As is true of similar programs today, the inmate self-government programs of the past were far from being perfect. Certain inmates simply do not benefit from such programs, and others use them to manipulate both the staff and other inmates. Nevertheless, modern corrections owes a debt to those reformers whose ideas and programs have served as positive examples to all other correctional innovators. All of them risked their jobs and reputations because of their commitment to what they believed to be right and humane.

THE MODERN GOAL OF REHABILITATION

An offender is usually considered to be rehabilitated if he successfully adjusts to community life and refrains from engaging in further criminal activities. The last twenty years have seen a great revival of interest in the development of rehabilitation programs. As a result of this interest, there are now more therapy, recreation, and education programs within correctional institutions than at any other time in our history.[39] There have also been significant improvements in classifying and segregating various types of prisoners, in creating special facilities for different types of offenders, and in the extended use of probation and parole.[40] Following the example of the federal government and the state of California, most states have established sophisticated governmental units (state departments of corrections) that control and coordinate all institutional and parole functions. Thus, services are administered more efficiently and duplication of effort is reduced. As will become evident in future chapters, there are still many unsolved problems in the field of corrections. Nevertheless, the advocates of rehabilitation have brought about significant changes within recent years.

Rehabilitation Under Attack

Today's correctional system is under attack from critics who, while they often bitterly disagree with each other, are united in their disagreement with the goal of rehabilitation and the techniques used to obtain that goal. "Law and order" advocates, disgusted with the amount of crime that still exists, vehemently object to what they call the "coddling" of criminals by do-gooders, and to the "country club" atmosphere within modern prisons. The majority of the inmates in many state and federal correctional facilities are members of minority groups—usually blacks or individuals of Hispanic origin. To many, this fact alone indicates that the white middle class majority in American society and its leaders are discriminating against minorities. The majority's representatives, so they contend, make the rules (laws) and force all others to obey or suffer the consequences. Correctional systems, it is said, are only instruments by which the white establishment maintains control over minority group members who either come into conflict with the law when they attempt to assert themselves as human beings or when they are forced to resort to criminal activity because few legitimate opportunities to become successful or, perhaps, even to survive, are available to them. Rehabilitation rhetoric, from their viewpoint, only camouflages this suppression and placates the public. Other critics, while they would not agree that American correctional systems are political tools of the dominant class, do maintain that corrections is being taken over by misguided therapists who desire to inflict their values on others. While such assertions are not new, their increasing popularity makes them more formidable challenges to rehabilitation advocates than they have been at any other time since the beginning of the 20th century.

Many of these same critics question the right of correctional officials to attempt to reform offenders who do not want to be reformed. In an age when chemical and psychological behavior modification techniques are close to being perfected, this is a particularly pertinent ethical consideration. "Consider," says Seymour L. Halleck, "the impact on our society if our prisons had succeeded in rehabilitating such convicted offenders as Henry Thoreau, Eugene Debs, Martin Luther King, or Malcolm X." These and many similarly inclined individuals "violate the law, out of conscience, or as part of a deliberate effort to change the society."[41]

If we had the authority to make all of our so called deviants into average citizens, say the new reformers, we would not only deprive our society of its vitality, but we would also create an environment in which a totalitarian government could obliterate all vestiges of human rights and use the law as an instrument of political coercion. This all could be accomplished under the guise of rehabilitation. Norval Morris and Gordon Hawkins maintain that "The jailer in a white coat with a doctorate remains a jailer, but with even larger powers over his fellows."[42]

A few short years ago reformers such as Carl Menninger and former Attorney General Ramsey Clark were greatly admired by the liberal community for their leadership in support of indeterminate sentence legislation and similar rehabilitation aids. Today, however, they are being rebuked for trying to create a system that could give "Big Brother" unlimited control over each and every one of us. Likewise, the new liberals are most adamant in their criticism of those very programs and facilities that past liberal reformers extolled as being the most progressive.

Extreme critics are calling for the total abolition of prisons.[43] A large and more restrained group of reformers still support such traditional correctional services as group and individual counseling and educational and recreational programs for prisoners. However, many are quick to maintain that refusing to participate in such activities should not lessen the inmates' chances of receiving parole or other privileges.

SUMMARY

Those facets of modern American corrections that are now considered progressive were actually based on the innovations proposed years ago by such pioneers as Alexander Maconochie and Sir Walter Crofton. Although they were not American, the techniques and philosophies developed by Maconochie and expanded by Crofton were to become the foundation for modern corrections programs. Maconochie's "mark" system was the forerunner of modern treatment and behavior modification programs, and perhaps more importantly his advocacy of rehabilitation was to result in its eventual recognition as a legitimate goal of correctional institutions.

Despite the efforts of the New York Prison Association and various Quaker individuals and organizations, most of the pre-Civil War correctional progress was only theoretical. The development and maintenance of prison industry and the associated lease system seemed to be the main concerns of penal administrators during the first half of the 19th century. However, some practical progress was made during this time period. The public became increasingly aware of the need to upgrade welfare and correctional services for children, both individuals and organizations developed programs to assist the ex-prisoner, and probation services were formally established.

In 1870 at the first national prison congress in Cincinnati, the National Prison Association (later to become the American Correctional Association) was founded and set forth a "Declaration of Principles" to guide all future reform efforts. While the participants in the congress did not succeed in bringing about the anticipated massive changes in the penal system, they were instrumental in producing legislation such as indeterminate sentence statutes, and correctional innovations such as reformatory programs and parole.

The early years of the 20th century brought the establishment of federal correctional facilities, the expansion of state-wide systems, the enlightened administration of some institutions for females, and the growth of private prison aid societies. Despite such progress, however, the first 40 years of the 20th century were characterized by the failure to use most of the progressive legislation that was available, the neglect of treatment and vocational training programs, poorly administered penal programs, and an over-emphasis on prison industry. The renewed interest in prison industry was thwarted by laws mandating "state-use systems," and only resulted in massive inmate idleness and unrest. During these "years of abuse," there were several administrators who distinguished themselves by being humane and progressive. Sanford Bates, the first director of the Federal Bureau of Prisons, and those great experimenters in inmate self-government, William Reuben George, Thomas Mott Osborne, Mordecai Plummer, and Howard B. Gill made valuable contributions to the correction systems.

A significant revival of interest in rehabilitation has occurred within the last 20 years. The growing emphasis on changing the offender, as opposed to punishing him, has resulted in the implementation of numerous innovative reform programs. The modern goal of rehabilitation has, however, been vehemently attacked by individuals of various political persuasions. Some maintain that we should deal more firmly with law violators, while others contend that while we talk of rehabilitation and mouth humanitarian sentiments, in general we are only disguising our attempts to suppress the rights of racial and/or political minorities. Concerned that a totalitarian type of government might use correctional agencies as means of political persuasion, many critics have challenged the legal and moral authority of those who would attempt to alter, in any way, the attitudes or personalities of those who do not want to be "reformed."

ENDNOTES

1. John Vincent Barry, "Alexander Maconochie" in *Pioneers in Criminology,* ed. Hermann Mannheim (Chicago: Quadrangle Books, Inc., 1960) pp. 68–69.

2. Ibid., p. 81. Also see John Vincent Barry, *Alexander Maconochie of Norfolk Island: A Study of a Pioneer in Penal Reform* (Melbourne and London: Oxford University Press, 1958).
3. Blake McKelvey, *American Prisons: A Study in American Social History Prior to 1915* (Montclair, N.J.: Paterson Smith Pub. Co., reprinted 1968) p. 29.
4. Ibid., p. 30.
5. Ibid., p. 42–45.
6. David Dressler, *Practice and Theory of Probation and Parole* (New York and London: Columbia University Press, 1951) pp. 52–56.
7. Ibid., p. 9.
8. Ibid., p. 18.
9. Joseph W. Eaton, *Stone Walls Not A Prison Make* (Springfield, Illinois: Charles C Thomas, Publisher, 1962) p. 9.
10. Ibid., pp. 9–20.
11. Ibid., p. 10.
12. In reality, many more individuals are incarcerated in mental institutions through various indeterminate type procedures than are sentenced to prisons and reformatories under indeterminate sentence laws. While such procedures raise serious moral and Constitutional questions, we will confine our comments, in this volume, to only those issues that are directly related to corrections.
13. The Borstal system was named after the town in which the system was first implemented. See Robert G. Caldwell, *Criminology* (New York: The Ronald Press, 1963) p. 516.
14. Harry Elmer Barnes and Negley K. Teeters, *New Horizons in Criminology* (Englewood Cliffs, N.J.: Prentice-Hall, Inc., 1959) pp. 425–28.
15. McKelvey, *American Prisons*, p. 141; Barnes and Teeters, *New Horizons in Criminology*, pp. 408–09.
16. McKelvey, *American Prisons*, p. 144.
17. Caldwell, *Criminology*, p. 517.
18. Ibid.
19. McKelvey, *American Prisons*, p. 211.
20. Ibid., p. 214.
21. Ibid., pp. 209–10.
22. Ibid., pp. 216–17.
23. Caldwell, *Criminology*, p. 518.
24. Ibid., pp. 626–29.

25. Barnes and Teeters, *New Horizons in Criminology,* pp. 378–81; McKelvey, *American Prisons,* pp. 224–26.
26. McKelvey, *American Prisons,* p. 223.
27. Christopher Hibbert, *The Roots of Evil: A Social History of Crime and Punishment* (Minerva Press, 1963) pp. 172–74.
28. Ibid., pp. 174–75.
29. Because it will be elaborated on in chapter four, the history of politically appointed wardens and the exploitation of prison populations by inmate leaders will only be briefly discussed in this chapter.
30. Barnes and Teeters, *New Horizons in Criminology,* p. 382.
31. Ibid., p. 388.
32. Ibid.
33. Walter Hartinger, Edward Eldefonso, and Alan Coffey, *Corrections: A Component of the Criminal Justice System* (Pacific Palisades, California: Goodyear Pub. Co. Inc., 1973) p. 93.
34. Eaton, *Stone Walls Not A Prison Make,* p. 73. See Sanford Bates, *Prisons and Beyond* (New York: The Macmillan Co., 1936).
35. Barnes and Teeters, *New Horizons in Criminology,* pp. 499–53.
36. Ibid. Also see Frank Tannenbaum, *Osborne of Sing Sing* (Chapel Hill: University of North Carolina Press, 1933).
37. See Robert G. Caldwell, *The New Castle County Workhouse* (Newark, Delaware: University of Delaware Press, 1940).
38. Fred E. Haynes, *The American Prison System* (New York: McGraw-Hill Co., 1939) pp. 59–87.
39. Caldwell, *Criminology,* 606–631.
40. Ibid.
41. Seymour L. Halleck, "Rehabilitation of Criminal Offenders—A Re-Assessment of the Concept," *Psychiatric Annals* 4:3, March, 1974, p. 63.
42. Norval Morris and Gordon Hawkins, "Attica Revisited: The Prospect for Prison Reform," *Psychiatric Annals* 4:3, March, 1974, p. 36.
43. See Jessica Mitford, *Kind and Usual Punishment* (New York: Alfred A. Knopf, 1973).

4

The Social Organization of the Prison

Some psychiatrists believe that the individual who is a behavior problem can be helped or rehabilitated only if he is in a state of anxiety and desires some relief from his emotional stress. To this type of person a free society presents an unstructured daily life that does not fulfill his deep seated need for security. He becomes anxious about uncertainties and subconsciously yearns to lead a more regimented existence. Psychiatrists believe that if this individual remains in the free community, he can be successfully treated because he will cooperate in attempts to alleviate his suffering. However, if he does not receive help, the individual may violate the law so as to be apprehended and placed in the highly structured (secure) environment that he subconsciously desires. The prison society reduces the anxiety, and thus the individual is no longer amenable to therapy because he perceives no need for it.

A more sociological point of view is that as the prisoner becomes institutionalized (conditioned to and by the regimented lifestyle of the institution), his personality becomes so altered that he is unable to readapt to a "normal" society. While experts disagree on such issues relating to prisoners, most contend that the unnatural living conditions peculiar to correctional institutions are not conducive to preparing a person for his eventual freedom. Therefore, a basic understanding of the problems related to the social organization of prisons is necessary if intelligent solutions to these problems are to be found.

THE FUNCTIONAL ANALYSIS OF THE SOCIAL ORGANIZATION OF THE PRISON

Social scientists have conducted numerous studies of the interpersonal relationships of prison inmates and the social interaction that develops between inmates and institutional staff members. Although there have been disagreements concerning the social organizations of prisons, all researchers have documented the existence of groups or subcultures within the general inmate population. These subcultures are distinguishable by the adherence of their members to the attitudes, values, and lifestyles of their fellow members.

There are two basic theoretical approaches—the functionalist and the diffusionist—to explain the development and features of inmate subcultures. An example of the functional explanation of the development of such subcultures has been presented by Gresham Sykes and Sheldon Messenger. Their theoretical position, based on the result of Sykes' three-year study of the New Jersey State Prison, is that the inmates' participation in the development and maintenance of subcultures that exclude staff members and others who support "legitimate" societal values represents their method of attempting to solve the problems they encounter in traditional maximum security institutions.

Correctional institutions by their nature, regardless of how progressive, deprive an individual of his liberty by confining him in a highly structured environment designed to control him. Societal rejection and the rigid bureaucratic control of the prisoners' lives deprives them of their autonomy or their ability to significantly control their own destinies.[1] In several ways the prisoners must revert back to a role reminiscent of the one they played as children. Prisoners are allowed to make few of the decisions affecting their welfare, and they have little knowledge of the plans that the staff may contemplate for them. This restoration to the realm of childhood is, however, incomplete. The authoritarian control exhibited by custodians is considerably dissimilar to the protective care of parents, and most likely represents authentic security only to a few psychologically disturbed inmates. To Sykes and Messenger, the inmate population represents a debased and humiliated mass who are subjected to seemingly nonsensical rules and regulations and whose humanity is far from acknowledged by officialdom.[2]

Another problem for the prisoner is maintaining a masculine identity. Except in extremely rare circumstances, American prisoners are totally isolated from heterosexual activity. While sexually arousing material is still available to the prisoner through the media, the inmate is, as Sykes proclaims, "figuratively castrated by his involuntary celibacy."[3] Perhaps the frequency of exaggerated attempts by prisoners to prove their masculinity through displays of phyiscal prowess is, in part, a reaction to their frustration over their inability to perform the complete masculine role. Such a deprivation may indirectly produce acute feelings of guilt or self-doubt.

In American society, extensive emphasis is placed on the attainment of material possessions, and in evaluating an individual's worth, undue consideration is frequently given to his economic status. Sykes and Messenger assert that in such a society, permitting an individual to retain only the bare necessities of life may indeed be psychologically distressing. In discussing the desires of the average American prisoner, Sykes states "He wants—or needs, if you will—not just the so-called necessities of life, but also the amenities: cigarettes and liquor as well as calories, interesting foods as well as sheer bulk, individual clothing as well as adequate clothing, individual furnishings for living quarters as well as shelter, privacy as well as space."[4] The inmate, then, is deprived of "goods and services" and, in most instances, he is forced to realize that his situation is a direct consequence of his own inadequacies. The individual's acceptance of such an assumption

An inmate pauses to show his purchase of a cigar and food.

serves to represent another assault on his sense of personal worth. It is only the exceptional captive, such as some of the draft evaders during the Vietnam conflict, who can find solace in the conviction that he is foregoing the material pleasures of life for what he believes to be superior moral satisfactions or for a justifiable purpose.

Another distasteful aspect of penal incarceration involves

what Sykes refers to as the "deprivation of security."[5] The realization that one is forced into relatively intimate daily interaction with thieves, rapists, murderers, and others whose mores and ethical standards differ from those accepted by "society" is inevitably discomforting, even to the inmate who is regarded by others as being dangerous. The degree to which prisoners suffer from or are threatened with cruelty by their peers depends on the conditions in particular institutions and the characteristics of their populations. Nevertheless, the new inmate in any American prison or reformatory must be prepared to meet the challenges of aggressive associates who feel compelled to demonstrate their manhood through physically coercing others into subservience, sexual or otherwise.

What are the responses that the inmates make to these deprivations of their liberty, autonomy, masculinity, goods and services and security? Some, defeated by the rigid bureaucratic control that is exerted over their lives, give in to various temptations. Deprived of their liberty and autonomy, prisoners occasionally strike out physically at their captors and openly violate the seemingly nonsensical rules and regulations. Such behavior, however, usually only tightens the administrative control and brings about other distasteful repercussions. Being unable to engage in heterosexual relationships within the institution, some inmates turn to homosexual activity. Some inmates may become what, in the argot of the prison, is termed "a merchant" or "peddler." Because of his "connections," his prison job placement, or his ability to outwit others, this type of prisoner has the opportunity to hoard candy, cigarettes, coffee, or even contraband materials such as liquor, narcotics, and weapons. He usually trades or sells these items to his associates, making as much profit as possible. Fearful for their own security, some prisoners align themselves with other aggressive or frightened inmates and as individuals or as a group engage in assaultive behavior that they hope will accord them reputations as individuals who are not to be meddled with.

The functionalists contend, however, that there is another more suitable solution to coping with the pains of imprisonment. The most frequent inmate response to the deprivations that he encounters is to create and participate in the development and maintenance of an antagonistic and defensive subculture in which he is able to attain status among his peers and to develop an adequate self-concept. To further understand the manner in which these people allegedly contend with their problems, let us reflect on the words of Sykes:

> But if the rigors of confinement cannot be completely removed, they can at least be mitigated by the patterns of social interactions established among the inmates themselves.
> Frustrated not as an individual but as many, the inmate finds two paths open. On the one hand, he can attempt to bind himself to his fellow captives with ties of mutual aid, loyalty, affection, and respect, firmly standing in opposition to the officials. On the other hand, he can enter into a war of all against all in which he seeks his own advantage without reference to the claims or needs of the other prisoners.[6]

INMATE JARGON

bad   pretty, nice
bandit   person who induces sex with same gender
bid or bit   conviction and/or sentence
boat   transfer of inmates between facilities
bomb   letter for information, interview slip
boss action   enjoyable
box   special housing, segregation unit
bug juice   medicine
bug off   get away from me
bug out   acting abnormal
bug report   report of prison psychiatrist
buggo   one who acts crazy
bum rapper   liar

SOCIAL ORGANIZATION OF PRISONS

Thus, say the functionalists, only by developing and maintaining a "collective" subgroup can the prisoners contend satisfactorily with the pains of imprisonment that they encounter. Only through mutual aid can they present a united front against their captors that will, to a degree at least, offset the degrading impact of their confinement.

What is the cohesive force that binds the inmates to each other and perpetuates a status system in which an inmate is able to elevate his own sense of self-worth to the extent that he actually regards himself as being superior to his keepers? This rallying point, according to Sykes and Messenger, is an unwritten but all-pervasive code of conduct which details how the inmate is expected to behave in his interpersonal relations with both peers and staff. This code includes the following tenets:

1. Don't interfere with inmate interests . . . never rat on a con . . . no qualifications or mitigating circumstance is recognizable . . . be loyal to your class—the cons.

bum wire	false information
busted	arrested
butch kid	aggressive youth
buy	segregation
C. R.	conditional release
cell time	time spent locked up in evenings or when no programs are scheduled during the day
chilly	cool, nice, aloof
cold turkey	to cut off completely from use of hard drugs
company	group of inmates in one gallery
compo fund	inmate's money account for commissary, stamps, etc.
con	inmate
cooker	items used to heat heroin prior to injection
cop	slang reference to correction officers

2. Play it cool and do your own time.
3. Don't break your word; don't steal from the cons; don't sell favors; don't be a racketeer; don't welsh on debts . . . share favors.
4. Don't weaken . . . the prisoner should be able to take it and maintain his integrity in the face of privation . . . be tough; be a man.
5. Don't be a sucker. Guards are hacks or screws and are to be treated with constant suspicion and distrust.[7]

From the inmate's perspective, this code is extremely functional and it directly relates to the deprivations he faces. If admonitions to "be loyal to your class" and "do your own time" are adhered to, the inmate can maintain a feeling, at least in his "society," of being able to control his own life (thus retaining at least a portion of his autonomy). These and other inmate norms such as "don't weaken" and "be a man" help him to preserve his sense

cop	to obtain drugs
cop a mope	get away from me
cop a plea	plea bargaining, admit to a lesser charge
cop out	confess, or give in
cracking shorts	stealing cars
crate	a carton of cigarettes
crib	cell
dead beat	"not into anything"
devil	a white person
digging and dying	hypocritical
ding him	to swing at him sneakily
doing a pound	serving a five year sentence
down	as in how much time done in prison
draft	transfer of inmates between facilities
drop a dime	snitch
dropper	a wired hook-up made out of copper coils that is used to heat water

of masculinity. Obviously, if prohibitions such as "never rat on a con" or those that dictate avoidance of guards are not given wide support in the inmate population, a sophisticated traffic in contraband will be impossible and, in turn, the goods and services that they desire will not be provided. Likewise, of course, if prisoners do not prohibit stealing from or interfering with each others' welfare, their security and sense of well being will be severely threatened.

While such a code is obviously not universally adhered to by the inmate population, the majority of inmates are said to at least lend verbal support to its tenets. Even for some who violate such doctrines, the code may still provide security, an access to goods and services, and even a source of status. For example, for various reasons such as personal revenge, an inmate may divulge information to officials regarding the illicit activities of one of his peers. However, this same individual may outwardly support the basic tenet of the code which dictates that one should "never

dub	pack of cigarettes
dude	person
fag, faggot	homosexual
feeb	lower on the inmate social scale
fired on him	to swing at him
fish, mark or chump	easily took
flat bit	definite sentence
flats	the gallery in ground floor of blocks
flic	movie
frisk	search
full deck	means that one's head is together
fuzz	correction officer
gallery	one set of cells within a block
gay people	homosexuals
get down	participate
give-me-five	brotherhood hand slap

rat on a con." He most certainly does not want others to inform on him, and he may also desire to take advantage of the prohibited traffic in contraband goods. Of course traffic in contraband goods could not usually exist if details of the operation were made known to officials by informants.

Functionalist theorists also maintain that a prisoner's status among his peers is largely determined by the degree to which he lives up to the dictates of the code. If the inmate rigorously adheres to all the principles of the code, he is said to be accorded great prestige and respect by his fellows and, at least in the New Jersey State Prison, Sykes relates, he is labeled as a "real man."[8] The real man aligns himself with the code in its totality. He "pulls his own time," bothering no one and most certainly not allowing anyone to interfere with his own interests. By never exhibiting any indication of weakening under the pains of imprisonment, (and thereby permitting the captors to strip him of his autonomy) he displays a quiet ability to "take anything they can dish out and

godfather	superintendent
gold bricking	faking illness
good time	time earned for good behavior
gopher	one who is gullible
grog	homemade wine or booze
Habe	writ of habeas corpus
hack	correction officer
hamster	a black person
half deck	means that one is mentally or emotionally unbalanced
hang up	not being truthful
heist	crime
hip	worldly wise, knowledgeable
hit	rejection by parole board
hooker	prostitute
hole	special housing

more," without physically striking out against members of the staff. To engage in such action could bring reprisals by the administration that would adversely affect others in the population. Such an individual is characterized by his aloof and unemotional countenance, which serves to indicate to inmate and staff member alike that he is mastering his own destiny.

On the opposite extreme of the prestige continuum is the "rat." This is the inmate who, either by trying to gain personal favor from the staff or by seeking revenge against other inmates, becomes an informant, violating every tenet of the code and threatening the very existence of the inmate social system. Yet even the rat serves a purpose, i.e., the aggression directed against him represents a method by which others can demonstrate their loyalty to the code. The rat also serves as a scapegoat, allowing the other inmates to vent their hostility.

Is there other evidence that would support the functionalist contention that the prison code and subcultures within the insti-

home boy, homie, honcho	someone from home town, buddy
honkey	white person
house	cell
I got your back	I'll back you on this fight
ice, short ice	movies with lots of sex
jacket	to label someone
jail house punk	made a homosexual in prison
jail house lawyer	an inmate who is up on the law
jitterbug	young gang fighter
jive	sharp, slick
jockers	aggressive homosexuals
joint	correctional facility
joint	cigarette
jones	habit
juggin	harassment

tution exist as a result of the inmates' reactions to the pains of imprisonment? While the exact precepts of the prison code differ depending on the institution, evidence does indicate that a sizeable proportion of American prisoners internalize values and attitudes which are contrary to those usually deemed socially acceptable by prison officials.[9] Furthermore, the inmate elite (leaders) tend to be the ones who most vehemently regard "legitimate" values as being foreign to their personal philosophies.[10] Donald Clemmer, in his classic analysis of prison life, discovered that the longer the inmate remains incarcerated, and the more he associates with his peers, the greater the chances are that he will adhere to the anti-staff attitudes that are represented in the code.[11] Such findings would indicate that the deprivations he faces do progressively alter the inmate's lifestyle and, from the perspective of legitimate society, have detrimental effects on his personality. More recent studies have revealed similar but not precisely the same results. For example, Stanton Wheeler, in his study of the Wash-

jump street	from the beginning
keep lock	disciplinary confinement
kite	illegal letter or note
legal beagle	an inmate that has a lot of legal action going
long dude	tall
long green	a lot of money
loot	property, usually illegal
main squeeze	wife, girl friend
main man	good friend
The Man	superintendent
max out	complete maximum sentence
mick	correctional officer
"Mothers Day"	day when welfare check arrives at inmate's home—mother to send him some money
narc	narcotic

ington State Reformatory, discovered that the socialization process experienced by prisoners is not necessarily linear. Of the inmates that he questioned, those who had been incarcerated for a period of six months or less, as well as those who had six months or less remaining prior to release, expressed more pro-social attitudes than did another group whose confinement time fell in between these extremes.[12] This process was typical, regardless of whether or not the individual in question had many or few close associates within the inmate population. Perhaps the tendency to be influenced by the outside culture remains for a short time after initial incarceration, and is rekindled in anticipation of imminent release. In explaining these findings, the functionalists would assert that the pains of imprisonment become more intense as the individual progressively experiences the impact of societal rejection and isolation. Thus, after the first six months or so of imprisonment, he attempts to solve his problems of adjustment by aligning himself with the protective subculture, and only decreases his al-

niggerstick	officer's baton
no less than the deep freeze	expresses a degree of aloofness
off the back	"good time" taken off of maximum time
on tape	to know by heart
on the clock	short
on the earie	eaves dropping
open date	date of release for parole
oreo cookie	black outside, white inside
over the humps	success
pack	refers to cigarette packs as a medium of exchange between inmates
pass	a piece of paper issued by an officer for travel in an institution from one place to another; a manner of rejecting something which is offered
pick-up time	first appearance before parole board for determination of eligibility, etc.
play chickee	to look out for

legiance to it when the pains decrease in anticipation of return to free society.

Studies by Garabedian and by Glasser and Stratton also indicate that inmates tend to participate in prison subcultures more extensively during the middle periods of their incarcerations.[13] However, some research has not substantiated these findings.[14]

According to functional theory, it would be unlikely to find the cohesive anti-staff subculture, as described by Sykes and Messenger, developing in institutions where the pains of imprisonment were not excessive. In "treatment" oriented institutions (where there is less reliance on degrading the offender, excessive physical or psychological punishment, or rigid control), inmates should find less need for maintaining the ego-saving subcultures. David Street's rather extensive research conducted in several institutions for juveniles supports this hypothesis. He found that inmates in treatment-oriented institutions more often "expressed positive attitudes toward the institution and staff, nonprisonized views of

police	correction officers
puddin'	light action, easy
punk	homosexual
put the squeeze on	pressure
quail, queen	passive homosexual
racket	occupation, motive
rap	to talk
rap sheet	arrest record
right on	agreement
rip off	rape, pull a job, robbed
rollers	squad
rollies	handmade cigarettes
rolling	rumble, fight
round on me	ignore
rule 5	when a parolee must abstain from alcohol
run off at the face	talking too much

adaptation to the institution, and positive images of self-change."¹⁵ Studies of minimum security adult reformatories largely support the findings of Street and can be offered as at least partial evidence in support of the functionalist position.¹⁶

Such evidence, however, is of little help in finding solutions to the many problems confronting the administrators of adult maximum security institutions. Granting extended freedom of movement within or outside an institution, and thus reducing some of the pains of imprisonment, is practically impossible in an institution where there is both a public demand for societal protection and a necessity to protect dangerous offenders from each other. Such demands and precautions are usually not evident or necessary when juveniles are involved. Therefore, officials responsible for their care and control feel justified in engaging in forms of therapeutic experimentation which involves granting a relatively high degree of freedom to their inmates. In fact, as we shall see, the modern penologist views the progressive lessening of limita-

---

runner inmate whose job is to deliver things around the prison
sap stupid
screw correction officer
seg segregation unit
sell a wolf ticket invitation to a fight
shakedown the searching of an area within the facility
shamming goofing off
shark inmate who loans to other inmates for his gain
short departure is imminent
short heist pornography
skinners plastic surgery
snuff to kill
solid right
spike needle used by addicts

tions on freedom of movement and the bestowing of systematic responsibilities as necessary prerequisites to the preparation for mature societal adjustment after release.

Some research findings, however, indicate that it is possible to ease or reduce the deprivations (pains of imprisonment) within maximum security institutions. Of particular interest is an investigation into aspects of the inmate culture and the organizational effectiveness of Patuxent Institution in the state of Maryland.[17] The population of this institution is made up of intellectually or emotionally "defective delinquent adults" and the total administration is reportedly treatment-oriented in the extreme. Because of the type of inmate confined in Patuxent, strict security is perceived as being a necessity. When the inmate displays genuine progress, as evidenced by attitudinal and behavioral changes, he is gradually accorded more positive rewards and privileges. Ultimately he is rewarded for his improvement by being placed in a section of the institution where he is allowed to participate in a

split bit	sentence with a set minimum and maximum
squeeze	fag
statch time	statutory release time
straight date	inmate has a parole program approved by Commissioner and is given a definite date to be released on
stretch	prison term served
stuff	dope, money
take him off the count	he's been killed
tip	to leave
turkey	square person
two counts running wild	two sentences to run consecutively
vic	interest on a loan
wasted	killed
waterman	inmate assigned to deliver hot water to each cell
wing waiter	inmate assigned to clean cell block

"therapeutic community" that includes twelve psychiatrists, nine psychologists, and fourteen social workers. Within the therapeutic community, the emphasis is on developing meaningful relationships between inmates and staff members. Thus, when an inmate faces a crisis, the therapists are there to help him. This, of course, is in contrast to the typical situations in both mental hospitals and correctional institutions where the "client" has to make and wait for an appointment.

In comparing 31 inmates who had participated in the therapeutic community experience with 34 inmates who had not, it was discovered that the former group was, in general, more accepting of legitimate societal values and less likely to conform to an anti-therapeutic subcultural code. Testing also revealed that such attitudinal dissimilarities could not be attributed to either sociological or psychological factors in the histories of the subjects. Of course, it would be premature to conclude on the basis of this study that a reduction in the pains of imprisonment lessened

---

wolf aggressive homosexual
works equipment used by addicts
yam a black person
zex careful, someone's coming
zip represents zero minimum time set by judge; e.g. zip 5 —zero to five years sentence

Source: *Guidelines to Volunteer Services,* New York State Department of Correctional Services, pp. 38–44.

inmate allegiance to an antagonistic code of behavior and resulted in the development of a population characterized by more socially acceptable philosophies of life.[18] This is particularly true in light of the fact that we have no knowledge concerning what motivated the therapeutic community sample to actively participate in their own reformation. However, it can be stated with certainty that the regimented confinement characteristic of our traditional institutions is not conductive to the development of socially acceptable lifestyles.

THE DIFFUSIONIST PERSPECTIVE

Most students of the social organization of prisons would agree that the circumstances of incarceration have a profound effect on the prisoner's personality and are, at least to some degree, related to his behavior within the institution. This is true regardless of his personality or social background. Dramatic evidence presented by Bruno Bettelheim demonstrated that even when law-abiding citizens are subjected to severe penal conditions, their frustrations may give vent to aggressive action. These internalized hostilities may be directed toward their oppressors, or they may be redirected toward the inmate population. When Bettelheim was incarcerated in two Nazi concentration camps, he carefully observed and recorded in his mind the reactions of the prisoners to the cruelties they suffered at the hands of their captors. He witnessed intelligent and responsible adults who, because they were completely deprived of any control over their own lives, deteriorated to the extent that they behaved as children. Their attention spans were shortened, some retreated into a fantasy world, and perhaps most distressing of all many of the prisoners who had been in the camps for extended periods began not only to admire their Nazi persecutors but also rivaled them in their inhuman treatment of newcomers.[19] Erving Goffman also convincingly relates how the inhabitants of many "total institutions" such as American prisons and mental hospitals retreat to childlike worlds of fantasy. Goffman contends, in an explanation that is similar to the one offered by Bettelheim, that this type of reaction is a result of depriving the captives of participating in almost all decisions that affect their destinies. When the individual is treated as a child over an extended period of time, he can eventually be expected to behave in a manner befitting a child.[20]

While the adherents to the diffusionist theory of prison organization realize that the pains of imprisonment and the general institutional environment can have a profound effect on the personality, they do assert that the functionalist should give more consideration to the inmates' personalities and social backgrounds that had developed prior to their incarceration. There is evidence to indicate that the impact of incarceration can sometimes dramatically alter attitudes and lifestyles, but it is uncertain how lasting these changes are.[21] Some research indicates that when previous behavior and backgrounds are taken into consideration, the type of penal organization that offenders were in makes little difference when evaluating recidivism.[22] In other words, while certain types of institutions may elicit particular kinds of subcultures and associated attitudes, criminal recidivism is not related to a particular type of institution.

As we have seen, some research has revealed that the inmate tends to become progressively deprisonized or is less influenced by the anti-staff subculture toward the end of his incarceration. This is further indication that the changes that occur during imprisonment are perhaps not permanent.

As far back as 1940, Donald Clemmer observed that the character of the prison subculture was determined to a large degree by the social world that the individuals participated in outside of the institution.[23] In analyzing his diffusionist position, Clemmer stated "we may use the term prisonization to indicate the taking on of the greater or less degree of the folkways, mores, customs, and general culture of the penitentiary."[24] Clemmer's contention was that all inmates become prisonized to some degree. To comfortably adjust to prison life, the individual must learn the proper language (prison argot), how to get a "good job" ("do easy time"), and the ways of obtaining desired goods and services. Most inmates participate in this educational process;

however, there are a multitude of other circumstances that determine the degree and speed of prisonization, and whether or not the inmate accepts the prison code. His accidental associations (e.g., those inmates he works and lives with) have a profound effect on his attitudes and behavior. More important, the diffusionists contend, is his personality development prior to imprisonment and the extent and nature of his association with people in free society. The beliefs and opinions held by many prisoners are often directly related to their racial or ethnic backgrounds. The majority of prisoners might "learn the ropes," within the institution, but they also react to their incarcerations as individuals who have been molded by their past experiences. The "diffusionist" feels that the social backgrounds and personality traits of the individual largely determine the mode of life in which they will engage after incarceration. Recent occurrences on the outside may also affect the behavior of the captive. For example, a man who unexpectedly has divorce action brought against him will probably view and react to prison life somewhat differently than will the inmate who is being given moral support by a loving and devoted wife.

Richard Irwin and Donald Cressey have expanded the diffusionist line of thinking by maintaining that the following three types of inmate subcultures are evident in most prisons: (1) The "convict" subculture which develops out of the pains of imprisonment, (2) the "thief" subculture which results when individuals who are involved in a criminal way of life on the outside bring their culture into the prison, and (3) the "legitimate" subculture which is also brought in from outside of the institution but by individuals who are more attuned to the values of the larger society.[25] These writers emphasize that both the convict and the thief subcultures are rooted in what might be referred to as the general lower-class subculture. Obviously, members of the "legitimate" subculture are more likely to have middle-class backgrounds.

A typical member of the convict subculture would be the politician or merchant who tries to attain status within the institution but, at the same time, attempts to manipulate fellow inmates and staff so that he will be able to obtain more luxuries and comforts than his peers. The convict's only reference group is the inmate population, and he seeks to attain importance, power, or recognition within that group. In a later study of felons within the California correctional system, Irwin discovered that this type usually had long histories of incarcerations dating back to their childhood. These "state-raised youths", as Irwin calls them, have been institutionalized or prisonized to such an extent that the social world of the prison is the only environment in which they feel comfortable, and the only one that is of importance to them.[26] This type of individual usually attaches a great deal more significance to obtaining goods and services than do other prisoners.

According to Irwin and Cressey, the previously discussed real man or "right guy" is a typical member of the thief subculture. While his reference group is the subculture of the professional or semi-professional criminal, he is admired for his "solid" character inside the walls. It is claimed that what has previously been thought of as the prison code is simply a set of ethical mandates developed by professional criminals in free society and has been diffused into the prison world. The thief, because his outside associates and the nonprison world are more important to him, does not concentrate on gaining status or goods and services through manipulative activities. He is usually accorded high status within the inmate population because of his relative expertise as a criminal and because of his other admired qualities (associated with his adherence to the code). However, the obtaining of prison luxuries is of little importance to him, for they appear inconsequential compared to the desired material possessions that can only be obtained on the outside. As an example of the differences between the values of the convicts and those of the thieves, Irwin and Cressey observed that in one institution they studied, members of the convict subculture expended a great deal of effort in developing "connections" in the prison laundry so that they could get their denims (prison clothing) starched. To them this was a way of "being sharp," and was a great source of prestige. The thieves, however, regarded such behavior with amusement and could not understand why anybody would go to such lengths to acquire, what seemed to them, unimportant privileges.[27]

It is also noted that despite the anti-social attitudes characteristic of both groups, neither the thieves nor convicts advocate rebelling against prison authorities or disrupting the status quo in any way. The member of the convict group does not want anything to interfere with the status-enhancing "rackets" in which he engages, and deliberately antagonizing the administration could result in a crackdown on his illicit activities. Likewise, the thief has a strong desire to "do easy time," or serve his sentence with minimal effort and without undue interference from prison officials. He realizes that if he does not cause trouble for the staff, they are less likely to interfere with his interests.

There are legitimate grounds for criticizing the diffusionist position. For example, some have asserted that Irwin and Cressey err by not considering the problems associated with adjusting to prison life that must be experienced by members of the thief subculture.[28] Nevertheless, there is little ground for doubting the validity of the diffusionist's basic contention that the social backgrounds, experiences, and personalities of individuals largely determine the type of behavior that they will engage in and the attitudes that they will hold during incarceration. The tendency for many prisoners to be deeply concerned with radical philosophies and to view themselves as political prisoners is an example of how outside attitudes and beliefs are diffused into the prison. (Radical politics and militancy within American prisons will be discussed in chapter six.)

In an effort to compare the contentions of both the functionalists and the diffusionists, consider the following question: If different types of offender populations encountered the same deprivations, would they develop and maintain similar subcultures? The results of one Norwegian study and the research involving the inmates in 15 other Scandinavian institutions may give us a partial answer to this question. An analysis of the social organization of these institutions revealed that American type prison subcultures simply did not exist. While many inmates expressed a strong dislike for prison officials, they did not represent a cohesive lot that was in any way organized in opposition to the staff. Violence was unheard of in these institutions and even those individuals who informed on others were, as a rule, not punished by the other inmates. Inmate codes and associated role playing were almost nonexistent. The difference in behavior patterns of these inmates and those in American prisons should be quite startling to the functionalist, because the Scandinavian prisons were very similar to American prisons, both architecturally and administratively. In fact, the Scandinavian prisons were patterned after the Pennsylvania system. These inmates faced many of the same pains of imprisonment as American prisoners, but they reacted differently. While such evidence appears to represent a damaging blow to functional theory, it must be acknowledged that the following circumstances may partially account for the differences.

1. Scandinavian inmates serve shorter sentences than do their American counterparts, and therefore have less time to organize antagonistic subcultures.
2. Scandinavian inmates are segregated to a greater degree than are American prisoners and do not have as much opportunity to communicate and organize.
3. The deprivations that were faced in the Scandinavian institutions were not as keenly felt because the prisoners were not accustomed to the material comforts that American offenders usually enjoy on the outside.

However, it is highly probable that the characteristics of Scandinavian culture are simply diffused into their prisons. Reportedly there is less emphasis in their society on toughness or proving one's manhood (from a physical point of view) and there is a tendency to be more psychologically isolated and not as involved in social relationships. These same characteristics are definitely in evidence within their correctional institutions.[29]

In Scandinavian institutions the degree to which inmates held anti-staff sentiments differed a great deal from one institution to another. (Similar research findings by Street, Berk, and others were mentioned above.) What seems to be important here, however, is not the type of institution or the extent of the deprivations encountered by the inmates, but the type of inmates incarcerated in the particular institutions. For example, the most important

Although the cells in maximum security institutions are often too small to be comfortable, inmates are usually allowed to decorate as they please.

factor associated with strong anti-staff attitudes was the median age of first arrest. Those who experienced arrest at a younger age were more likely to harbor deep resentments toward prison officials than did those who were arrested at later ages.[30]

There is a great deal of additional evidence indicating that the attitudes and conduct of prisoners are molded by outside influences. A 1968 study of juveniles in Massachusetts institutions revealed that inmates attached a great deal of importance to life on the outside and were concerned about visits from friends and relatives as well as about how they would be accepted upon their return to the community.[31] In contrast, Sykes did not find prisoners to be preoccupied by interests in individuals and conditions outside of the institution. Forty percent of the population had no visitors during their entire incarceration periods.[32] While such lack of concern for and contact with outside interests was not found to be characteristic of the adult offenders studied by Glasser in a much more extensive research project, it is easy to understand why the New Jersey prisoners accorded a great deal of importance to maintaining and participating in the inmate subculture. When the prisoner has no outside resources, he may justifiably feel compelled to rely on the subculture for status, security, and rationalizations.

The functionalists' position does appear to be logical when explaining the development of the social organization of prisons that primarily house individuals who have long histories of incarceration and few outside contacts. However, even when discussing the social conditions that exist in most maximum security institutions only, there seems to be a great deal more evidence to support the diffusionist position. Inmate leaders certainly have an influence on the social organization of the prison and, in some institutions, the most anti-social inmates are the ones that are likely to become the leaders.[33] In choosing leaders, social backgrounds and experiences are of great importance; prisoners tend to choose as leaders those individuals who have committed offenses resembling their own, are similar in intelligence, and are assigned quarters in close proximity to their own. As in free society, individuals with similar interests and personalities seek each other out and maintain close associations. Educated prisoners, aggressive prisoners, homosexual ones, as well as many other types befriend those with analogous characteristics and lifestyles. Clarence Schrag, in his examination of role playing within the Washington State Prison, found this to be true in general, but also discovered that there was an overriding inmate preference for leaders who had committed crimes of violence. Leaders usually had spent more time in prison, were regarded as troublemakers by the staff, and were likely to be "officially diagnosed as homosexual, psychoneurotic, or psychopathic."³⁴ Thus, contrary to what Sykes found, the type of inmate that was admired by his peers was not the "real man," but the agitator with a history of violent behavior prior to commitment. Obviously when the most serious offenders are the leaders and molders of inmate opinion, there exists an anti-social climate that is bound to have an adverse influence on the younger prisoner.

Peter Garabedian's research can be offered as at least partial evidence in support of functional theory, since like Wheeler he found that prisoners tended to support anti-staff values and became more affiliated with the inmate group during the middle period of confinement when they were most psychologically removed from free society. However, while this was true for the majority of inmates, when Garabedian categorized them into role types, he discovered that role playing within the institution was definitely related to conduct prior to incarceration. The following are some examples. Prisoners referred to as "politicians" typically interact with both staff and inmates, to a greater or lesser degree, depending on the particular stage of incarceration that they are in, and try to manipulate both factions to their own advantage. Usually such individuals have committed crimes that require similar sophistication of manipulative abilities and wit. Like the politician, the "outlaw" exhibits a high degree of self interest, but the latter remains relatively isolated from both staff and inmates through all stages of confinement. This type of individual is likely to have participated in crimes of violence on the outside, and he continues to rely on physical force to get what he wants within the institution. The "right guy," as other researchers have noted, remains isolated from the staff, especially during the middle stage of imprisonment, and tends to be affiliated with the world of the professional criminal on the outside. The "square John" interacts with staff members more than do other types, and usually does not have an extended history of criminal behavior.³⁵

Also of interest is a study conducted by Elmer Johnson of fifty individuals who were labeled as rats and had been assaulted or at least threatened with physical retaliation from their peers. Curiously, this research indicated that it was not only those individuals who divulged information to staff members who were in danger of being categorized as rats, but also those who evidenced certain characteristics such as dependent personalities or middle-class value orientations that were in variance with the philosophies held by the majority of the prison populations.[36] Johnson's study, of course, is relevant to the present discussion because it reveals how the cultural milieu of an individual in free society affects his prison life. The emotional weakling who, while not philosophically aligned with either the inmate population or officialdom, was sometimes marked as a rat after seeking emotional support or solace through interacting with prison officials. This type of prisoner can sometimes get himself into serious trouble with his peers by behaving the way that the staff encourages him to. Prisoners with middle-class attitudes or orientations are likely to be ignorant of "the prison way of life." Johnson found that some inmates did not know that they were violating inmate standards by being friendly to guards. While certainly not trying to incur the wrath of their fellow inmates, they did so because of their naivete.[37]

Much more could be said regarding the analysis of role types, or as Sykes refers to them, "argot roles," as they have been presented by various writers, but such material is frequently founded on abstractions that have little basis in reality and therefore lend an artificiality to the description of prison life. Garabedian discerned various roles on the basis of attitudinal tests. One certainly can classify types by this method, but as other researchers can attest, when asking inmates about certain individuals, it is most difficult to obtain a concensus of opinion regarding the role playing activities of their peers even though they will be able to fit some into the ideal types. For example, most prisoners could name several politicians but there most likely would be disagreements as to whether or not a specific individual could be categorized as such.[38] Obviously, every member of the inmate population is not given a label (argot role) and those who are so categorized frequently reverse character and are thus regarded differently by their peers. Likewise, differing roles are often played simultaneously by the same individuals. A prisoner, for example, may be noted for playing both the role of a "gorilla" (an aggressive bully who victimizes the weaker inmates) and a "wolf" (an individual who aggressively plays the male role in homosexual relationships). The reader should be cautioned that the same difficulties associated with role type analysis in male institutions apply to the discussion of role playing in women's institutions.

MALE SEXUAL BEHAVIOR WITHIN THE PRISON SETTING

While no completely accurate statement can be made regarding the extent to which overt homosexuality is practiced in the average maximum security institution for men, observers of the correctional scene agree that the practice is quite extensive in almost all institutions.[39] The frequency of such behavior varies in accordance with the type of custodial and surveillance methods used by officials, the years spent in prison, and the social histories of inmates. Nevertheless, when the estimates of various authorities are taken into consideration, the evidence indicates that between 30 and 45 percent of our male inmate population have experienced overt homosexual contact while in prison.[40] There is documented evidence that, in a few mismanaged and decadent jails and prisons, the percentages run much higher than this.[41] Such figures may seem disturbingly high to some, but when considering sexual behavior in general, it is clear that the sexual activity of the average offender is substantially reduced after he is imprisoned. In other words, his sexual contacts, whether they are of a heterosexual or homosexual nature, are likely to have been more extensive in free society.

To assume, as do some functionalists, that homosexual activity within the prison is simply a natural consequence of being deprived of heterosexual contacts and being confined in close proximity to members of their own sex, is clearly an oversimplification of the problem. Prior life experiences also pattern the type of sexual response that the male will have to his incarceration. Research by Alfred Kinsey revealed that incarcerated offenders are more likely to have histories that indicate a variety of sexual experiences than are nonoffenders. This was shown to be true even when the inmate and noninmate sample groups came from the same social class. Social class is a very important factor, since the majority of prisoners come from the lower social classes. Sexologists maintain that members of the lower social classes tend to develop inner prohibitions against masturbation (one alternative source of sexual release within the institutional setting), and those who do engage in the practice seldom undergo sexual fantasizing during masturbation. According to Gagnon and Simon, "unlike the middle-class male who learns and rehearses sexual styles in the context of masturbation, the usual prisoner is drawn from a population in which sexual experience is concrete and not symbolic, in which there is a taboo on masturbation, and finally, in which much of heterosexual experience is structured around the need to have sexual encounters that validate his masculinity among other men."[42] If these authorities are accurate, then it is easy to understand why the lower-class prisoner sometimes resorts to "concrete" sexual acts of a homosexual nature, while another individual may be better prepared to release his sexual desires through masturbation and accompanying sexual fantasies.

It is quite evident that homosexual activity within the prison is usually not patterned after homosexual lifestyles on the outside, but on heterosexual role models. As with heterosexual relationships in the free community, in prison the masculine and feminine roles are clearly defined, and few individuals indulge in activities that are associated with both.[43] Most participants regard themselves as being purely heterosexual. Of those who engage in homosexual activity, the one who is best able to maintain his masculine self-concept is the "wolf." The wolf coerces others, physically or otherwise, into engaging in sexual activity, but he always insists on performing the male role in such relationships. In his own estimation, he is extremely manly and sees his behavior as a temporary substitute activity that allows him to fulfill basic sexual needs that would ordinarily be satisfied by females. Primarily as a result of his outward masculinity (physical aggressiveness), the lack of evident emotional involvement with his partner, and the fact that he invariably performs the masculine role in the sexual relationships, he is not scorned by the majority of his peers. He does not behave in any way that would imply there are romantic or emotional feelings associated with his sexual relationships. To disclose any hint that he regards his partner as anything more than an object of sexual release would place his masculinity in question. Whether or not the relationship involves masturbation or oral or anal intercourse, the wolf plays the dominant male role, and while he ejaculates, he does not actively or purposely stimulate his partner. Among certain groups of lower-class adolescents, behavior that is characteristic of the wolf is not necessarily considered abnormal. If a youngster allows a homosexual to perform fellatio on him for a sum of money, neither he nor his fellow gang members question his masculinity.[44] If the prisoner happens to come from a subculture where such a practice was common, he would probably have few moral reservations about engaging in homosexuality while incarcerated. Also, it must be realized that many offenders have led impoverished lives and, in terms of proving their manhood through self or family support, they have been failures. Many, if not most, have proved unsuccessful even in their criminal endeavors. Sexual conquest may have been their primary status source. Only by sexually exploiting women could some derive a sense of power or masculinity. Thus, the wolf's preoccupation with sexual exploitation may be directly related to his former lifestyle.[45]

No matter how manly the wolf's behavior, he must always have a gnawing realization that his sex life is not normal. If he cannot maintain a strong set of rationalizations for his behavior, it is always possible that he will be beset by homosexual panic. If he is apprehensive about becoming a true homosexual, he may either discontinue his homosexual activities or adopt a more passive role in such relationships. The latter reaction may eventually result in his self-confirmation as a homosexual, and his acceptance of a lifestyle appropriate to such an identiy.[46]

The wolf may bribe, coax, threaten, or actually physically assault other inmates in an effort to get them to comply with his wishes. Those who resort to extreme brutality to accomplish their goals should be given special mention, for their pathology exceeds that of the average wolf. Based on an extensive research project in which polygraphs (lie-detectors) were used during the interviews, Allan J. Davis "conservatively estimated" that there were at least 2,000 homosexual assaults within a 26-month period within the Philadelphia Prison system.[47] Sixty thousand prisoners passed through the system during that time period. This figure did not include the consensual or even semi-voluntary homosexual activity (where subtle pressures were involved) that was engaged in during this time period, but represented brutally sadistic rapes, frequently of a gang nature, that were physically painful as well as psychologically humiliating to the victims. Fortunately, such behavior does not typically occur as often as in this particular case and is seldom found where institutions are administered by competent officials. If officials in other systems were as lax as the ones in the institutions studied were alleged to be, similar deviant activity would quite possibly be the result. The aggressors tended to be individuals who were convicted of violent crimes. The aggressors not only viewed themselves as heterosexuals, but they also did not consider their sexual activity to be homosexual in nature. To their way of thinking, only the passive participant was engaging in homosexuality. Davis is convinced that the "conquest and degradation of his victim, and not sexual release, is the major goal of the aggressor." As with the average wolf, it is believed that the desire to degrade and humiliate others is born out of the frustrations associated with being socialized in a subculture where the only means of asserting one's masculinity and pride is through aggressiveness or sexual prowess. Racial hatreds seemed to be another precipitating factor in the Philadelphia sexual assault cases. There was also reason to believe that a number of those individuals who participated in gang rapes did so primarily to establish themselves as members of aggressive groups and, therefore, to lessen the likelihood that they would be chosen as victims.[48]

One of the most blatant examples of an individual who has weakened or given in to the pains of imprisonment is the type of inmate commonly referred to as a "punk." The punk assumes the role of the submissive partner in the homosexual relationship, not because he receives any genuine sexual or psychological satisfaction from doing so, but because he is intimidated by the aggressive wolf. The punk permits himself to be degraded in such a manner, usually either out of fear for his own physical safety or because the wolf has agreed to protect him from the ravages of other ruthless members of the population. Not only is this type of individual held in disrespect by his fellows because they regard his behavior as being repugnant, but they also regard him as a weakling and a coward. (Of course, the inmate is not necessarily regarded as a punk in those instances when, for example, he is viciously beaten and raped by a group after a gallant defense for his honor.)

There is a third type of homosexual participant who, in the language of the prison, is referred to as the "fag." This kind of person identified himself as a homosexual prior to his entry into the institution and continues to practice this form of sexuality after he is released. The fag receives true erotic satisfaction from engaging in the submissive role in sexual relationships. While he is regarded with contempt by most inmates, he is usually not felt to be as despicable as the punk. Certainly, from the viewpoint of the average prisoner, he cannot be respected as a man, but he does not engage in sexual abnormalities out of fear or cowardice. Thus, some are of the opinion that he should not be unduly persecuted for acting out desires over which he has little control.[49]

It should be noted that, as with argot roles in general, the sexual roles with which prisoners associate each other are differently labeled in various institutions. As examples, the wolf might also be called "daddy," or "jocker." Punks and fags are sometimes placed into the same category and labeled as "kids," "gal boys," "fruits," "cannibals," "head hunters," "brats," etc.[50]

Thus far, prison homosexual alliances have been characterized as cold, impassionate, and usually exploitative relationships. Most authorities would agree that this description is accurate and that such concepts as love, romance, affection, or even consideration are unimportant to most individuals who engage in sexual relationships in prison. However, there are others who have strong emotional needs for love and affection and attempt to fulfill these needs through the formation of homosexual liaisons. Others may bring warmth and affection to their sexual relationships in an attempt to, at least in a limited way, show some inmate solidarity in the face of prison adversities.[51] Research by Morris G. Caldwell disclosed the existence of courtships bearing similarities to heterosexual relationships and even marital-type ceremonies within institutions.[52] It is not unheard of for an inmate to proclaim that he does not desire a parole unless his "friend" can obtain one also, or for a prisoner to be injured or even slain as a result of a dispute stemming from a love triangle. Thus, there is evidence that shows that such relationships are not always outside the realm of emotionality. As one resident of a decadent prison system exclaimed, "I saw men learn to love boys harder than they could any woman."[53]

As far as controlling sexual behavior within the prison walls is concerned, it should not be assumed that the progressive educational upgrading of correctional personnel that has occurred within recent years will necessarily reduce the homosexual activity of inmates and, in fact, in many instances the very opposite results might be expected. Progressive prison administrators have come to the realization that prohibiting relatively free movement within the institutions and confining individuals in diminutive living quarters may be both demoralizing and dangerous to their mental health. As a result, prisoners usually are not as subjected to arbitrary restrictions as they were in the past, and are now more at liberty within the institutions. However, since architecturally most prisons and reformatories are relics of a past age, they are not equipped with the necessary surveillance facilities that would enable custodial officers to constantly view the activities of inmates as they take advantage of their institutional freedom. Thus, sexual perversion as well as brutality in its various forms are even more likely to go undetected than in the past. The functionalist might conclude that the more repressive regimes of the past may very well have furthered aggressive homosexuality by discouraging self-expression, thereby making the inmates more aware of the threats to their manhood. Thus, as a reaction to this particular deprivation, some would exploit others sexually. While this is probably true to a degree, many impoverished offenders, hostile and frustrated by societal barriers to success (manhood), would sexually exploit the more timid and weaker inmates, regardless of prison conditions.

Prison homosexuality is a subject that officials sometimes perceive as being relatively unimportant. They realize that associated jealousies and the exploitative nature of many of these relationships may lead to disruptive violence. While they are concerned about such dangers, they should also realize that even when violence is not blatantly evident, some inmates are being coerced into engaging in behavior that is foreign to their nature. The full significance of being degraded in such a manner may not be comprehended by the inmate himself until after release, but his self-concept and sexual identity may be permanently affected by the humiliations that he suffered. He may take his disgrace and self-hatred with him when he returns to free society, and thus be less prepared to cope with life situations than he was before imprisonment. Unfortunately, those most susceptible to sexual exploitation in the institutions are the weaker, and frequently less-serious criminals. Many show excellent potential for reform, but such a goal is certainly not furthered by allowing them to be preyed upon sexually.[54]

THE SOCIAL ORGANIZATION OF THE WOMEN'S PRISON

The developmental and maintenance processes that account for the specific characteristics common to the social organization of women's prisons in many respects resemble those that produce and support the inmate subcultures within male institutions. As is the case with the male offender, women tend to react in predictable ways to the institutional environment. Perhaps more significantly, however, much of the behavior that they exhibit after their imprisonment can only be attributed to the socialization and personality development that occurred in free society. The unique status of women in American society must be considered if we are to understand the women in prison. The functional theorist is quick to point out that females, like males, are forced to contend with the problems that are brought about by incarceration. However, their experiences on the outside pattern (sometimes in subtle ways) their response to such difficulties.

In contrast to the male offender, the female is usually not regarded as a serious danger to society. Therefore, the administrators of institutions for females are less concerned with external and internal security precautions than are those officials charged with the control of male prisoners. As was indicated in chapter three, female institutions are usually smaller than their male counterparts, are constructed on the cottage plan, and commonly provide individual quarters that can be decorated to suit the tastes of the occupant. Staff members, perhaps because they have no reason to fear for their personal safety, usually attempt to promote friendly interaction with the prisoners. In their study of the largest women's institution in the country, The California Reformatory for Women, David Ward and Gene Kassebaum discovered that most of the prisoners were quite surprised and pleased by their pleasant surroundings and by the friendliness of both staff members and inmates. Such circumstances were indeed comforting, since many inmates initially expected to be mistreated by officials and by their peers. While the professional expertise of those who administer women's institutions is usually no better than their counterparts in men's institutions, the female facilities are more likely to be characterized by a relaxed atmosphere and the adherence to humane treatment principles. Of course, like any other generalization, there are some documented exceptions. On occasion, women prisoners have been subjected to extreme brutality at the hands of sadistic and aggressive inmates as well as corrupt staff members.[55]

Despite the fact that the average female prisoner may be incarcerated in relative comfort, when the status of women in American society is taken into consideration, it is not difficult to conclude that the trauma associated with imprisonment is more severe for the female than for the male. To be separated from home and family in our culture is generally more painful for the female. For many women the husband, children, parents, or boyfriend are such integral parts of their existence that separation may result in serious depression or at least a gnawing anxiety regarding the welfare and behavior of their loved ones. These feelings may be especially intense for the woman with children who must be cared for by others during her period of confinement.

The American male, of course, has similar problems but, from an early age, he is taught to be more self-reliant. His prime interests are less likely to revolve around the home and family and he plays only a secondary role in the child-rearing process. Long term imprisonment is generally a more unique and, therefore, more disturbing experience for the female. Statistics vary from one jurisdiction to another, but there is evidence to indicate that inmates in women's institutions are less likely than male prisoners to have prior commitments, and their prior criminal involvement is considerably less extensive.[56] There is little empirical evidence to support the logical assumption made by some authors that because we tend to be more protective toward women in our society, we only incarcerate them for relatively serious offenses.[57]

It appears clear that the pains of imprisonment are quite different for women and relate more to outside conditions than to the deprivations that are encountered within the institutions. Likewise, the nature and character of the inmate code (when it exists among women inmates) is considerably different from the one adhered to by male prisoners. The admonitions to "be tough" or "be a man" are, of course, usually meaningless to women in or outside of the institutional setting. To maintain one's autonomy and to "do your own time" is not consistent with the dependent nature of women that has been cultivated in our society. Therefore, with one notable exception, role types such as "toughs," "gorillas," and "real men" that emphasize certain American male virtues are seldom if ever detected in institutions for females. The dependency and submissiveness that seem to be characteristic of American women probably represent the major reason why female prisoners rely on staff members for help and counsel to a much greater extent than do their male counterparts. Unlike the situation in men's institutions, where anti-staff feelings and group solidarity appear to be most extensive during the middle stages of incarceration, such sentiments, when they do exist in female institutions, are usually associated with early age of arrest and lengthy criminal careers.[58]

As in male prisons, there does seem to be an inmate prohibition against divulging information about their peers to officials in almost all women's institutions. However, the mandate that forbids ratting is much more frequently violated by female inmates, and those who are known rats are usually in no danger of physical retaliation. For example, Rose Giallombardo, in conducting her excellent study of the federal reformatory in Alderson, West Virginia, discovered that while women usually verbally indicate that ratting is about the worst thing a woman can do, the practice is extensive and the informer's safety is almost never in danger.[59] As in other women's institutions, there was so much ratting in Alderson that it became a problem for the institutional staff. For example, officials had no desire to discipline either the excellent typist who occasionally stole some office supplies for her own personal use or the productive worker in the dress shop who would procure a little material to make an article of clothing for herself. To remove such people from their jobs or even to reprimand them could create low morale or interfere with production quotas. However, when it became known that such individuals had been ratted on, the staff usually felt obligated either to take punitive action or at least investigate the situation. In the latter case, which was the most common staff response, officials frequently conducted pseudo-searches of the subject's room in which they would purposely overlook the stolen goods. Giallombardo contends that, because the inmates were usually aware that such contraband could have been uncovered if the staff really desired to do so, officials, by allowing rule infractions to go unpunished, were actually encouraging deviancy within the institution.[60]

It has been established that the inmate is profoundly affected by her socialization into womanhood and by the close ties to friends and relatives in the outside community. The greater the degree of her emotional affiliation with outside sources, the more likely she is to experience psychological discomfort and strife during her confinement.[61] Some women find that if they are to alleviate the feeling of loneliness and longing for an outside existence, they must learn to, at least temporarily, break the emotional ties that bind them to the outside world and participate in a "substitute universe" within the institution. This involves a resolution on the part of the individual to psychologically cut herself off from past or future concerns or commitments. The substitute universe, though artificial, is quite similar to the social world that the women participated in, or desired to, in free society, and revolves around an imitation family structure and an elaborate set of role types. Thus while the code as it exists in male institutions is virtually unknown in female institutions, group solidarity is also of the greatest importance to female inmates; for to adjust to the emotional deprivations that they encounter, they often have to rely on support from their peers. There is substantial evidence to indicate that in some institutions the major response to the pains of imprisonment is the establishment of homosexual alliances similar to the heterosexual relationships that they had previously maintained in free society. The extent of homosexual activity in women's prisons is unknown. Some writers, with no empirical support, reason that women in American society are better prepared to withstand sexual deprivation and, therefore, one would expect that less overt sexual behavior such as masturbation and homosexuality would be practiced in women's prisons than would be the case in institutions populated by men.[62] However, in the two major studies of women's institutions, when various staff and inmate groups were interviewed, no group estimated that less than fifty percent of the prisoner population participated in overt homosexuality, and one group (those who admitted that they participated) maintained that ninety to ninety-five percent of the women engaged in this type of behavior.[63]

When discussing prison homosexuality, it is important to distinguish the "true homosexual" from the "jailhouse turnout" or the woman who is primarily heterosexual, but engages in sexual activity with members of her own sex only because she is prevented from securing a male partner. It is probably easier for the true homosexual to adjust to prison life, since she does not have to adapt a new set of rationalizations that justify a change in sexual behavior. The confirmed lesbian usually adjusts relatively well to prison life, and frequently makes her confinement comfortable, "does easy time," by manipulating the environment and those in it. This is evidenced by the fact that the few politician and merchant types that are found in female prisons are usually true homosexuals.[64]

The true homosexual (in prison) usually adopts the role of the "stud" in homosexual alliances. Depending on the institution or the social group involved, she may also be referred to as a "butch," "daddy," or some other title indicating that she performs the dominant role in sexual and social relationships. Regardless of what she is called, she is expected to act and even look like a man. In attempting to maintain a male appearance, she usually wears short, cropped hair, uses no makeup, does not shave her legs, and walks with a manly gait. Her role expectations include opening doors for and helping the "girl friend" on with her coat as well as escorting her to various functions such as movies and recreational activities. If she is to be considered successful in this role, she must be prepared to defend her mate and never to exhibit any of the coquettishness and dependency that has been traditionally associated with the female. In fact, in Alderson, when a woman attempts to play this role but reveals feminine mannerisms and characteristics, she is labeled a "punk" and subjected to much ridicule by other inmates. While women who adopt the stud way of life in a free society are frequently regarded with scorn or at least amusement, this type of person is generally accepted and even appreciated by the institutional population. She is respected because she has mastered a role that few others have the ability or the inclination to play; but, more importantly, she supplies the desired male image in the institution.

The "femme" or "mommy," on the other hand, adopts a role similar to the one she engaged in on the outside. She attempts to maintain her femininity and physical attractiveness in a way that will prove to be pleasing to the stud. When possible she performs typical housewife duties such as cleaning, making her "husband's" bed, and washing "his" clothes. When engaging in overt sexual activity, she plays the passive role and, in general, is the more submissive and dependent partner. Her reliance on the male substitute is one way of attempting to cope with the threatening impact of her incarceration, and if she is able to view herself as bisexual, she has a better chance upon release of readapting to a heterosexual lifestyle with little emotional difficulty. Whether or not an individual finds this type of arrangement to be the easiest way of adjusting to imprisonment, of course, depends on the sort of life that she had in free society and the nature of her previous sexual behavior.

Unlike their counterparts in male institutions, female homosexuals usually advocate "sincere" love relationships with all the romantic trappings. Thus, even though the courtships and pseudo-marriages that take place within the institutions are of short duration, such argot types as the "chippie" (who indiscriminately jumps from one relationship to another) and the "turnabout" (who is also not sincere as evidenced by her willingness to play both male and female roles) are held in low esteem by others.

Within the federal reformatory at Alderson, as is the case in many other women's institutions, the formation of pseudo-marital units appeared to be the most common method of adjusting to the pains of imprisonment. However, marital partners were frequently only part of the total family configurations that were maintained there. As in male institutions, inmate cooperation was viewed as a necessity in Alderson in order to develop the type of stable and comfortable lifestyle that they desired—and to avoid exploitation by one another. This cooperation was most evident in the establishment of an elaborate set of kinship relationships. Two women, for example, may form a close friendship, but as a result of personal prohibitions or simply because they have no romantic inclinations toward each other, may not choose to become romantically or sexually involved. In such a situation they would generally accept one another as "sisters" (or, if they happen to play stud roles in other relationships, as "brothers"). By defining each other as close relatives, they will inform other inmates that no romantic involvement exists between them, thereby avoiding the jealousy, gossip, and bickering that often accompany sexual alliances. As indicated previously, the family constellations are sometimes quite elaborate at Alderson with some units consisting not only of "fathers," "mothers," "sisters," and "brothers," but also "grandparents."[65]

Of interest also is the relationship that is established between "homeys." If a girl enters Alderson who is from another inmate's home town or neighborhood, the two usually remain close friends during their incarceration. Giallombardo hypothesizes that these relationships are formed in order to maintain one's good reputation in the outside community. Homeys maintain amicable relationships with each other in hopes that neither will inform mutual acquaintances in the home community about their homosexual or other deviant activities within the institution. As a rule, homeys refrain from selecting each other as homosexual partners.

Women's prisons have not been the subject of many extensive research projects; therefore, it is by no means claimed that the above represents an adequate description of the average women's institution. In fact, while it has been well established that family constellations similar to the ones in Alderson do exist in other institutions, they most certainly cannot be found in all prisons that house females.[66] Women do, however, typically react to their imprisonment in ways that are consistent with the feminine role they play in free society. They usually attempt to maintain an adjustment that will, at least in part, satisfy their dependency and other socially defined female needs. This is accomplished mainly by adopting a submissive role model similar to the one adhered to on the outside. Even when the woman imitates the masculine role model within the institutional setting, she may still be meeting her needs in the way that she has been conditioned to in society. If she is a product of a broken or unstable home environment, and such circumstances are often part of the histories of female offenders, she may compensate through involving herself in a prison family. Perhaps, also, while the male finds security and satisfaction in membership in subcultures, the woman seeks the fulfillment of these needs through family membership and involvement.[67]

SUMMARY

Both the functionalist and the diffusionist can contribute to our theoretical understanding of the social organization of the prison. However, any analysis of prison life that takes only one of these positions into consideration proves to be incomplete and artificial. Evidence supports the functionalist's claims that the institutional environment can adversely affect the personalities of many inmates, and that some are irreparably corrupted or made dependent by their prison experiences. It has also been established that in order for the inmate to adequately adjust to the institution, he must usually learn to cope with the "pains of imprisonment" in prescribed ways. Some research evidence also indicates that for the average prisoner, many of the harmful effects of prisonization are not lasting, for even before he is released, he begins to readapt to an "outside" existence.

To be stigmatized as a criminal is disruptive to one's ego and personality development. However, we cannot refute the diffusionist's assertion that an individual's lifestyle is well developed prior to incarceration and determines, to a large degree, the type of behavior that he will engage in within the institution.

It is important to understand that while reducing or even eliminating many of the pains of imprisonment and becoming more humane in our dealings with prisoners are worthwhile goals, even if they are accomplished, little will have been done to reduce recidivism. Most experts in the field of corrections feel that a necessary prerequisite to the reform of the criminal is an in-depth analysis of his personality. Any evaluation that does not take into consideration an individual's family, social, and general environmental background is, of course, incomplete. The prison experience is just one factor that may contribute to a person's inability to adjust to legitimate societal norms. Regimented prison life may stunt independence and creativity. Can this be remedied by granting inmates more control over their own affairs and those of the institution?

At least in some prisons, the most dangerous offenders are the ones most likely to be chosen as leaders by their associates. Should the less dangerous criminal be sheltered from their corrupting powers? One would logically assume so, but if various types of offenders were segregated from each other, who would provide a pro-social stabilizing influence in a population comprised of hardcore offenders? Are certain rehabilitative techniques more successful with particular types of offenders than with others, and at what stages in the incarceration period are they most effective? While such questions will be considered in detail in chapter seven, the reader should now be prepared to offer some logical and constructive answers and comments.

ENDNOTES

1. Of course if we accept the psychiatric explanation previously alluded to, we would conclude that prisoners have found the ideal situation which they sought on a subconscious level and now reside in an environment which provides the life controls that they themselves could not. This explanation of criminality deserves consideration, but need not be dwelt on in this chapter since even many of those who espouse it concede that it does not apply to the majority of those who comprise our institutional populations.
2. Gresham M. Sykes and Sheldon L. Messenger, "The Inmate Social System," *Theoretical Studies in the Social Organization of the Prison* N.Y., Pamphlet #15, Social Science Research Council, 1960, pp. 5–19.
3. Gresham M. Sykes, *The Society of Captives: A Study of a Maximum Security Prison* N.Y., Atheneum Press, 1968.
4. Sykes and Messenger, *Theoretical Studies in the Social Organization of the Prison,* p. 72.
5. Ibid., p. 68.
6. Sykes, *Society of Captives,* p. 72.
7. Sykes and Messenger, *Theoretical Studies in the Social Organization of the Prison,* p. 5.
8. Ibid., p. 9.
9. Clarence Schrag, "Leadership Among Prison Inmates," *American Sociological Review* Vol. 19, 1954. Also see "A Preliminary Criminal Typology," *Pacific Sociological Review* Vol. 4, 1961.
10. Ibid.
11. Donald Clemmer, *The Prison Community* Holt, Rinehart and Winston Company, Incorporated, N.Y., 1958, pp. 298–304.
12. Stanton Wheeler, "Socialization in Correctional Institutions," *The Criminal in Confinement.* Leon Radzinowicz and Marvin E. Wolfgang, eds. (New York: Basic Books, Inc., 1971) pp. 97–116.
13. Peter G. Garabedian, "Social Roles and Processes of Socialization in the Prison Community," *Social Problems* 11:2, Fall 1963, pp. 140–152. Also see Daniel Glaser and John R. Stratton, "Measuring Inmate Change in Prison," *The Prison: Studies in Institutional*

Organization and Change. Donald R. Cressey, ed. (New York: Holt, Rinehart and Winston, Inc., 1961) pp. 381–392.
14. Robert C. Atchley and M. Patrick McCabe, "Socialization in Correctional Communities: A Replication," *American Sociological Review* Vol. 33, 1968.
15. David Street, "The Inmate Group in Custodial and Treatment Settings," *American Sociological Review* Vol. XXX, Jan. 1965; reprinted in *Prison Within Society: A Reader in Penology* edited by Lawrence Hazelrigg, N.Y., Doubleday and Co., 1968, pp. 199–228.
16. B. B. Berk, "Organizational Goals and Inmate Organization," *American Journal of Sociology* Vol. 71, March 1966, pp. 522–534.
17. John M. Wilson and Jon D. Snodgrass, "The Prison Code in a Therapeutic Community," *Journal of Criminal Law, Criminology, and Police Science* Vol. 60 Dec. 1969, pp. 472–478.
18. Ibid., p. 473.
19. For an extreme example of this, see the classic study by Bruno Bettelheim, "Individual and Mass Behavior in Extreme Situations," *Journal of Abnormal and Social Psychology* 1943, XXXVIII, pp. 417–452, and condensed in *Readings in Social Psychology,* edited by Eleanor E. Maccoly, Theodore M. Newcomb, and Eugene L. Hartley; Holt, Rinehart and Winston, N.Y., 1958, pp. 300–310.
20. See Erving Goffman's *Asylums: Essays on the Social Situation of Mental Patients and Other Inmates* Anchor Books, Doubleday and Company, Inc., N.Y., Chapter 1: Also see Gresham M. Sykes' *Society of Captives,* Chapter 4.
21. David Street, R. D. Vinter, and Charles Perrow, *Organization for Treatment* (New York: Free Press, 1966).
22. Wheeler, *The Criminal in Confinement,* p. 113.
23. Clemmer, *The Prison Community,* pp. 298–304.
24. Ibid., p. 298.
25. John Irwin and Donald R. Cressey, "Thieves, Convicts and the Inmate Culture," *The Other Side: Perspectives on Deviance* edited by Howard S. Becker, N.Y. The Free Press, 1964, pp. 225–245.
26. John Irwin, *The Felon* Englewood Cliffs, N.J., Prentice-Hall Inc., 1970, pp. 26–29.
27. Irwin and Cressey, *The Other Side: Perspectives on Deviance* pp. 225–245.

28. For an elaboration on this point, see Julian Roeback's "A Critique of 'Thieves, Convicts and the Inmate Culture,' " *Social Problems* II (Fall, 1963) pp. 193–200.
29. Wheeler, *The Criminal In Confinement* pp. 102–108.
30. Ibid., p. 106.
31. Ibid., p. 108.
32. Sykes, *Society of Captives*.
33. See Clarence Schrag, "Leadership Among Prison Inmates," *American Sociological Review* 19, 1954, pp. 37–42. And Peter G. Garabedian, "Social Roles and Processes of Socialization in the Prison Community," *Social Problems* 11:2, Fall, 1963, pp. 140–152.
34. *American Sociological Review* 19, pp. 37–42.
35. *Social Problems* 11:2, pp. 140–152.
36. Elmer H. Johnson, "Sociology of Confinement: Assimilation and the Prison Rat," *Journal of Criminal Law, Criminology and Police Science* Vol. 51, Jan.-Feb. 1961, pp. 528–533.
37. An interesting side light as far as this particular research is concerned is that it was generally discovered that after an individual had been labeled as a RAT by others in the population, his rate of rule and regulation infraction would diminish dramatically.
38. Daniel Glaser and John R. Stratton, "Measuring Inmate Change in Prison," *The Prison: Studies in Institutional Organization and Change* ed. Donald R. Cressey (New York: Holt, Rinehart and Winston, Inc., 1961) pp. 381–392.
39. In a letter to criminologists Harry Elmer Barnes and Negley K. Teeters, Alfred Kinsey states, "In regard to the incidence of the homosexual in penal institutions, I may indicate that we have never gathered histories from any male institution in which fewer than 35% of the inmates were involved in homosexual relations while they were in the institution. We have never secured histories from any long-term institution in which fewer than 60% of the men were engaged in such activity, and in one such institution we have over 90% of the inmates admit such experiences within the institution." Harry Elmer Barnes and Negley K. Teeters, *New Horizons in Criminology*, Englewood Cliffs, N.J.: Prentice-Hall, Inc., 1960, p. 373.
40. Gagnon and Simon, *Correctional Institutions* p. 225.
41. See Alan J. Davis, "Sexual Assault in the Philadelphia Prisons and Sheriff's Vans," *Trans-action*, (Dec. 1968) pp. 8–16.
42. Gagnon and Simon, *Correctional Institutions* p. 224.

43. Ibid., p. 225.
44. See Albert J. Reiss, "The Social Integration of Queers and Peers," *Social Problems* IX 1961, pp. 118–119.
45. Gagnon and Simon, *Correctional Institutions* p. 226.
46. Ibid.
47. *Trans-action*, p. 13.
48. Ibid., p. 16.
49. Sykes, *Society of Captives*.
50. See Clyde B. Vedder and Patricia King, *Problems of Homosexuality in Corrections* (Springfield: Charles C Thomas Pub. 1967), p. 18.
51. Gagnon and Simon, *Correctional Institutions* pp. 226–227.
52. Morris G. Caldwell, "Group Dynamics in the Prison Community," *Journal of Criminal Law* Vol. 46, No. 5 (Jan.-Feb. 1955) pp. 648–657.
53. Hayward Patterson and Earl Conrad, *Scottsboro Boy* (New York: Doubleday and Co., Inc., 1950) p. 82.
54. *Trans-action*, p. 9.
55. See Dorthy West, "I Was Afraid to Shut My Eyes," *The Saturday Evening Post* 241 (July 13, 1968), p. 23; Virginia Kellogg, "Inside Women's Prisons," *Collier's* Vol. 125, No. 22, (June 3, 1950), p. 15, and Kate O'Hare, *In Prison* (New York: Knopf, 1923).
56. David A. Ward and Gene G. Kassebaum, *Women's Prison: Sex and Social Structure,* (Chicago: Aldine Co., 1967) pp. 66–67.
57. John H. Gagnon and William Simon, "The Social Meaning of Prison Homosexuality," *Federal Probation* XXXII (March 1968) pp. 22–29; reprinted in *Correctional Institutions* edited by Robert M. Carter, Daniel Glaser, and Leslie T. Wilkins (New York: J. B. Lippincott Co., 1972), p. 229.
58. Ward and Kassebaum, *Women's Prison: Sex and Social Structure* pp. 56–79.
59. Rose Giallombardo, *Society of Women: A Study of a Women's Prison* (New York: John Wiley & Sons, Inc., 1966), pp. 105–115.
60. Ibid.
61. Ward and Kassebaum, *Women's Prison: Sex and Social Structure* pp. 1–29.
62. Gagnon and Simon, *Correctional Institutions* p. 229.
63. Giallombardo, *Society of Women: A Study of a Women's Prison*

p. 151; Ward and Kassebaum, *Women's Prison: Sex and Social Structure* p. 90.
64. Ward and Kassebaum, *Women's Prison: Sex and Social Structure* pp. 118–126.
65. Giallombardo, *Society of Women: A Study of a Women's Prison* pp. 158–188.
66. Also see Seymour L. Halleck and Marvin Hersko, "Homosexual Behavior in a Correctional School for Adolescent Girls," *American Journal of Orthopsychiatry* 32, 5 (1962) pp. 911–917.
67. Gagnon and Simon, *Correctional Institutions* p. 230.

5

Correctional Institutions in Transition

One of the most frequent criticisms of American prison systems is that they are opposed to change and progressive innovation. Twenty-five prisons in this country are over 100 years old, and many of our recently constructed institutions are architecturally obsolete.[1] While such circumstances are, indeed, distressing to the casual observer, the impression created may be somewhat false. Although the buildings are antiquated, the correctional programs used are not necessarily outdated. Some of our correctional institutions are very progressive, and we are justified in taking pride in them, but the majority of American prisons are, in fact, the "monstrous, inhuman dungeons, schools for crime, and centers for sexual abuse" described in the popular press and by concerned politicians.[2]

In recent years, correctional systems have employed many highly trained and talented practitioners of the social sciences who have initiated significant reforms. Along with this progress, however, many problems and conflicts have arisen. As innovation occurs, conflicts are created between new and old personnel, professionals and nonprofessionals. Long existent misunderstandings come to the forefront, and there is always the possibility of creating inmate unrest.

Along with alterations in the philosophical and educational backgrounds of correctional staffs, there has also been a change in the type of person who is incarcerated. The prison has, to a degree, become a microcosm of American society. The more socially conscious and revolutionary prisoner demands more enlightened correctional administration.

In this chapter the transformation of the social organization of American prisons will be discussed in light of the effects it has had on those directly involved and on society as a whole.

THE EMERGENCE OF A TREATMENT EMPHASIS

To both those who are employed in correctional work and much of the general public, it has been obvious that in the past decade a great deal of emphasis has been placed on the treatment or rehabilitation of criminals, as opposed to retribution and punishment. Along with this humanitarian trend has come an economic upgrading and increased prestige for correctional work. Because of this alteration in philosophy and the accompanying economic benefits for personnel, corrections can now, at least in a limited way, compete with other treatment organizations (such as private social service agencies and mental health clinics) for the services of trained social workers, clinical psychologists, and psychiatrists. Of all those in the "helping professions," social workers have found careers in corrections to be the most appealing. Having educational backgrounds that are superior to those of most other correctional employees, being supported by the influential American Association of Social Workers, and having been caught up in the challenge of revamping what seems to them to be a decadent system, many from this profession have demanded and obtained key policy making positions in state correctional organizations.

However, just as the academic and practical training acquired by social workers has qualified them for these important positions within correctional systems, this same training has in several ways prevented them from accepting less prestigious employment in the institutions. From an economic perspective, it is understandable that few professional social workers accept employment in and spend years working toward high positions in institutions. For example, a 1967 report indicated that median salaries of superintendents of juvenile detention homes ranged from $7,000 to $8,000 per year, and wardens (superintendents) of adult correctional institutions received median salaries ranging from $10,000 to $11,000.[3] Undoubtedly, salaries have significantly increased within the last few years, but unfortunately the economic upgrading of correctional work has not affected institutional positions to the extent that such employment is now regarded as attractive by the professionally trained worker.[4]

Accreditation concerns have also precluded consideration of institutional employment for many young social workers. After receiving a master's degree in social work, it is necessary to work for a two-year period under the direct supervision of an accredited social worker in order to be certified as an accredited social worker. Relatively few prisons have professional social workers on their staffs; therefore, it is frequently impossible for the novice to become accredited while performing institutional work. It should also be noted that in the eyes of the social worker (partially because of the nature of his education) the authoritarian atmosphere that exists within maximum security prisons is hardly conducive to the accomplishment of a rehabilitative goal.

However, many experienced social workers and other professionally educated and treatment-oriented individuals have accepted "headquarter executive" positions in state Divisions of Corrections (which govern state correctional bodies). Therefore, in some states correctional policy is made by individuals of one particular background, and presumably carried out by others who have not been schooled in the same philosophy.[5]

The literature and public statements from various "social work" oriented divisions of corrections often portray admirable, but unjustified, images of existing penal conditions.[6] Such material often outlines rehabilitative programs of all types—vocational, psychological, academic, and social—that are allegedly in progress. Such phrases as "helping the inmate help himself," "total staff approach," and "therapeutic community" are used, but no verbal emphasis is given to custody or the deterrent and retributive aspects of incarceration. Instead, the important roles played by social workers, psychologists, special therapists, and counselors are emphasized, even though there are few of these professionals actually employed in the institutions. The correctional facilities always seem to have an abundance of unfilled professional positions. There is little doubt that these statements by upper echelon officials represent honestly conceived plans for the future, and that reforms would be undertaken if the requisite funds and staff were available. Nevertheless, to understand the reality of the situation requires an in-depth examination of operating policies and practices of the actual institutions.

OFFICIAL AND OPERATIVE GOALS

When analyzing a correctional system, it is important to examine the discrepancies between the organization's "official" goals and its "operative" goals. As defined by Perrow, "official goals are the general purposes of the organization as put forth in the charter, annual reports, public statements by key executives, and other authorities . . . Operative goals designate the ends sought through the actual operating policies of the organization; they tell us what the organization actually is trying to do, regardless of what the official goals say are the aims."[7]

In evaluating the effectiveness of any prison or reformatory program there are two basic questions that must be asked. First, do the officials goals of the institution, as formalized by the Division of Corrections, coincide with its operative goals? Secondly, if they do not coincide, what is the possibility of the official goals becoming a reality?

With regard to the first question, a glance at the organizational chart of a maximum security institution (directed predominately by executives with professional social work backgrounds) would lead one to believe that treatment, the official goal, is of

CORRECTIONAL INSTITUTIONS IN TRANSITION 153

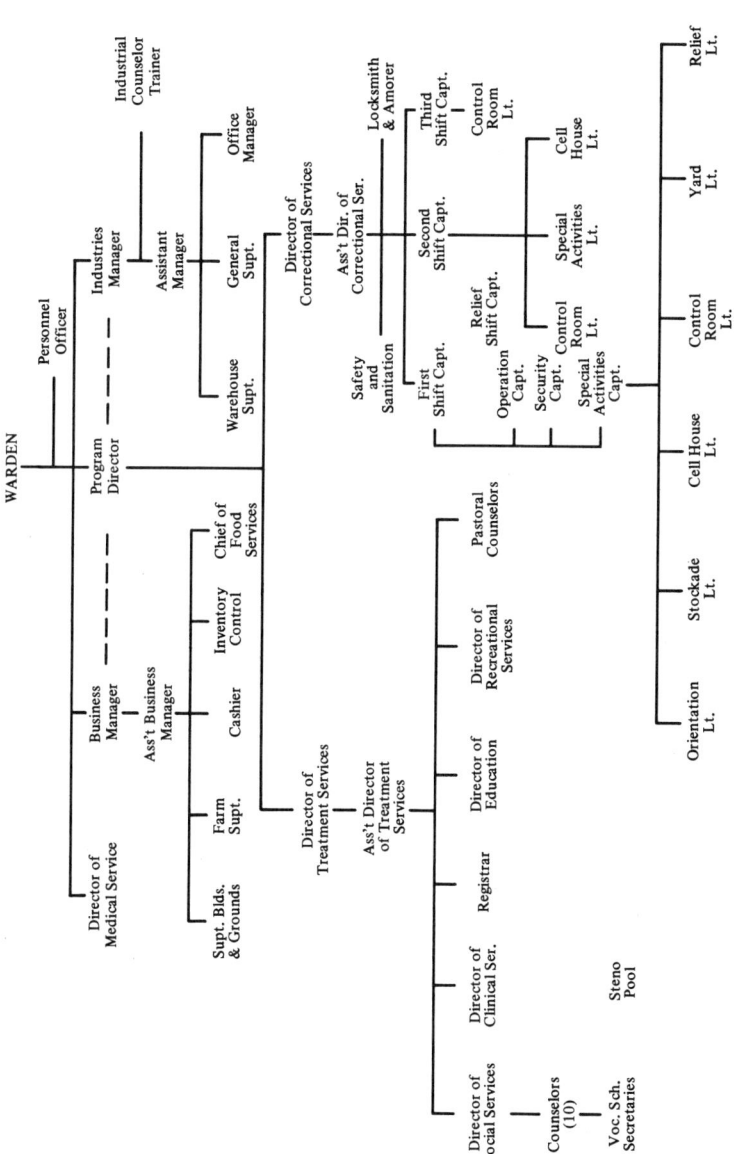

Figure 5.1 Organizational Chart of a Maximum Security Institution

secondary importance in comparison with custody (control of the inmate population). Only eight of the fifty employment categories have functions primarily aimed at treatment. Of course, the relative degree to which rehabilitation is emphasized cannot adequately be determined by looking at an organizational chart. However, to those familiar with this type of institution, the lack of direct concern with treatment efforts, outside of the relatively small social service departments, is quite evident. While we are presently concerned with correctional institutions that are externally governed by social work oriented executives, obviously, all correctional facilities do not fall into this category. Nevertheless, it is interesting to note that on a nation-wide basis only 12.7 percent of all employees in adult institutions have specific "treatment and training" responsibilities. The treatment emphasis appears to be more extensive in juvenile establishments, where 25.9 percent of their personnel function in treatment and training capacities.[8] Furthermore, and most regrettably, even in the social service departments, where treatment is considered the primary objective, the lack of expertise on the part of most staff members makes their rehabilitative efforts almost futile.

In addition, key personnel in charge of custodial or security services are quite often more experienced, knowledgeable, and respected than their counterparts in the treatment branches of the organization. For example, from viewing the organizational chart, one would assume that the director of treatment services (or associate warden of treatment) and the director of correctional services (or associate warden of custody) hold equally prestigious positions. However, in many institutions, because of his more extensive experience and his superior knowledge regarding correctional affairs, the director of correctional services is viewed as the higher official.

Observation does indicate then that the official goals of many institutions are not always realized, and we can agree with Perrow when he states that "the type of goals most relevant to understanding organizational behavior are not the official goals, but those embedded in major operating policies and the daily decision of personnel."[9] An institution's operational goals seem to be directly related to the pertinent problems and concerns of its organization and the backgrounds and orientations of its personnel. To many prison and reformatory employees, the official goals are commonly regarded as either unrealistic and unobtainable, or based on an unsound philosophy. Frequently, only the minority who are directly involved in treatment programs give credence to them. As will be evident, such circumstances often result in antagonism between the treatment staff and the majority who emphasize the importance of the custodial aspects of imprisonment. The more clever inmates sometimes successfully add fuel to intra-staff hostilities by persistently drawing further employee attention to and exaggerating the philosophical differences between "treatment" and "custody" personnel.

In summation, the official policy may indicate that the goal of the institution is treatment. However, the operative goal, which is in actuality reached, frequently is primarily concerned with custody, and the organizational structure itself gives little emphasis to treatment. In other words, the operative goals which coincide with the interests of the majority of the institutional staff may bear no relation to the official goals and may develop into standard institutional policy.

THE POSSIBILITY OF CHANGE

The second question to be answered is: What is the possibility of the official goals ever becoming a reality? As indicated, the operative goals will be directly related to the values and orientations of the dominant group and to the organizational structure itself.[10] Usually the dominant groups in prisons and reformatories are primarily concerned with custody. However, there is a real possibility that the social work philosophy, the official goals, eventually will become dominant in American correctional institutions.

At the present time, in most correctional institutions across the country, it is virtually impossible for those with a social work philosophy to initiate their "progressive" programs. Most individuals in key positions in these institutions would not give support to what they regard as one-sided social work ideals. However, if social workers were placed in key positions they could, and have in some instances, develop lines of promotion that would eventually result in placing other social workers in such vital administrative positions as warden or associate warden. If this became common practice, the direction of policy development would eventually be dictated by this group.

The rapidity with which the social work philosophy could gain acceptance can also be examined from another point of view. According to Price, when the social system allocates decision making to "role," "rational legal" decision making results.[11] Those in the chain of command believe the person occupying a role to have the legal and rational right to play the role of superior and they have a sense of duty to conform to his demands. Formal rank and ability are thought of as being closely related, and so those social workers filling key positions or roles will have an added advantage in promoting their ideas.[12]

In studying the prison as a formal organization we may not be accurate if we assume that it is analagous to all other such organizations. For example, the expert in social work, psychology, or psychiatry is not automatically accorded prestige by his underlings in the same manner that an engineer in a modern factory is likely to be. The behavioral scientist is seldom viewed as a true scientist, but many times as little more than a classroom theorist. Also, while empirical evidence, except on a limited scale, is lacking, practical observations would support the conclusion that social work administrators have considerable difficulty in eliciting cooperation from line personnel.

As more staff with social work backgrounds is recruited for institutional work, their influence will, of course, increase. With this in mind, a major obstacle that social workers may encounter in their attempts to dictate correctional policy should be mentioned. An extreme emphasis on treatment may be supported by the changing values of society. However, more probably, the public will not only find fault with the "profession's" seeming lack of concern for societal protection, but also with its emphasis on a type of specialization (involving casework techniques) which many feel conceals the correctional process from public scrutiny. These problems may be at least partially alleviated by the increasing number of individuals who are entering the field after receiving graduate training in corrections. Many of these new academic programs in corrections will produce treatment oriented administrators who not only have mastered casework techniques, but understand progressive security procedures and are knowledgeable in the disciplines of penology, criminology, criminal justice, psychology, and sociology.[13] Unfortunately, in a few states whose correctional systems are completely controlled by professional social workers, regulations still prohibit the hiring of holders of master's degrees in corrections (unless they also have advanced degrees in social work) for supervisory positions. Such uncompromising policies are not only illogical, but they are in direct opposition to the recommendations of almost every official correctional organization, including The Joint Commission On Correctional Manpower and Training.[14]

In conclusion, the point that the official goals of the Division of Corrections in many states do not coincide with the operative goals of the individual correctional institutions should not, of course, be generalized to include all correctional institutions in the United States. For example, as Sykes indicated in his study of the New Jersey penal system, the correctional philosophy that formed the basis for this system assumed that an individual could not be expected to obey the rules of society if he were not forced to conform to the discipline of the institution. In the New Jersey prison that Sykes studied, social work or treatment was given a very minor role and the official goals seemed to be the maintenance of proper segregation of offenders, the protecting of inmates from each other, and strict custodial practice.[15] Of course, it is easy to find a great deal of fault with this type of system, but it is obvious that because their official goals coincided with their operative goals, there was limited confusion and a relative lack of public misunderstanding of their position.

INTERNAL CONFLICT: AN INCREASING PROBLEM

As Cressey indicates, society traditionally expects the administrators of its correctional institutions to emphasize the goals of "incapacitation, retribution, deterrence, and reformation."[16] Reformation has been an increasing concern in recent years, and there is evidence to show that such changing attitudes towards prisons and their inhabitants are, to a degree, uniform throughout the country.[17] Of course, the extent to which humanitarian sentiments are activated into concrete programs differs enormously not only from state to state, but from institution to institution within the same political boundaries. The various differences in the goals of correctional systems, the attitudinal and background characteristics of institutional staffs, and the availability of sufficient funds to support institutional programs (something over which correctional administrators usually have little control) account for the lack of national uniformity in correctional practices.

We have analyzed how philosophical differences between "headquarter executives" and institutional staffs may result in reduced organizational effectiveness and public misunderstanding. Those who have examined the correctional scene have discovered that the value orientations of the administrators and the lower echelon personnel are particularly relevant to determining the directions that institutional policy will take. Staff attitudes are, of course, usually the end products of both education and experience. Zald's analysis of five correctional institutions for juveniles indicated that the power wielded by various interest groups was directly related to whether or not each group's philosophy coincided with the dominant goals of the institution in question.[18] For example, in the type of institution that gives prime emphasis to societal protection and internal security (custody), guards (correctional officers) either control the organization or are at least more influential than counsellors, social workers, or other treatment specialists. The reverse is found to be true in treatment-oriented establishments.

High caseloads, the inmate code, and intrastaff conflict often reduce the correctional counselors' effectiveness.

Zald, on the basis of his studies, also concluded something of which correctional practitioners are increasingly aware—that there is more intrastaff conflict in treatment oriented institutions than in institutions that emphasize the goal of custody. Quite understandably, when cottage parents, teachers, counselors, and others have divergent views regarding correctional philosophy, hard feelings and intense competition are likely to develop between the group that actually controls the institution and other employee groups who are less powerful. Conflict between staff echelons usually develops within institutions where older ("longtime") security oriented employees work under the direction of treatment oriented administrators. To a lesser extent, serious conflict between treatment oriented employees can arise when there is disagreement over what type of rehabilitation program and/or techniques should be implemented.

Also, Zald found that serious conflicts arise only where there is intercommunication between groups. As a case in point, the administrators of one of the institutions in his study held societal protection to be their primary objective, but this position did not coincide with the philosophy of the institutional school teachers. Nevertheless, because the teachers were not included in any decision-making processes concerning policy, were not consulted regarding administrative matters, and held no authority outside the classroom, their antagonism was of little importance to the institutional elite and was not disruptive to the organization.

Another of Zald's observations is appropriate as it relates to the organizational effectiveness of treatment oriented institutions. He asserts that if conflict between staff members is to be avoided, lower echelon personnel must be allowed to participate in the decision making that affects organizational problems. The professionals who administered the treatment institutions did not seem to realize that if guards, house parents, industrial supervisors, and other nonprofessionals were not included, in any real sense, when institutional policies were being developed, they could not be expected to exhibit unbridled enthusiasm about their role in an organization they regarded as being based on an unsound philosophy.[19] Even where circumstances enable professionals to carefully screen potential custodial employees, the problem is by no means alleviated. Unlike experts in many fields, the "expert" in the behavioral sciences is not necessarily respected by those with less formal education.

What Zald fails to mention is that, usually, professionals are, in fact, explicitly schooled in a philosophy that advocates the necessity of permitting lower staff members to become active in the decision-making processes. In actuality, however, it frequently becomes obvious that the professionals are in no way prepared to let the untrained nonprofessionals determine, in any vital manner, administrative policies. Most nonprofessionals are quick to realize the farcicality in the upper level personnel's pretended attempts to gain their involvement.

DIFFERING VALUE ORIENTATIONS

Additional empirical evidence supports the assertion by many correctional workers that, especially in recent years, there are great hostilities between professionals and nonprofessionals. After his extensive examination of a number of institutions for juveniles, Weber enumerated the differing value orientations which all too often brought about disagreements between the two personnel types.[20] The professionals interviewed in this study tended to see themselves as humanitarians who were obliged, because of their superior education, to scrutinize and guide all administrative and rehabilitative efforts. The nonprofessionals, in return, considered themselves the "backbone" of the organizations, and they evaluated the usually less experienced professionals as being much too theoretical and as "pseudointellectuals." The nonprofessionals had little academic comprehension of the etiology of delinquency, and regarded common sense along with kind but firm treatment as the most desirable method of handling their charges. They voiced little sympathy for or agreement with the diagnoses and treatment schemes devised by the professionals who had substantially less contact with the individual delinquents. Also, as Weber states "Many nonprofessionals assumed that all surface behavior had the same dynamics or meaning. Thus, they were confused when the professionals recommended dissimilar attitudes and activities for what the nonprofessionals thought were like delinquents."[21] In other words, any attempts to individualize treatment (treat youngsters on the basis of their personality makeup or sociological background, irrespective of their offense or rule violation) were viewed by the nonprofessionals as examples of injustice and inconsistency. Interestingly enough, there is evidence to indicate that delinquents tend to concur with the nonprofessionals in such evaluations.[22] The professionals were disgruntled because they felt that the lower staff members disregarded their recommendations, were too strict, and did not try to understand the youngsters. While both groups perceived the necessity of establishing some form of control over the deviant activities practiced by the juveniles, the nonprofessionals were more likely to evaluate misbehavior from a moralistic perspective.

The following quote by a farm employee at an institution for juveniles represents an attitude that is not atypical of nonprofessionals.

> I work with boys all day long, every day. I know a boy, what he is like and what he's not like, what he can do and can't do. Just the other day, without me saying a thing, a boy told me about his home and cried. I can't put it in the language that those people in the administration building can— that is, put it up so nobody but them can understand it—but I know this boy. That outfit up in the administration sees a boy for a few hours and they think they know the whole story and then they want to tell us in language we can't understand. And besides the kids come back to us all upset about these tests they give 'em.[23]

As indicated, in many juvenile and adult institutions, vital decisions concerning the welfare of the inmates are made on the basis of extremely superficial relationships between professionals and inmates. The nonprofessionals, who are more familiar with the daily activities of the prisoners, do not in reality have a significant role in the decision-making processes.

THE BREAKDOWN OF ORGANIZATIONAL EFFECTIVENESS

Naturally, such divergent attitudes make coordinated efforts between various staff members next to impossible. The resulting breakdown in organizational effectiveness is magnified when some staff members withdraw from interaction with their peers or secretly turn to "headquarters" officials in hopes of removing personnel toward whom they are particularly antagonistic.[24] Such behavior presents an ideal opportunity for the more intelligent and devious inmates to manipulate staff members and further turn them against each other.

In a highly bureaucratic institution, formal staff positions involve specific role expectations and, therefore, changes in personnel seldom disturb the overall functioning of the organization. However, because there is no universally sanctioned training for correctional administrators, many differing disciplines and philosophies are represented in the field. Despite the formality that is characteristic of many correctional facilities, conflict is destined to arise when institutional goals are changed abruptly by new administrative officials. Likewise, conflict will arise when a newly appointed administrator is viewed by some as being opposed to their rehabilitation efforts. A prime example of such a situation was evidenced in Grusky's study of a small midwestern prison camp in which severe antagonism developed between the custody oriented staff members and the treatment oriented employees. These potentially explosive conditions originally were controlled by a chief administrator who assumed a relatively neutral position. When this official was replaced by one who emphasized custody, staff conflict became more overt and was reflected in increased hostility and rebellion on the part of the inmates. According to Grusky's analysis:

> Three general factors within the camp's staff contributed to the organizational strain: (1) the decline of the old informal group among the staff, (2) the inability of the new supervisor to enlist the staff's cooperation in enforcing the new policies because of his overcommitment to the custodial goal, and (3) the lack of direct communication channels from the inmates to the guards to the supervisor, resulting in a lack of immediate knowledge by the chief policy maker of the impact of his decisions.[25]

As Grusky indicates, the problem of disturbances and riots within the walls of correctional institutions is, at least in some cases, directly related to staff conflict. This assertion is supported by the extensive investigations conducted by the authors of *Riots and Disturbances in Correctional Institutions,* who maintain that "there does appear to be an identifiable causal relationship between inmate disturbances and staff conflict. There must be a consistent policy through the institution in dealing with the inmates, and the philosophy and goals of the institution must be reflected by all staff members."[26]

The social organization of a prison basically consists of three power groups: administrative personnel, line personnel, and the inmate population. Conflict between staff echelons may result in the reduced effectiveness of programs initiated by either group. Some inmates understandably become disillusioned and cynical when they observe one employee group attempting to prevent an-

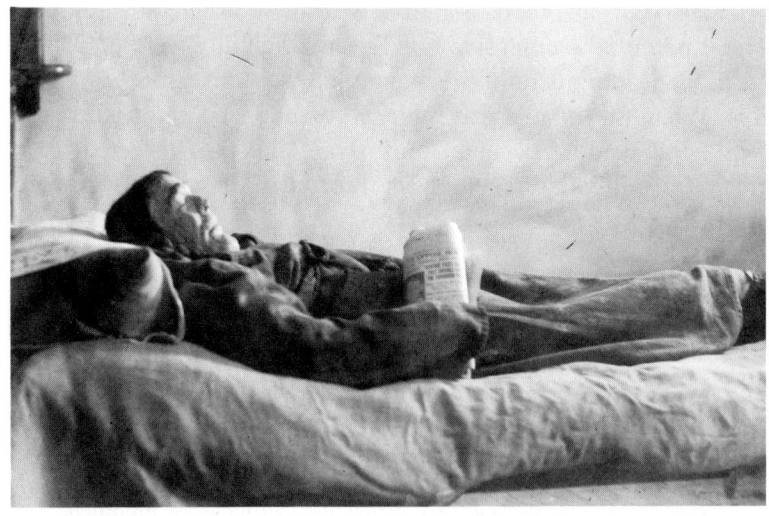

Escape Attempts. An inmate was successful in fooling the guards with this look-alike dummy that he made, but he ultimately failed in his attempt to escape.

other group from developing programs that inmates generally approve of. For example, counselors may attempt to initiate more evening programs where guests and entertainers from the outside are brought into the institution. Corrections officers may vehemently oppose such programs because they entail the maintenance of extra security precautions and more supervision. The prevention or cancellation of such activities is often interpreted by inmates to mean that the staff is generally not concerned about their welfare. Unfortunately, planning programs that would be beneficial to prisoners and then not following through with these plans may be more disappointing and frustrating to inmates than doing nothing in the first place.[27]

DISORDER IN A CHANGING PRISON WORLD

Because the prison is a closed community, conflictual and anxiety-producing situations are difficult to avoid, and, in fact, are perhaps experienced more intensely than they would be in normal society. In such an atmosphere, crises develop rapidly and sometimes prove disastrous for both the inmates and staff members. Rumors and incidents associated with changes in administration, intrastaff disputes, warring inmate factions, the arrival of a famous underworld figure, the granting of a pardon, or the winning of an appeal, all can produce emotionally explosive conditions.[28] However, the most grievous and, of course, dramatic of all crises is the riot. While the literature on the subject indicates that riots have always disrupted or threatened correctional systems, it is difficult to define exactly what a riot is, or at what stage an inmate-created disturbance reaches riot proportions. This discussion will subjectively be confined to those incidents where a number of prisoners have (1) temporarily seized control of a portion of an institution and represented threats to the safety or lives of hostages, or (2) created excessive physical damage to institutional property. For example, such cases existed in the

1952–53 disorders in Michigan, Pennsylvania, and Ohio, accounting for approximately $2,000,000 in damages in each instance.[29]

In 1952 at Jackson State Prison in Michigan, "the worst wave of riots in history," began and spread in "epidemic" form to 15 other institutions throughout the country by the end of that year. The years 1952–53 witnessed 25 major prison disturbances.[30] Beginning in Walla Walla, Washington and ending in Deer Lodge, Montana, where the deputy warden was shot to death by an inmate leader, another tragic but less extensive series of riots occurred in 1959.[31] Violent prison disturbances such as the incident at San Quentin Prison that resulted in the deaths of self-styled revolutionary George Jackson, three guards, and two other inmates, and a number of isolated disturbances have been common within recent years.[32] The catastrophe at the Attica Correctional Facility in New York, which left 32 inmates and 10 correctional employees dead, fortunately, did not set in motion another sequence of major outbursts.[33]

"BRUTAL" RIOTS

Hartung and Floch, in their analysis of the 1952 disturbances, differentiated between (1) "brutal riots—those whose origin appears to have been mainly in what can be regarded as the historical causes of prison riots and (2) collective riots—those whose origin appears to have been mainly in a combination of certain penal advances and the nature of the maximum custody prison."[34] Hartung and Floch contend that the brutal riot represents the "overwhelming majority" of all riots, and that this type will occur as long as hatred and frustration-breeding conditions remain in some institutions. According to them, those conditions are:

1. poor, insufficient, or contaminated food
2. inadequate, unsanitary, or dirty housing

3. sadistic brutality by prison officials
4. some combination of the first three.[35]

However, this list of "common sense" precipitating factors should be expanded considerably in order to fully comprehend the brutal riot.[36] Also, while inadequate food, unsanitary living conditions, and staff-initiated physical brutality does in fact exist in a few institutions, such conditions are relatively rare today. This appears to be the case, even though rebelling inmates still frequently demand changes in personnel, better food, and adequate medication.[37] There is ample reason to believe that such demands reflect ex post facto rationalizations and are often conjured up after the riot has reached full intensity.[38]

The authors of *Riots and Disturbances in Correctional Institutions* list unnatural institutional environment and antisocial characteristics of inmates as general causes of prison riots. It is a logical contention that the anxiety and emotional stress that is brought about by regimentation, exploitation, deprivation, and general dehumanizing surroundings become intolerable preludes to open rebellion, even though the actual disturbances are sometimes ignited by lesser grievances such as specific incidences of staff ineptness, insensitivity, conflict, or over-reaction to small disciplinary problems.[39]

The "antisocial characteristics of inmates" as they relate to racial and/or political militancy will be discussed later, but it should be noted here that violent careers do not necessarily terminate upon entrance into the confines of a correctional institution. Obviously, it is true that "correctional institutions have a disproportionate share of individuals who are mentally deficient, emotionally unstable, and prone to violent and other socially deviant behavior."[40] In fact, more researchers should be concerned with ascertaining why such individuals do not sieze control from their usually unarmed and defenseless captors more often than they do. It should also be understood that in the past the vast majority of prisoners were not physically aggressive or violence-prone individuals. Usually, in progressive systems today, only those who are considered to be a threat to the safety of others are confined in maximum-security institutions. Most other of-

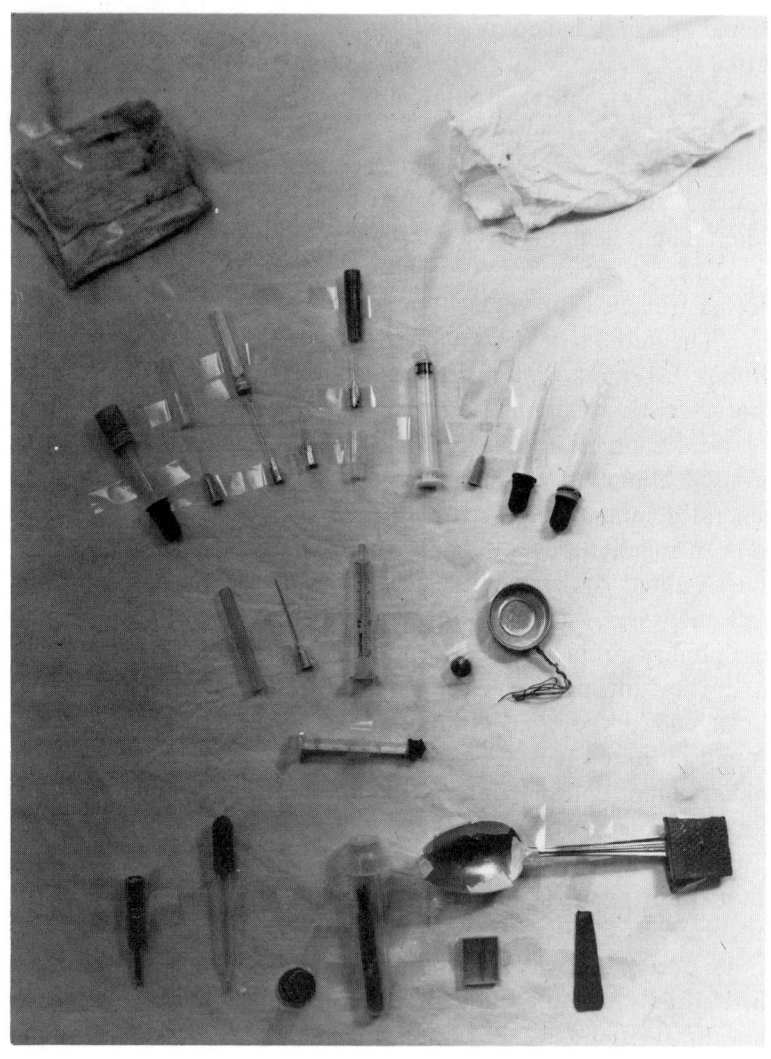

CORRECTIONAL INSTITUTIONS IN TRANSITION 169

Contraband. These weapons and drug paraphernalia were discovered during a "shakedown" of cells at a maximum security institution.

fenders are allowed to remain in the community on probation or parole. Therefore, today a larger proportion of our prison population is made up of dangerous offenders than at any other time during our history. Obviously, it was easier to administer an institution where the dangerous offender was the one who deviated from the norm than it is to administer an institution in which the nonaggressive inmate is the one who is considered to be abnormal.[41]

It is tempting for the academic penologist to enumerate and elaborate on the relationship of riots to inept officials and decadent correctional practices which promote favoritism, forbid fraternization of staff with inmates (and thus preclude the establishment of productive communication between the two groups), and fail to communicate policy changes adequately to either staff member or inmate. While officials obviously should not be immune from criticism, it should be noted that the causal process usually originates outside the walls of the institution and beyond the realistic control of correctional administrators. The bulk of the problem is rooted in public apathy or punitive societal attitudes. Some contend that prisoners perceive of rioting as the only method of bringing about societal concern through the publicizing of their grievances.

"The riots result, we believe, not from bad prison conditions or practices but from the belief of prison inmates that the only way in which they can gain public interest in improving such conditions is by rioting. Nonviolent protests or requests for remedial action, prisoners believe, never accomplish anything. Riots sometimes do."[42]

Public disinterest has been reflected in the failure of its elected representatives to provide the requisite finances that would upgrade an underpaid, understaffed, and poorly trained correctional work force. For the same reason, we are plagued with outmoded and overcrowded physical structures in which exists an atmosphere of gloom, despair, and thus, potential rebellion. As noted previously, such institutions usually do not have the proper facilities to segregate various types of offenders, provide adequate therapeutic programs, or even to use constructive labor. With

The prison labor problem is complicated by legislation that severely limits the sale of prison-made goods on the open market.

regard to prison labor, the problem is further complicated by legislation, promoted by competition-fearing community pressure groups, that severely limits the sale of prison-made goods on the open market.[43] As a consequence, prison industries seldom teach useful skills and many of the inmates are idle.[44]

Lastly, when searching for "common sense" explanations, it must be realized that the "inequities and complexities in the criminal justice system," which exist apart from and unrelated to the institutions, breed a smoldering resentment that affects the attitudes of the incarcerated.[45] Blatant disparities in sentencing procedures and parole practices may offend the inmate's sense of justice and increase his antiestablishment feelings.

All of the above circumstances have at one time or another appeared to be causally related to prison riots or disturbances. However, where one or many of these conditions exist, it does not necessarily follow that rebellion will be the result.

ATTICA: THE ANATOMY OF AMERICA'S
MOST BRUTAL RIOT

The report of the New York State Special Commission on Attica referred to the riot that took place at the Attica New York Correctional Facility from September 9–13, 1971, as "the bloodiest one-day encounter between Americans in this century."[46] During those five days, world-wide attention focused on that institution, located in a rural section of the state, as 43 men were killed and scores of others were injured. Thirty-nine people, 28 inmates and 11 correctional employees, were slain in a 15 minute fusillade conducted by State Police and some corrections officers as they overwhelmed both the inmates and their hostages.

Because of their complexity and their relationship to philosophical and moral concerns that exceed the scope of this discussion, several controversial issues associated with the Attica uprising will not be covered here. When considering important questions that relate to the negotiating that took place between Commissioner Oswald and inmate leaders, his final actions, and Nelson Rockefeller's refusal to come to Attica, the reader is encouraged to consult the source material that is available before drawing any conclusions.[47] Also, because we are more concerned with determining causal factors, the pros and cons of the attack on the inmate stronghold will not be dealt with in detail. It should be mentioned, however, that it was an extremely vicious and poorly planned assault. As the Special Commission's investigation revealed, no precautions were taken to avoid injuring hostages or peaceful inmates; numerous "scatter" weapons, such as shotguns (which could hardly be expected to hit only those inmates who were thought to be assigned the role of executioners and not hit the hostages or other inmates) were employed, and some corrections officers, using weapons, took part in the attack even though they were not authorized to do so.

The best information available indicates that several of the conditions that were identified as precipitating factors in brutal riots existed at Attica prior to the inmate uprising. Attica was an institution that had little to offer inmates in terms of vocational training, academic schooling, or therapeutic services. Reportedly, inmates spent as many as 16 to 18 hours a day in their cells and were subjected to, perhaps to an even greater degree than are most prisoners in other maximum security institutions, intensified regimentation and pains of imprisonment similar to those previously discussed.

Other contributing factors were related to the growing number of politically sophisticated and anti-authoritarian inmates, who were gaining more influence among the captive population. Many of these antiauthoritarian inmates had been transferred to Attica from other institutions because of their disruptive activities. Sensing a lack of support from headquarters and from the courts, the all-white officer corps (most of whom were from rural backgrounds) was puzzled and threatened by this new breed of prisoner. The officials found it difficult to deal with these prisoners, many of whom had participated in and were strongly influenced by the urban riots of the 1960s, and who seemingly refused to accept official authority.

THE CHAIN OF EVENTS

On September 8, a dispute occurred in one of the yards between an officer and an inmate. This dispute came precariously close to blossoming into a much larger and more serious confrontation, but the outnumbered officers backed down. This was the first major link in the chain of events that culminated in the insurrection. That same night, two of the inmates who allegedly had been involved in the afternoon flare-up were removed from their cells and placed in solitary confinement. Both of the inmates were believed by the rest of the cell block population to be innocent of any wrongdoing. While they were perhaps not entirely blameless, the two inmates were, in fact, victimized because officers were mistaken as to who they were and what type of activity they had engaged in.

The inmates assumed, primarily because they misinterpreted

the noises that one of the resisting inmates made when he was being removed from his cell, that he was being beaten by officers. While this assumption was later shown to be completely false, it aroused emotions within the cell block and further solidified the inmate population in opposition to the administration. They perceived themselves as being betrayed, and they were convinced that their "brother" was being tortured unjustly.

The second man was removed from the unit that housed most of the inmates who were regarded as "troublemakers." While the inmate put up relatively little resistance as he was taken from his cell, other prisoners hurled various objects and shouted epithets at officers as they escorted the inmate to solitary confinement. Many vowed to gain revenge for this injustice.

One of the objects that was thrown by an angry inmate was a can of soup, which struck an officer in the head and injured him to the extent that several stitches were required. The inmate whom the officers regarded as the culprit was keep-locked (locked in his own cell when he normally would be engaging in activities outside of his individual quarters). However, in direct defiance of official authority, the individual was released from keep-lock by another prisoner, and he joined the other inmates at breakfast. As the company of inmates returned from breakfast, they passed through the central section known as Times Square, where there is access to all four major divisions of the institution, and continued on into one of the adjacent corridors as one of the Times Square gates locked behind them. They expected to be released through another gate into the yard, but officials, who were disturbed about the release of the inmate from keep-lock, had different plans for them.

While opinion varies regarding what the exact order was and who gave it, the authorities decided to return the company of inmates to their cells. A lieutenant, who had been involved in the confrontation in the yard the day before and whom the inmates had mistakenly believed to be responsible for placing the second inmate in solitary confinement, calmly approached the inmate group with the intention of persuading them to return to their cells. Several of the inmates became enraged when they saw the lieutenant and viciously attacked him. Two other officers came to the lieutenant's aid, causing such a commotion that another group of inmates who were in the yard became aroused and attacked two officers and obtained their keys to the inside corridor.

The original group of rebelling inmates, joined by those from the yard, armed themselves with make-shift weapons, mostly athletic equipment, and began to yell to the inmates in other parts of the institution (who at that time showed no interest in becoming involved) to unite with them in revolt. In a seemingly futile effort, the inmates rushed the Times Square gate. To the surprise and horror of the officers who were stationed in Times Square, a defective bolt in the gate gave way and the inmates were soon in control of the central section of the institution, with access to the rest of the prison population.

The Special Commission was convinced that the riot was a spontaneous one and was not the result, as some have suggested, of a conspiracy designed by revolutionaries. When the importance of the defective bolt is taken into consideration, the Commission's argument is quite persuasive. If they had intended to revolt, the logical time would have been either in the mess hall or after they had left and entered into Times Square. As things were, they rushed Times Square, the area that they had just left, in a seemingly vain attempt to knock down the steel gate. If it were not for the defective bolt, a riot of major proportions would not have occurred when it did.

While the majority of the inmates had nothing to do with either instigating or prolonging the riot, they were all affected by it in one way or another. Some treated their captive officers brutally, while others, particularly the Muslims, attempted to protect them from any physical abuse. Likewise, testimony revealed that vindictive and atrocious punishments were inflicted on many inmates by some officers and troopers after they had regained control. The unfounded rumors about both officer- and inmate-initiated brutalities most likely excited and enraged everyone to the extent that many over-reacted when they were placed in dominant positions over their adversaries.

The bloody retaking of the institution occurred after a period of extended negotiating over a list of 25 demands that were presented by inmate leaders. Russell G. Oswald, the State Commissioner of Correctional Services, agreed to all but two of the demands. He maintained that he did not have the authority to grant amnesty from criminal prosecution or to arrange for transporting the inmates to a "nonimperialist" country. By the fifth day of their takeover, the inmates still insisted that these conditions must be met. The authorities then moved in.

The pros and cons of the decision to forceably retake the institution, and the controversies that are associated with the subsequent behavior of police and corrections officers, will be debated for years to come. However, at least a few facts were divulged by the Attica investigations. Officials are quite certain that the Attica uprising was not the result of a conspiracy, but was at least partially a consequence of frustration and resentment-producing prison conditions. Likewise, the inability of employees to control or understand the primarily ghetto-bred, but politically and racially conscious, group of inmates was another significant causative factor in making the institutional environment potentially explosive.

It is misleading to over-emphasize the importance of the roles that the revolutionary type prisoners played in the riot. The inmate demand for transportation to a nonimperialist country has, perhaps, been given too much attention. Most of the demands were traditional reform-related ones similar to those made by inmates in other prison riots throughout our history. In many instances, they were simply demanding the implementation of a number of the same "common sense" remedies to adverse prison conditions that Commissioner Oswald, in a speech that was piped into the cells several weeks prior to the riot, had promised to pursue.

THE DYNAMICS OF THE COLLECTIVE RIOT

What Hartung and Floch have labeled the collective riot, though less understood than the brutal riot, is much more predictable. In discussing this particular type, the focal point will be the riots of 1952–53. The relevancy of these particular riots rests in the fact that many of the disturbances that occurred then were directly related to well intended but mismanaged "progressive" innovations that suddenly and violently upset the status quo. One of America's foremost penologists comments:

> Why prison riots? This question is impossible to answer if we adopt a strict definition of 'cause.' Generally speaking, a background of frustration and deadening routine is probably always present. Pent-up energy, then, like a charge of powder in a hair-trigger rifle may be set off by the slightest stimulus, perhaps a chance remark by an unwary guard. Food may be good; medical care of high grade; parole boards may be respected; and yet riots may rage.[48]

Hartung and Floch, Ohlin, Sykes, and others maintain that in many instances a more logical and systematic explanation can be offered if there is proper understanding of the social organization of (or more specifically, the balance of power that tends to exist in) the "traditional" institution. Because this type of facility provides the setting in which most collective riots occur, further discussion of the social organization and role playing within is needed.

In the traditional institution, the key staff member, yet prestigiously the lowest, is the guard (custodial or correctional officer). While his primary responsibilities are to follow the orders of his immediate supervisors and to enforce the standardized institutional rules, his job is complicated by the fact that if he forces conformity to regulations too rigidly, the inmates may become rebellious. If this should happen, the guard, of course, is held responsible. The guard's dilemma is perhaps best analyzed by Sykes in his classic study of the New Jersey State Prison. He discovered, contrary to popular belief, that the custodial officer is seldom capable of exercising total authority over the captive population. To maintain total authority, Sykes contends, there must be "a rightful or legitimate effort to exercise control on the one hand and an inner, moral compulsion to obey, by those who are to be controlled, on the other."[49] Unlike the conditions existing in many other formal organizations, the prison environment provides a situation in which the typical inmate acknowledges that the officials have a legitimate right to control him, but he seldom feels morally bound to conform to their wishes. Only in extreme cases is the reliance on physical force effective in gaining inmate conformity. That this is so is not only due to the fact that physically coercive methods employed by guards might result in vehement retaliation, but also because such tactics are not conducive to encouraging their charges to perform their everyday tasks, for the completion of which the guards are, again, held responsible.

Sykes also contends, and he is supported by other expert opinion, that the officially sanctioned rewards and punishments that the guard has at his disposal are not sufficient to motivate inmates to comply with his demands for the conscientious performance of work duties and to obey institutional rules and regulations.[50] With regard to punishment, the prisoner is unlikely to consider the few privileges that he can be deprived of, and the relatively inconsequential penalties that the guard can impose, as a genuine threat to his ultimate welfare. In fact, punishment at the hands of the staff may cause the inmate to view himself as a hero or martyr and give him that identity with his fellows.

Adding to the dilemma, what the staff considers rewards or incentives to conformity such as visiting privileges, good time, recreation, and the use of the commissary are regarded by the prisoners as their "inalienable rights," not favors to be earned through good behavior. This, of course, is a logical assumption on the part of the inmates when one understands that these so-called privileges are bestowed on them when they enter the institution, and are withdrawn only when conformity is not maintained.[51]

Thus, being unable to rely on a legitimate system of rewards and punishments "the pivotal figure on which the custodial bureaucracy turns," the guard, is plagued with obstacles to effective control over his "subordinates." He is the middle man between higher officialdom and the world of convicts, and is to a significant degree evaluated in terms of the conduct of those under his control. As indicated, the guard does not have complete authority over the prisoners and if he feels the necessity to resort to continually reporting rule infractions to his superior, he will not only be adding to inmate antagonism, but he will also be acknowledging his inability to perform the control function upon which institutional stability is so dependent. Again, Sykes shows how the guard's authority is frequently corrupted:

> The guard, then, is under pressure to achieve a smoothly running tour of duty not with the stick but with the carrot, but here again his legitimate stock is limited. Facing demands from above that he achieve compliance, and stalemated from below, he finds that one of the most meaningful rewards he can offer is to ignore certain offenses or make sure that he never places himself in a position where he will discover them. Thus the guard, backed by all the power of the State, close to armed men who will run to his aid, and aware that any prisoner who disobeys him can be punished if he presses charges against him, often discovers that his best path of action is to make "deals" or "trades" with the captives in his power. In effect, the guard buys compliance or obedience in certain areas at the cost of tolerating disobedience elsewhere.[52]

Thus, with no significant means at his disposal of legitimately rewarding his charges and at the same time being expected to attain a degree of inmate "compliance," the guard must resort to illegitimate or semilegitimate measures such as tolerating certain inmate transgressions. The guard's generosity ranges from minor considerations such as allowing some inmates to keep food in their cells to permitting or even contributing to the illicit traffic in contraband liquor, drugs, or other luxuries. Thus the guard is, to some extent, corrupted by the very nature of his job, and his capacity to enforce obedience is eroded and frequently transferred to a group of inmate elite who in return compensate the guard by preventing others from disrupting the status quo. In the New Jersey State Prison prior to 1950, Sykes relates that influential inmates rose to positions of dominance because they were sources of privileges such as contraband goods, preferential job or cell assignments, and even the occasional granting of trusty status. These powerful prisoners progressively took over the actual duties of the guards, as their counterparts in some other institutions continue to do today. For example, it was not uncommon for an inmate who was assigned to a particular guard as a "runner" (a prisoner who delivers messages or performs other errands) to, within a short time, be granted additional privileges such as locking cells or aiding in the "count" (the periodic checking of the whereabouts of all inmates). This relationship between the guard and the favored inmate should not be interpreted to be a "friendly" one. It represents a mutually rewarding business agreement, with a minimum of conversation involved and no social "niceties" attached. When talking with his peers, the prisoner usually voices utter contempt for his benefactor, for to do otherwise would be to run the risk of being regarded as a rat or "center man."[53]

When the situation reaches the point that inmates are actually performing the guard's function, the stage has then been set for blackmail. The corrupted guard is rendered even more subservient to his captives by the knowledge that it is within their power to report his disciplinary laxity to administrative officials.

While some observers of the correctional scene recognize similar developments in a number of institutions today, such conditions were manifest throughout the country in the late 1930s through the mid 1940s. These problems were compounded by many penologically ignorant and politically appointed wardens who were satisfied to have a "smooth running" prison no matter who did the running or what methods were used. Some conditions were worse than others, but the following example is a description of what MacCormick has labeled the "paragoric prison:"[54]

> Women could be brought in for sexual purposes by paying a fee to the inmate leaders. The prisoner would be sent to the hospital; when his woman came to visit him there, the attendants would kindly enclose his bed with screens. When she left, the prisoner-patient would undergo a speedy recovery! Liquor was quite easily smuggled in. Even narcotics found their way into this prison in relatively large

quantities. Inmates on favored outside-the-walls assignments were able to form friendships among citizens of the surrounding cities. Some were entertained by their girlfriends in the latter's homes. In addition, prisoners who had been racketeers in civilian life, and therefore retained a measure of importance, were able to secure some very good concessions within the walls, which in many instances provided annual incomes to be envied by modest citizens on the outside.[55]

In order to understand the etiology of the collective riot, it is necessary to have an appreciation of what Sykes refers to as "the shifting status of the semi-official self government exercised by the inmate population."[56] This can best be accomplished by viewing the subject from an historical perspective. As indicated, by the mid 1940s, inmates in many prisons had gained control over such institutional affairs as issuing of job and cell assignments and the granting of numerous privileges—even the exercising of discipline. By allowing the most powerful prisoners to informally govern the institution, many incompetent officials found a solution to their control problems.

As the public became more knowledgeable regarding the corruption of penal authority, and, in turn, were shocked by the discovery that incarcerated criminals were going unpunished and not being rehabilitated, pressures for change were stimulated. As a result, reforms were instituted across the country, including the removal of many unqualified politically appointed officials, the replacement of numerous inmates in semiadministrative positions by civil service personnel, and a general "crackdown" on the illicit activities of inmates. Thus, in many instances, the prison elite were shorn of their power and inmate self-governments were destroyed. In the New Jersey State Prison, for example, the former leaders emphasized inmate cohesion and could induce their fellow captives to "get along" or at least avoid an open conflict with the staff; a confrontation of this nature would interfere with their "easygoing" existence. However, when the members of this previously prestigious group were deprived of their power, their following diminished, simply because they had lost the authority to grant privileges and indulgences. A new, more aggressive and violence prone elite, using the frustrations and resentments characteristic of prison populations as a lever, gained authority, and eventually precipitated a costly revolt.

As Ohlin indicates, the collective riot occurred in institutions where there was "a movement in the direction of reasserting traditional penal organization and procedures."[57] A number of authorities accept the general framework of such an explanation, but offer differing opinions regarding the leadership roles played by certain types of inmates and the variety of precipitating factors. Of course, several different institutions were studied, and no exact formula that can be applied to all collective riots should be expected. Differences between such possibly related factors as the characteristics of inmate populations and general penal conditions are too great.

Hartung and Floch, for example, based on their knowledge of the riots that took place at several institutions, explain that prison populations usually consist of two basic types of individuals: (1) the overtly aggressive, and (2) the covertly passive. The former type represents an aggressive and, to a degree, creative individual who finds the self-expression that is required by his personality by assuming control within the inmate group. During the decade prior to the mid 1940s, this type of prisoner attained satisfactory self-fulfillment through nonviolent control and manipulation of both staff and inmates. However, the nationwide "crackdown" severely curtailed their activities and left them with no reason to maintain the status quo by restraining their fellow prisoners. They then chose an alternative outlet for their aggression which placed them in direct and violent conflict with officials.[58]

THE NEW MILITANCY

You saw it every afternoon. There would be the Black Muslims, heads cleanly shaved, trousers creased, praying or doing calisthenics.

> Then there were the Puerto Rican cons, all from New York City, . . . gathering around the Young Lords members sometimes confined there. They had been transferred from Sing Sing and were angry at the tougher conditions.
>
> And the Black Panthers, suspicious, slipping into glowering silence whenever a white prisoner approached, keeping their own counsel.[59]

In the words of the ex-inmate, this was a typical scene in Cell Block D of Attica State Prison prior to the "worst riot in prison history."[60] Such self-imposed, tension-producing segregation of inmates along racial and quasipolitical lines is, of course, in evidence in many other institutions throughout the country. A journalist, who was at one time employed as a teacher at San Quentin Prison, related his astonishment, after a return visit, at the changes in the philosophical and political climate that had occurred within the institution in just a few years.

> Rage and frustration made themselves known in San Quentin that very evening. It started when a Chicano prisoner known as a Nazi stabbed a black prisoner. A Chicano prisoner known as a Nazi—there, surely, is a clue to the strange structure of racial politics in prisons today. In my days at the prison there were distinctions enough, but they were anything but political. There were blacks and whites and Mexicans; older men and young toughs; mainliners (not drugusers but regular prisoners receiving standard treatment) and those under special regimes; jockers (aggressive homosexuals) and punks (passive homosexuals).[61]

It would be naive to suggest that serious racial hatreds and associated violence have only recently become evident within correctional institutions; however, it appears that such attitudes and behavior have become significantly more sophisticated and organized within the last few years. The bigot, regardless of his racial or ethnic background, usually has no difficulty in gaining admittance into an established inmate clique that will provide group support and/or rationalizations for his racist activities. For example, usually because of his intense hatred of blacks, a white prisoner at San Quentin may choose to join the "Nazis" (White People's National Socialist Party). Participation in this organization involves engagement in guerilla warfare with other quasipolitical groups within the walls of the institution. This type of hit-and-run combat has recently resulted in 17 stabbings within a three-month period at San Quentin. Such battle tactics, as opposed to mass confrontations or gang fights, obviously, pose a more serious administrative control problem than has ever been encountered in the past.[62]

Racial conflict does not always reach this level of intensity, even in San Quentin. A caste system based on both political and racial activism is emerging in our prisons, and if the political fervor is prevalent it can, to a degree, mitigate racial hatreds. United in allegiance to leaders such as Che Guavara, Frantz Fanon, and Mao Tse-tung, and encouraged by a number of atypical offenders who were civil disobedients and revolutionaries prior to their incarceration, various racial groups collaborated in instigating disturbances in San Quentin, Soledad, and Folsom prisons in 1970.[63] Some are of the opinion that they (prisoners in general) are an oppressed minority, and that they develop a kind of loyalty to others who are forced to endure similar conditions.[64]

Many of the leading spokesmen for radical causes began to develop their political consciousness while serving prison sentences.[65] A partial list of prison-spawned militants includes Malcolm X, Eldridge Cleaver, Huey Newton, and George Jackson. These men have become heroes and martyrs to inmates and to various protest groups, some of which have been active in picketing state and federal institutions throughout the country, endeavoring to show their sympathy for and support of prisoners in general.[66]

The current New Left interest in American prisons has been reciprocated and is reflected in the statements made by volatile radical elements within the prison walls. This became evident when Attica rioters demanded "asylum and safe passage to some nonimperialist country," and asked for and were granted meetings with a number of left-leaning figures.[67]

An extensive investigation and subjective evaluation of American judicial practices would provide little support for the contention that the United States Government imprisons people solely on the basis of their political beliefs. It can be argued, nevertheless, that because of their adherance to revolutionary philosophies, prisoners have remained incarcerated for unreasonable periods of time under indeterminate sentence legislation (where the time of release is determined by correctional officials). Whether or not a person is considered to be a "political prisoner" is usually related to the political disposition of the individual who is doing the categorizing.

Few give credence to Eldridge Cleaver's assertion that he raped white women because he was antagonized by the racism that allegedly characterizes American society and was thus a "political prisoner."[68] Nor could many justify some white radicals' view of shoplifting, "ripping off the establishment", as being politically motivated.[69] Our skepticism over these claims must not, however, hide the fact that many prisoners steadfastly believe that a racist capitalistic political and economic system has given them no alternative to a life of crime. Many no longer view themselves as criminals, but have developed racial, ethnic, and/or political identities that, in their own minds, absolve them of any guilt or responsibility for their behavior. How is it possible to "rehabilitate" a person who is convinced that he is morally and philosophically virtuous, and that those who control him are only pawns of the corrupt "establishment?" George Jackson, for example, rejected all efforts of prison officials to make him into what he termed "a good nigger."[70]

That minority group members do, on occasion, refuse to participate in various prison programs is hardly surprising. In many instances a nonwhite inmate majority is governed by a small number of white staff members. Official speech and behavior frequently confirm the belief of the nonwhite prisoner that whites are insensitive to his plight. Minority group members sometimes regard themselves as representatives of an alien society who are in no way obligated to adhere to the advice (counseling) or desires of their "oppressors."

The new militancy, then, is significantly changing the cor-

A black solidarity meeting at Sing Sing.

rectional scene, and it is possible that inmate leadership throughout the country is gravitating toward this new breed of convict. However, research has yet to determine the pervasiveness of these revolutionary attitudes and behavior. In truth, the personalities and social backgrounds of the men confined to our correctional institutions are still so varied that they defy generalization. Some who were reared in poverty and socially pathological home environments are not articulate enough to advocate any particular philosophical doctrine. The incarcerated members of the middle class usually still support traditional American values, and possibly, despite other differences in opinion, the average prisoner does also. Irwin, after an extensive study of a group of California inmates, concluded that:

> The revolutionary styles are poorly accepted among the general criminal population. They irritate a deep and sensitive conservative nerve in most convicts. Though the

criminal, especially the white criminal, is deviant and in many respects antiestablishment, he usually feels that he is an "American." When America is under criticism from without or from malcontents within—from communists, socialists or militant Negroes—he shifts from his deviant identity to a more deeply founded conservative American identity and becomes the defender of certain sacred American traditions and institutions, especially private property, racial discrimination, and capitalism.[71]

SUMMARY

Most of the innovations that have taken place in recent years have proven to be beneficial. The last two decades have witnessed a significantly greater emphasis on the rehabilitation of the offender, stricter control over illicit inmate activities, and a growing tendency to assign the socially nondangerous criminal to community based programs in lieu of incarceration. Such progress, while indeed welcome, has been accompanied by numerous difficulties. Unfortunately, rehabilitation sometimes fosters intense conflict between "treatment" and "custody" personnel. Situations of this nature are detrimental to inmates in that they are unable to benefit from staff cooperation. Likewise, official pronouncements and literature emanating from treatment oriented state departments of corrections are often unrealistic, and they generate public misunderstanding regarding the direction of correctional goals.

Preventing prisoners from continuing to control institutional affairs, when such control involves the exploitation of others, is, of course, advisable. Historically, however, many administrators, in regaining control, have so severely restricted inmate activities that the former cohesively oriented leaders were left with no way of rewarding followers for maintaining the status quo. Thus, in some cases, a more violence-prone elite has come into prominence, and chaos has often been the result. In other similar circumstances, leadership did not change but aggressive elites, no longer having any outlets for their energies, resorted to disrputive conduct.

Undoubtedly, outside radical ideologies, drastic societal changes, and the incarcerating of some self-styled revolutionaries have affected the attitudes and behavior of many prisoners. However, we should not be blinded to the fact that more enlightened methods of treating the nondangerous offender outside of institutions have sometimes created a situation of having hard core rebellious offenders within the institutions, without the stabilizing influences of "normal" criminals.

ENDNOTES

1. "The Shame of the Prisons," *Time,* January 18, 1971, p. 53.
2. "Prisons: The Way to Reform," *Time,* September 27, 1971, p. 26.
3. Figures from 1968 indicate that only 11 percent of the supervisors (including those in charge of educational and casework services) in adult institutions and 13 percent of the similarly employed personnel in juvenile institutions earned more than $12,000 per year. Fifty-three percent of the administrators (included in this category are wardens and superintendents as well as assistant/associate wardens and superintendents) of adult institutions and 68 percent of the administrators of juvenile institutions make less than $14,000 per year. *Task Force Report: Corrections,* Task Force on Corrections, The President's Commission on Law Enforcement and Administration of Justice; U.S. Government Printing Office, p. 95.
4. *A Time to Act: Final Report of the Joint Commission on Correctional Manpower and Training,* October, 1969, p. 19.
5. While such circumstances are certainly not claimed to be true of every state, national statistics do indicate that "headquarters executives" are the most highly educated of all correctional employees (nearly one third of this group hold doctoral degrees) while the administrators of adult prisons and reformatories are the least well educated of the correctional administrators and also have generally inferior educational backgrounds to the administrators of juvenile institutions and probation and parole services. See "Developing Correctional Administrators," *Research Report of the Joint Commission on Correctional Manpower and Training* November, 1969.

6. In referring to "social work" here, it should not be inferred that the personnel that make up the type of Divisions of Corrections under discussion are always exclusively professional social workers. Other treatment oriented individuals such as psychiatrists, psychologists, and criminologists are also included.
7. Charles Perrow, "The Analysis of Goals in Complex Organizations," *American Sociological Review* December, 1961, Vol. 26, p. 855.
8. "Manpower and Training in Correctional Institutions," *Staff Report of the Joint Commission on Correctional Manpower and Training* December, 1969, p. 11.
9. Perrow, "Analysis of Goals in Complex Organizations," p. 855.
10. Ibid., pp. 856, 857.
11. James L. Price, *Organizational Effectiveness* (Homewood, Ill.: Richard D. Irwin, Inc., 1968) p. 55.
12. Ibid., pp. 55–60.
13. *A Time to Act: Final Report of Joint Commission on Correctional Manpower and Training* October, 1969, pp. 24–32.
14. Ibid., p. 29.
15. Gresham Sykes, *Society of Captives: A Study of a Maximum Security Prison* (New York: Atheneum, 1970).
16. Donald R. Cressey, "Achievement of an Unstated Organizational Goal," *Pacific Sociological Review* Vol. I, 1958; in *Prison Within Society: A Reader in Penology,* edited by Lawrence Hazelrigg (New York: Doubleday and Co., 1968), p. 50.
17. Louis Harris, "Changing Public Attitudes Toward Crime and Corrections," *Federal Probation* December, 1968, pp. 6–16.
18. Mayer N. Zald, "Power Balance and Staff Conflict in Correctional Institutions," *Administrative Science Quarterly* Vol. VI, June, 1962; in *Prison Within Society: A Reader in Penology,* edited by Lawrence Hazelrigg (New York: Doubleday and Co., 1968), p. 398.
19. Ibid., p. 407.
20. George H. Weber, "Conflicts Between Professional and Non-Professional Personnel in Institutional Delinquency Treatment," *Journal of Criminal Law, Criminology and Police Science;* in *Prison Within Society: A Reader in Penology,* edited by Lawrence Hazelrigg (New York: Doubleday and Co., 1968), p. 440.
21. Ibid., p. 436.
22. David Matza, *Delinquency and Drift* (New York: John Wiley and Sons, Inc., 1967), chapter 4.

23. Weber, "Conflicts Between Professional and Non-Professional Personnel in Institutional Delinquency Treatment," p. 436.
24. Ibid.
25. Oscar Grusky, "Role Conflict in Organization: A Study of Prison Camp Officials," *Administrative Science Quarterly* Vol. III, 1959, p. 465.
26. *Riots and Disturbances in Correctional Institutions* prepared by The American Correctional Association, October, 1970, p. 11.
27. Ibid., p. 4.
28. Sykes, *The Society of Captives* (New York: Atheneum, 1970), pp. 109–111.
29. *Riots and Disturbances in Correctional Institutions* p. 6.
30. According to Ohlin, riots frequently occur in series because prisoners all over the country identify with each others' plights. Lloyd E. Ohlin, *Sociology and the Field of Corrections* Russell Sage Foundation, 1956, p. 23. Also see Frank T. Flynn, "Behind the Prison Riots," *Social Science Review* Vol. 27, 1953, p. 73.
31. Walter B. Jones, Jr., and Lee Bruce, "How We Broke the Montana Prison Riot," *Saturday Evening Post* June 13, 1959.
32. "Death in San Quentin," *Time* September 6, 1971, pp. 17–18.
33. "War at Attica: Was There No Other Way?" *Time* September 27, 1971, pp. 18–26.
34. Frank E. Hartung and Maurice Floch, "A Social-Psychological Analysis of Prison Riots: An Hypothesis," *Journal of Criminal Law, Criminology, and Police Science* May-June, 1956, p. 51.
35. Ibid.
36. An unpublished 1966 California study listed 94 causes of prison riots. *Behavior Today* Vol. 2, No. 40, October 4, 1971, p. 1.
37. Ruth Shonle Cavan, *Criminology* (New York: Crowell Co., 1962), pp. 436–437.
38. Ohlin, *Sociology and the Field of Corrections* p. 24.
39. *Riots and Disturbances in Correctional Institutions* pp. 3–12.
40. Ibid., p. 3.
41. See Kenneth Lamott, "The San Quentin Story—The Prisons are Getting a Tougher Class of Convicts," *The New York Times Magazine* Vol. XLI, No. 4; May 2, 1971. © 1971 by The New York Times Company. Reprinted by permission.
42. "What Do the Prison Riots Signify?" *Christian Century* Vol. 72, p. 148, quoted in *Riots and Disturbances in Correctional Institutions* prepared by The American Correctional Association, Washington, D.C., October, 1970.

43. See Robert G. Caldwell, *Criminology* (New York: The Ronald Press Co., 1965).
44. As indicated in chapter one, a disinterested public has traditionally shown little concern as one inept official after another was appointed to key positions as political favors. See Austin H. MacCormick, "Behind the Prison Riots," *The Annals of the American Academy of Political and Social Science* Vol. 1, 1954.
45. *Riots and Disturbances in Correctional Institutions* p. 1.
46. *Attica: The Official Report of the New York State Special Commission on Attica,* September, 1972.
47. Russell G. Oswald, *Attica: My Story* (New York: Doubleday and Co., 1972).
48. Vernon Fox, *Violence Behind Bars* (New York: Vantage Press, 1956), p. 36.
49. Sykes, *Society of Captives* p. 52.
50. See MacCormick, "Behind the Prison Riots."
51. Sykes, *Society of Captives* p. 52.
52. Ibid., pp. 56–57.
53. The advent of the somewhat recent emphasis on prisoner reform has definite implications for all correctional staff members and most assuredly for the guard. In the past, this type of employee knew what was expected of him; in other words, he fit securely into his bureaucratic niche. As penological philosophy changed, no longer was he universally expected to function solely as an enforcer of rules and regulations. In some of our more treatment oriented establishments, the guard is regarded as an asset to the rehabilitative process and is called upon to individualize justice and use discretion in his disciplinary practices. Unfortunately, such freedom has often resulted in inmate claims of discriminatory practices on the part of the guard. Also, having fewer concrete and binding rules and regulations to fall back on during times of crisis, the guard's job has, manifestly, become more frustrating. To reiterate, traditionally, the guard has been assigned the unenviable task of maintaining control over the prisoners and enforcing rules without unduly arousing their hostility. More recently, in some institutions, while he is still required to perform these functions, he is allotted the additional burdens of becoming concerned with the personal problems and social adjustment of members of the inmate population. As one can imagine, these directives are in some ways contradictory and are indeed confusing to the custodial personnel.

54. See MacCormick, "Behind the Prison Riots."
55. Hartung and Floch, "A Social-Psychological Analysis of Prison Riots: An Hypothesis," p. 54.
56. Sykes, *Society of Captives* p. 46.
57. Ohlin, *Sociology and the Field of Corrections* pp. 22–26.
58. Hartung and Flock, "A Social-Psychological Analysis of Prison Riots: An Hypothesis," pp. 51–57.
59. "Social, Racial, Political Tensions Helped Foster Attica Rebellion," *Minneapolis Tribune* September 19, 1971, p. 1. Reprinted by permission of *AP Newsfeatures*.
60. Ibid.
61. Lamott, "The San Quentin Story—The Prisons are Getting a Tougher Class of Convicts," p. 83.
62. Ibid., p. 86.
63. Jessica Mitford, "Kind and Usual Punishment," *Atlantic* March, 1971, p. 52.
64. John Irwin, *The Felon* (Englewood Cliffs, N.J.: Prentice-Hall, Inc.; 1970), p. 82. © 1970, Prentice-Hall, Inc., Englewood Cliffs, New Jersey.
65. Jack Waugh, "Prisons Fuel Radical Politics," *The Christian Science Monitor* September 14, 1971, p. 1.
66. "U.S. Prison Conditions Protested," *Minneapolis Tribune* October 3, 1971, p. 6.
67. Waugh, "Prisons Fuel Radical Politics," p. 4.
68. As reported in "Who (and What) is a Political Prisoner?" *Time* September 6, 1971, p. 19.
69. Ibid.
70. Ibid.
71. Irwin, *The Felon* p. 100.

6

Juveniles in Trouble

The following two chapters will focus on the constitutionally guaranteed rights of the individual as he passes from the court to the correctional system. The traditional symbol of our justice system is a scale of justice on which evidence is weighed in order to make a finding of guilt or innocence. The fulcrum point for this balance is provided by a woman whose eyes have been shielded so that she weighs only the evidence, not the characteristics of the defendant. Chapter one pointed out that this conception of the justice system is far from accurate. Trials are infrequent, and the background characteristics of the defendant frequently do play a part in our justice system.

However, while the adult system of justice conceives of itself as operating according to the principals of this "due process" model, the juvenile justice system has never conceived of itself in such a manner. In fact, the juvenile justice system grew in part out of discontent with this legalistic orientation.

This chapter will look more closely at the juvenile justice system and, in particular, at recent appellate court decisions that relate to young offenders. Chapter seven will analyze the legal rights of the adult probationer, inmate, and parolee.

THE BACKGROUND OF JUVENILE JUSTICE

F. Wines, in 1895, expressed as clearly as anyone the philosophical basis upon which the juvenile justice system is built when he stated:

> Most children who commit criminal acts and are arrested on account of them, may be said to have acted without proper discernment; they are only partially responsible, in a legal sense; certainly they have not reached a stage in the development of criminal character such as to exclude the hope of their reformation, under proper treatment and influence.[1]

Juvenile justice bases its foundation on the tenets expressed in Wine's statement. Youths are seen as being less accountable for their behavior, and thus they are less appropriate targets for punishment. Secondly, youths are seen as being more amenable to rehabilitation through "proper treatment and influences."[2]

With this perspective as its base, the first juvenile court was established in 1899 in Illinois. By 1925, all but two states had established similar courts.[3] The foundation for the juvenile court is well summarized by Vaughn Stapleton and Lee E. Teitelbaum:

> Those who articulated the need for a juvenile court intended to create a new kind of forum which recognized a responsibility generally to provide guidance for errant youths and place them on the path to "good, sound, adult citizenship." Specifically, the new court would prevent crime by reforming the child who was in danger of becoming criminal. Obviously a parent is free to, and indeed should, act authoritatively when he feels it necessary for the proper development of his child, and not only when the child has done a particularly heinous act. Parental responsibility includes the guid-

ance of children toward becoming good and useful citizens; when the parent fails, it becomes the duty of the state to assume that role. It was assumed that properly constituted adult authority could and should diagnose and treat symptoms of deviance as well as deviant acts. Thus delinquency proceedings were described as "investigations into serious conditions which if unchecked may lead to the making of its children into criminals instead of law-abiding citizens."[4]

As part of the juvenile court's attempt "to provide guidance for errant youths," states expanded the concept of delinquency, beyond behaviors that were offenses for adults, to include behaviors that were suggestive of a misdirected youngster. Such youngsters were peculiarly suited to the juvenile court because the court would be able to assess not the "badness" of the behavior, but the social psychological environment that gave rise to this threatening behavior. For example, Stapleton and Teitelbaum, in discussing the development of juvenile court statutes, point out that the 1907 amendment to the Illinois statute expanded an already broad statute to read as follows:

> The words "delinquent child" shall mean any male child who while under the age of seventeen years or any female child who while under the age of eighteen years, violates any law of the State; or is incorrigible, or knowingly associates with thieves, vicious or immoral persons; or without just cause and without [the] consent of its parents, guardian or custodian absents itself from its home or place of abode, or is growing up in idleness or crime, or knowingly frequents a house of ill-repute; or knowingly frequents any policy shop or place where any gaming device is operated; or frequents any saloon or dram shop where intoxicating liquors are sold; or patronizes or visits any public pool room or bucket shop; or wanders the streets in the night time without being on [any] lawful business or lawful occupation; or habitually wanders about any railroad yard or tracks or jumps or attempts to jump on any car or engine without lawful authority; or uses vile, obscene, vulgar, profane or indecent language in [any] public place or about any school house; or is guilty of indecent or lascivious conduct; . . .[5]

Before the juvenile court, children were seen as dependents, not defendants, and thus the juvenile court until the recent past did not provide the youngster due process.

The original purpose of the juvenile court was to "treat" and protect, as opposed to punish. Establishing procedures to safeguard the due process rights of the child was not viewed as essential and the juvenile judge was entrusted with, seemingly in many instances, unrestricted discretion in exercising his immense "nonpunitive" powers. History has affirmed, however, that juvenile court judges have not always conducted themselves in a manner appropriate to the kindly figures envisoned by the court movements pioneers. Traditionally, there have been few legal safeguards to protect the child from the tyrannical judge or other court officials. Even when judges have endeavored to handle cases in accordance with the best interests of the children involved (it would be grossly unfair to assume that in the majority of instances that they have not attempted to do so), their lack of expertise regarding child care techniques, their limited knowledge of the behavioral sciences, and even their inadequate understanding of the law has only worked to the detriment of those unfortunates who appeared before them. The fact that juvenile court judges seldom measure up to the ideal was blatantly evidenced by a 1963 survey of 1,564 such judges which revealed that only 51 percent had bachelor's degrees, 24 percent had no formal legal education, and 72 percent indicated that juvenile court functions occupied less than one fourth of their time.[6]

The authoritative 1967 report by the President's Commission on Law Enforcement and the Administration of Justice divulged that "studies conducted by the Commission, legislative inquiries in various states, and reports by informed observers compel the conclusion that the great hopes originally held for the juvenile court have not been fulfilled. It has not succeeded significantly in rehabilitating delinquent youth, in reducing or even stemming the tide of delinquency, or in bringing justice and compassion to the child offender."[7]

It appears that America's lawmakers would have benefitted manifestly by heeding many of the lessons voiced so articulately by the legal philosopher, Cesare Beccaria, in his monumental 1764

Essay on Crime and Punishment.[8] As this brief yet profound volume indicates, a standardized code of law need not necessarily be repressive and such legal machinery is, in fact, mandatory if we are to be protected from not only dictatorial and incompetent judges, but from the well-intentioned yet penologically naive judge, probation officer, and social worker as well. It was such a problem that led such scholars as Paul Tappan to exclaim, "Who is going to save these kids from their saviors?"[9] Robert G. Caldwell decried "the tyranny of the expert." Frederic Wertham coined the term "psychoauthoritarianism." The brilliant Roscoe Round accurately perceived the problem as far back as 1937, when he protested that "the powers of the Star Chamber were a trifle in comparison with those of our juvenile courts."[10]

Even academic theorists have, on occasion, commented on the practical absurdity of our judicial methods of handling children. As a case in point, David Matza observes that probation officers and social workers, as well as other types of professional caretakers (including judges) frequently, by spouting their "humanitarian" rhetoric, have offended the perceptive juvenile's sense of justice.[11] By indicating to the youngster, either directly or through communication with others in the context of the court proceedings that he is deviant through no fault of his own but as a result of a poor environment or adverse family conditions, the professional confirms what the delinquent believed all along: namely, if he is in fact delinquent, his condition is a result of circumstances beyond his control and for which, most obviously, he is blameless. After mouthing these sentiments, his caretakers appear, indeed, hypocritical and unjust in the eyes of the juvenile, since they usually play an active part in administering his punishment. Of course, being placed on probation or even being incarcerated in an institution is not regarded as punishment by many "treatment oriented" officials. Having experienced the reality of having his freedom severely curtailed, the adjudicated delinquent is not that naive. Such frustration is apparent in the words of one inmate of an institution for juveniles. "The judge kept telling me how horrible this place (the reform school) was, and he was gonna send me here if I didn't straighten out. . . . Then when he finally decided I was bad enough to send up, he told me that it wasn't such an awful place after all, and that he was really helping me. What a jerk!"[12]

The process of individualizing justice has traditionally been associated with the workings of the juvenile court, and includes the practice of treating various individuals differently (in accordance with their supposed psychological or sociological needs), even if they have engaged in similar offensive behavior. Matza also observes that such a practice again results in portraying officials as being unfair and unworthy of the trust and confidence so vital to the rehabilitation process. Understandably, a youngster can have little confidence in a system that inflicts harsher punishment on him than it does on his associates who were equally guilty of the same offense.

JUVENILE CORRECTIONS: ITS FOIBLES AND FAILURES

To comprehend the significance of the relationship of the law to juvenile corrections it becomes necessary to comment on certain unfortunate penal practices in the juvenile justice system; however, the following brief yet well-documented description of how our juvenile judicial and correctional systems have run amuck should not be interpreted as a general polemic against all officials who participate in these processes. Needless to say, hundreds of judges, probation and parole agents, as well as institutional personnel are selflessly dedicating themselves to salvaging aberrant youths. As we shall see, at least in some instances, correctional agencies are administered by progressive and innovative practitioners of the behavioral sciences who, despite the fact that they are frequently maligned (or possibly worse, ignored) by members of the press, politicians, and citizens alike, are developing exciting rehabilitation programs.[13] Nevertheless, an objective analysis of the bleaker aspects of our methods of handling juveniles becomes mandatory, for not to remedy some of the tragic conditions that in fact do exist is to make a mockery of the whole concept of justice.

The situation, when examined in its totality, appears even more repugnant when one realizes that it could be greatly improved if many officials who are demanding strict allegiance to our legal and moral codes should abide by the tenets of the law themselves.

Historically, under the guise of social welfare and humanitarianism, this country has developed an incredible "legal system," which tolerates the placement of children in some of the most decadent bastions of brutality, homosexuality, and filth imaginable. This has been done not solely as punishment for wrongdoings that represent threats to societal safety, but as a means of disposing of youngsters who are defined by their parents as being "uncontrollable," who are "dependent" or "neglected," or who perhaps violate some legal principle peculiar to juveniles, such as truancy or drinking under age. As unbelievable as it seems, many are even deprived of their "day in court."[14] As a case in point, investigation has revealed that less than ten percent of the children in the Rhode Island training school were committed there from court. As recorded, "their status was a kind of limbo called 'FOC'—further order of the court—for months."[15]

Possibly, the importance of this topic can be more adequately emphasized if a few examples are given, as documented by reporters from the *Christian Science Monitor*. The abhorrent correctional conditions that must be tolerated by many of the approximately 100,000 children (ages 7 through 17) who are incarcerated annually will be cited.

In the state of Washington, children confined in what is considered one of the "better" detention centers spend an average of 20 hours a day in solitary confinement, where they are deprived of even such amenities as reading material.

Indiana and Florida officials openly admitted that flogging recalcitrant youngsters represented authorized policy, and corporal punishment was still permitted in Tennessee, Idaho, Montana, and a few other states.

Five boys in a Delaware institution were found to have incurred punctured eardrums as a result of the "slapping" they received from institutional personnel.

A reporter proclaimed, "In a South Carolina reform school I found, among other things, boys being beaten with fists, rubber hoses, ropes, broken hose handles, and broom handles, and other weapons. Beatings were administered by staff members and by large bully-boys appointed to do the job."[16]

Such examples should serve to indicate that atrocious conditions do, at least on occasion, persist in some juvenile correctional institutions, but the reader desiring more explicit documentation is referred to the original source.

TYPES OF FACILITIES

The most recent objective investigation into the status of juvenile institutions was recounted in the Staff Report of the Joint Commission on Correctional Manpower and Training.[17] Referring to juvenile correctional institutions only (excluding detention centers, mental health clinics, and various other places of confinement), the Commission labeled 41 percent of all correctional establishments as "special purpose facilities." Included in this category are "reception centers," "camps," "security institutions," and "other specialized facilities." The programs characteristic of these differing types of institutions represent ameliorative attempts, though frequently abortive ones, to meet the individual needs of the youths through various rehabilitation programs, and at the same time insure societal protection. Yet, despite the abundance of such establishments, only 16 percent of the "legally" incarcerated youngsters in this country are confined in such institutions. Eighty-four percent of our "juvenile delinquents" are housed in what are referred to as "multipurpose" institutions. This type of facility represents 59 percent of all juvenile correctional institutions. In the words of the Commission, "such institutions handle a fairly wide spectrum of juvenile offenders and provide a diverse program, rather than one narrowly focused on a particular activity . . . and many include among the offender population security risks, persons with severe educational deficiencies, and those who are mentally retarded, emotionally disturbed, or chronically ill. To the extent that juvenile corrections has its Big House, this type

The Robert F. Kennedy Federal Youth Center in Morgantown, West Virginia.

of institution would merit the label."[18] Usually understaffed and overcrowded (the average inmate population is 263), most of these institutions are ill equipped to perform a rehabilitative function.

The "Kids"

A more selective and personal view of some of the "kids" in correctional institutions is, of course, required if one is to develop a feeling for their perplexing situations. As a Milwaukee judge, upon discovering that an eleven year old boy had been confined and forgotten in a detention center ("a jail for children"), exclaimed disgustedly, "Somebody should teach the welfare department a lesson by charging them with neglect."

Tina, whose only "crime" was that she was the victim of a

child molester was placed in the same depressing Washington institution previously alluded to "for her own protection."

John, aged 14, found himself with his twelve year old brother in a Georgia detention center for allegedly stealing a pair of gloves.

Sally, unwanted and neglected, but never convicted of any crime, was placed in a Maine reform school from which she ran away 14 times. Such behavior resulted in her eventual transfer to the adult women's reformatory.[19]

The case of Sally is an example of the ultimate in legal absurdity. In over one-half of the states, it is permissible to transfer a boy or girl who is incarcerated in a juvenile correctional institution to an adult facility, even if he or she has never violated either the adult or juvenile penal codes.[20]

Obviously, there are many situations in which the judge is presented with no viable alternatives. Even in cases where children do not commit serious delinquent acts or are the victims of crimes, the court is often expected to intervene. If the court determines that a child is developing a behavior pattern that will eventually result in harm to the community or to the child himself, it is expected to take direct action. Remember, the juvenile court, because it has traditionally adhered to a treatment philosophy (as opposed to a punishment philosophy), has been given extraordinary powers to determine what is best for the child. In many cases the judge has only two alternatives. He can either place the child in an institution or leave him with his family. If the family does not want the child, or if the court feels that they cannot control him, then the court's options are seriously restricted. In many respects, the decisions of the juvenile court do not always reflect the desired one, but the available one.

In Re Gault

While situations such as Sally's are fortunately far from prevalent, it is common to discover in both detention centers and correctional institutions that the dependent and neglected (welfare cases) as well as minor offenders are integrated into populations consisting of the more hardened juvenile criminals as well as emotionally disturbed youths. Aside from the adverse influences that such companions may represent, the fact that such innocent young people must, at least in part, bear the stigma of delinquency should be an affront to our collective sense of decency.

Since this does not seem to be the case, the judicial reaction to the alleged behavior of a fifteen year old boy by the name of Gerald Francis Gault deserves particular consideration. The United States Supreme court decision in this case represents the only realistic remedy for the injustices characteristically encountered by juveniles in our judicial and correctional systems. That many of the individual states have given little heed to these 1967 Supreme Court mandates will soon be evidenced, but first some of the details of the case should be presented. Young Gault was taken into custody on the basis of a complaint by a woman who was the recipient of a "lewd" phone call and supposed Gerald to be the caller. His parents were notified of his confinement, a petition was never served, and the complainant was not present at the hearings. In fact, the judge determined Gault's fate without ever conferring with the woman who made the allegation. The boy was sentenced to a juvenile correctional institution and informed that he would remain there until his twenty-first birthday "unless sooner discharged by due process of law." (It is of passing interest to note that an examination of the Arizona penal code reveals that if an adult were convicted of the crime for which Gault was imprisoned, he would be subject only to a fine of from five to fifty dollars.)

On a writ of habeas corpus,[21] the case eventually reached the United States Supreme Court. Gault charged that the following basic procedural due process rights were denied him:

1. notice of the charges
2. right to counsel
3. right to confrontation and cross-examination
4. privilege against self incrimination

5. right to a transcript of the proceedings
6. right to appellate review.[22]

Basing its verdict on the first four claims (five and six, while perhaps legitimate assertions, were not, in the opinion of the Court, relevant to the case), the Court reversed the original decision. Thus the Supreme Court extended the mandates laid down in *Kent v. United States,* 1966, in which due process rights were granted to juveniles appearing in criminal (adult) courts; and for all intents and purposes invalidated its 1955 opinion, voiced in *In Re Homes,* which asserted that since juvenile courts were not in fact elements of the criminal judicial process, the safeguarding of "constitutional rights" was not mandatory in such proceedings.[23]

The Gault Decision's Potential For Positive Change

If taken seriously, which evidently is not always the case, the *Gault* decision has certain obvious ramifications for corrections, other than preventing dependent and neglected children from being subjected to the delinquency-producing conditions that are sometimes associated with juvenile correctional institutions. A primary point of emphasis, that was so evident in the Supreme Court's conclusions regarding the *Gault* case, was that juveniles should benefit from the same constitutionally guaranteed safeguards that adults do. Does it not logically follow that, as a result of the Supreme Court action, juvenile institutions should now be used to house only those relatively serious offenders who have been adjudicated, after being accorded all of their legal rights? It has been argued that some of our adult laws, particularly those pertaining to the mentally ill and such vague crimes as conspiracy, are as constitutionally questionable as such juvenile "offenses" as truancy and incorrigibility. Such arguments are usually quite persuasive, and certainly indicate a need for the reform of the criminal (adult) codes also. Nevertheless, we have gone to the extreme in incarcerating the morally blameless when we lock up juveniles who have committed no offenses, but are dependent and/or neglected.

Adherence to the principles enumerated in the *Gault* decision has created additional responsibilities for juvenile court personnel. Nevertheless, since welfare cases should be referred elsewhere and the requirement to conform to somewhat formal legal procedure should inhibit chances of conviction, institutional populations could be reduced in size, and adequate segregation of various types of offenders could become a reality. Thus, abiding by *Gault* could result in conditions long desired by correctional authorities, which would reduce overcrowding and unmanageably large caseloads, and thereby be conducive to penological experimentation and innovation. While no preventative or rehabilitative program can claim overwhelming success, as we shall observe in future chapters, those projects that involve working with relatively small groups (such as the guided group interaction programs that first enjoyed nationwide attention at Highfields and Essexfields) have proven to be statistically more successful than more traditional correctional ventures. The original rehabilitation objectives of the juvenile court have been found to be quite unrealistic. This has been due, at least partially, to a lack of resources, including trained personnel and adequate treatment facilities, and the continual adherence to the unsubstantiated assumption that individual therapy will be successful in the majority of cases. The courts have also failed to recognize that the official labeling of a youngster as delinquent may adversely stigmatize him and thereby work counter to the rehabilitation goal. Realizing this, the President's Commission recommends that: "The formal sanctioning system and pronouncement of delinquency should be used only as a last resort. In place of the formal system, dispositional alternatives to adjudication must be developed for dealing with juveniles, including agencies to provide and coordinate services and procedures to achieve necessary control without unnecessary stigma . . . The range of conduct for which court intervention is authorized should be narrowed."[24]

If we are to continue to support a system of juvenile justice that grants court personnel an immense degree of discretion in dealing with our youngsters, it would seemingly behoove us to attempt to determine whether or not the general public is sufficiently concerned with the welfare of children to take it upon itself to prevent officials from taking unfair advantage of their power. A substantial proportion of our citizenry must also feel obligated to scutinize the workings of juvenile corrections. In the past, investigations such as the Harris poll indicated that much of the public voiced support for progressive rehabilitation programs for juveniles and agreed that public spending should be increased in this area. It seems that at least part of the public will philosophically and perhaps even economically support humanitarian innovations.[25]

It also seems clear that study of the history of the juvenile court simply reveals evidence indicating that societal humanitarianism or bureaucratic social engineering, when relied on in lieu of more exacting legal standards and procedures, does not always result in justice. We cannot rely on humanitarian love and understanding because where they do not exist, disaster often results. Such legal systems that have relied on intangible concepts in the past, and some that continue to do so, accomplish little other than removing authoritarianism further from the eyes of the public.

Many "professional caretakers" sincerely hold to the opinion that granting due process rights to juveniles—such as access to an attorney—hampers the development of a therapeutic relationship between the correctional worker and the client, and that it is generally detrimental to the hopes of ultimate reformation. Investigation by Edwin M. Lemert into the California Juvenile Court system, which presumably since 1961 has been required to advise juveniles of their right to counsel, has revealed that there has in fact been an increase in the use of attorneys in juvenile proceedings. However, their use has only been extended from 3 percent to 15 percent of their cases. His research also indicated that the use of attorneys, despite problems involving inexperience and the enormous backlog of cases, did prove beneficial in that "a comparison of cases with and without attorneys showed that the former had a higher percentage of dismissals, fewer wardships declared, and more sentences to the California Youth Authority suspended."[26] Despite this evidence, Lemert was of the opinion that "the main conclusion reached was that the major contribution of attorneys in the juvenile court lay in their ability to mitigate the severity of dispositions rather than disproving allegations of the petitions."[27]

The most extensive experiment testing the impact of attorneys in the juvenile court was performed by W. Vaughan Stapleton and Lee Teitelbaum.[28] In an excellent study funded by the Russell Sage Foundation in two northern metropolitan areas (referred to as Zenith and Gotham in their study), the researchers randomly assigned youths charged with delinquency to an experimental group and a control group. The experimental group provided the youngster with lawyers specially trained for juvenile court work and whose caseloads were much smaller than those of the traditional legal counselors' available to youngsters charged with delinquency. The control group had only the regular legal services available in the particular cities being studied. Table 6.1 indicates that in Zenith, the experimental group was likely to receive a less severe sentence than the control group, but in Gotham, the advantage rests with the control group, although the advantage is slight. This study indicates that in Gotham, those represented by "special" counsel are more likely to receive a more severe disposition than those not represented by counsel at all or by regular counsel. In Zenith, the reverse was true. When Stapleton and Teitelbaum examined the data, it appeared that characteristics of the two courts were the basis for the different impacts of the experiment. The judges in Gotham appeared to be less legalistic in orientation (more in keeping with traditional juvenile court philosophy) than Zenith. The authors summed up their interpretation of the differences between the courts by indicating:

> The differential impact of the project in Zenith and Gotham may be explained, then, by the fact that the more radical threat to judicial organization was posed in Gotham—a threat successfully met and countered by the court during the course of the project.[29]

Thus, the authors view the introduction of defense counsel in

Table 6.1 Outcomes of Cases

	Zenith				Gotham			
	Experimental Group		Control Group		Experimental Group		Control Group	
Disposition	%	(N)	%	(N)	%	(N)	%	(N)
Case dismissed	49.8	(161)	40.0	(124)	18.5	(45)	19.2	(49)
Delinquency not formally entered, case continued under court supervision for a limited time	9.9	(32)	3.9	(12)	30.5	(74)	34.5	(88)
Probation	31.6	(102)	43.9	(136)	40.3	(98)	40.4	(103)
Commitment	8.7	(28)	12.3	(38)	10.7	(26)	5.9	(15)
	100.0	(323)	100.1[a]	(310)	100.0	(243)	100.0	(255)

$x^2 = 20.008, p < .01$ $x^2 = 4.169, n.s.$

[a] Per cents do not add up to 100 due to rounding.

Source: W. Vaughan Stapleton and Lee E. Teitelbaum, *In Defense of Youth* (New York: Russell Sage Foundation), p. 66.

Gotham as threatening the traditional welfare approach of the court (this was post-*Gault*) while Zenith was not so threatened.

THE IMPACT OF THE GAULT DECISION

That *Gault* represents no panacea must, of course, be conceded. Difficulties do arise. For instance, the move toward adversarial proceedings for juveniles has, on occasion, pitted parent against child, when the main objective should be to settle their differences and thereby bring them closer together. Likewise, when attorneys engage in plea bargaining and other types of legal maneuvers, they may serve only to make themselves appear dishonest in the eyes of the juvenile. It will be recalled, however, that the Supreme Court never prohibited informal proceedings or experimentations, but only insisted on securing basic constitutionally guaranteed rights for juveniles.

Problems arising from over rigidity in court proceedings can usually be attributed to personnel threatened by legal constraints and not the Supreme Court's rulings. Likewise, in jurisdiction where the *Gault* decision is adhered to, practical remedies must be sought for the problems encountered by understaffed legal aid associations that have been severely taxed by the demands placed upon them.[30]

Writing in *Federal Probation,* Fred D. Fant, a New Jersey probation official, appears convinced that probation officers should be grateful that the *Gault* decision (when observed) holds the potential of relieving them of many of their prosecutional functions. He acknowledges further that "a significant decrease in adjudications, because of the insufficiency of evidence to sustain a finding of delinquency, could bring about a period of relief from the rather persistent increase in the volume of work received from the juvenile court in recent years."[31]

However, despite the potential that the *Gault* decision holds, Fant accurately indicated that a substantial proportion of both the judiciary and probation officials have neglected to abide by all its mandates. He explains: "Refusal of cooperation appears to be based on current belief that the *Gault* decision is not relevant or applicable to this part of the process because of the nature and purpose of the function itself, and the presence and/or participation of counsel at such a critical time could be inimical to developing the kinds of interpersonal relationships needed by probation personnel for appropriate data gathering and planning for later possible supervision of the youth."[32]

Constitutionality aside, evidence indicates that the rejection of *Gault* on the part of officials does not always emanate from such lofty motives as the above. The investigation conducted by the *Christian Science Monitor* concluded that: "In a majority of states, the judges interviewed have never read the *Gault* decision handed down in 1967 by the Supreme Court of the United States to protect juveniles. Or else they ignore it." Unfortunately, not atypical is the following statement by a judge who presides over an Arkansas juvenile court, who had never "studied" the *Gault* decision, and was even ignorant of where the reform schools in his state were located: "I'm not compensated sufficiently to handle all that detail work... Besides, it takes so much time, I couldn't get anything else done. And it's not punishment anyway."[33] A study of three court systems that represent "juvenile courts at their best" reveals that, although improvements have occurred, numerous examples of blatant disregard for the rights of children are evident. Those who conducted the study suggested that the courts will totally conform to the mandates of *Gault* only when more legalistically oriented officials assume control from their parens patriae schooled colleagues who are now in command.[34] While numerous law enforcement officials regard many of the Supreme Court's decisions handed down in the last decade as being unrealistic and dysfunctional, research does indicate that the majority abide by the edicts of these decisions.[35] Unfortunately, juvenile court personnel, who are usually better educated and presumably more sophisticated than law enforcement officials, have frequently been unwilling to follow the directives of *Gault*. While many court and probation officials view themselves as civil libertarians and support other Court rulings such as *Miranda* v. *Arizona*, they regard a decision such as *Gault* as curbing their creativity and freedom, and therefore do not necessarily obey it. Until these "professionals," and their less idealistic and educated colleagues, find themselves capable of respecting the law at least as diligently as does the average policeman (whom they frequently subject to derision and misunderstanding), our system of juvenile justice and corrections will continue to work to the detriment of both the child and society. We can ill afford to wait another 65 years for humanitarianism to mysteriously evolve in our juvenile court system, the occurrence of which would far from alleviate many of our judicial and correctional problems in the first place. Our only recourse now is to thoroughly and dramatically publicize the necessity of adhering to a just but standardized legal procedure. Perhaps doing so will result in pressures, both public and private, similar to those directed at law enforcement organizations within recent times, the result of which would be a more enlightened system of juvenile justice.

THE RETURN TO A
PRE-*GAULT* PHILOSOPHY

It must be kept in mind that one of the most important lessons to be learned from the *Gault* decision is that the juvenile is now to be accorded the same basic constitutional rights as the adult. Therefore, many of the principles to be discussed in chapter seven are relevant to juvenile justice also, and it may be only a matter of time before courts apply them to juveniles. However, change does come about slowly, and many relatively recent court decisions still seemingly represent a pre-*Gault* philosophy. The 1971 *Harwin* v. *United States* decision, handed down by the Court of Appeals for the District of Columbia Circuit, represents a case in point. Upon being convicted of the crime of unlawful entry, Augustus Harwin was sentenced under the District of Columbia Youth Corrections Act. In reality, this meant that young Harwin could possibly have been kept under the control of the correctional authorities for a maximum of six years. An adult, for being convicted of the same crime, would receive a maximum of six months in jail. Harwin claimed that he was prosecuted for an "infamous" crime and, therefore, he should have initially been indicted by a grand jury, as required by the Fifth Amendment to the United States Constitution. It is generally understood that an "infamous" crime is one that carries a penalty of one year or more in a correctional institution. The Court of Appeals decided, however, that despite the long sentence imposed on the juvenile, his crime could not be considered "infamous" because it carried only a six-month sentence for adults. The court then rationalized its decision by expounding on the rehabilitative and "nonpunitive" goals of the juvenile commitment proceedings.[36] In reality, however, this case represents another example of how a juvenile, simply because of his status as a minor, was treated more severely than an adult would have been who violated the same law.

Those less concerned with the individual delinquent and more disturbed about the need for societal protection may take issue with the same court's ruling in another case. In the *United States* v. *Howard,* the Court of Appeals for the District of Columbia Circuit determined that instead of sentencing a youngster to life in prison after he was convicted of first degree murder, the lower court should have considered committing him under the Youth Corrections Act. This would mean that he could possibly be released immediately after conviction or anytime thereafter when correctional officials saw fit to do so.[37] Perhaps if all the factors involved in this particular case were known, the decision would appear to be a wise one. Nevertheless, the fortuitous and seemingly haphazard methods of dealing with youthful offenders evidenced in both these decisions may cause some observers to suggest that the courts could more satisfactorily meet both the needs of rehabilitation and societal protection by adhering to more set and systematic legal standards.

SUMMARY

Without giving a blanket criticism of court and correctional officials, in this chapter correctional facilities and programs, past and present, were described as being, by and large, inadequate. Our analysis of the difficulties faced by juveniles within the criminal justice system revealed that, since 1899, we have been incarcerating youngsters in understaffed, overcrowded, and frequently poorly administered institutions. Tragically, these juvenile prisons have housed not only the seriously delinquent, but many dependent and neglected children as well.

Gaining impetus from the social welfare movement, we have defined our juvenile courts and institutions as treatment facilities, and have supposed that they are staffed by enlightened humanitarians. The verbal emphasis on helping as opposed to punishing has lead many to assume that because we are placing children in the care of so-called experts, we no longer have to be concerned about safeguarding their constitutionally guaranteed rights. History should have taught us that individualized treatment may, in some cases, result in injustice from the juvenile's own perspective and, more importantly, when the humanitarianism and enlightenment that we rely on do not exist, tyranny often does. Therefore, stricter legal controls over court and correctional authorities must be adhered to if we are to really protect all of our children.

The *Gault* decision, which dictates that juveniles must be accorded basic due process rights, has provided us with the necessary standards. Nevertheless, many officials refuse to abide by the mandates of *Gault*. Universal allegiance to the mandates of *Gault* would certainly prove beneficial to corrections. Probation officers would be relieved of many of their prosecutional functions, institutions would be reserved only for seriously delinquent youngsters, and institutional populations would be reduced to manageable sizes.

ENDNOTES

1. F. Wines, *Punishment and Reformation* (New York: T. Y. Crowell and Co., 1895), p. 302 as quoted in W. Vaughan Stapleton and Lee E. Teitelbaum, *In Defense of Youth* (New York: Russell Sage Foundation, 1972), p. 8.
2. Ibid., p. 8.
3. The President's Commission on Law Enforcement and Administration of Justice, *Task Force Report: Juvenile Delinquency and Youth Crime* (Washington, D.C., U.S. Government Printing Office, 1967) p. 3.
4. W. Vaughan Stapleton and Lee E. Teitelbaum, *In Defense of Youth* (New York: Russell Sage Foundation, 1972), pp. 13–14. © 1972 by Russell Sage Foundation.
5. Ibid., p. 22.
6. Shirley D. McCune and Daniel Q. Skolen, "Juvenile Court Judges in the United States, Part I. A National Profile," *Crime and Delinquency* XI, April, 1965, pp. 121–131.
7. President's Commission, Juvenile Delinquency.
8. See Cesare Beccaria, *On Crimes and Punishments* trans. Henry Paolucci (Indianapolis: The Bobbs-Merrill Co. Inc., 1963).
9. See Paul Lehman, "A Juvenile's Right to Counsel in a Delinquency Hearing," *Juvenile Court Judge's Journal* 17, 1966.
10. See the majority opinion in In Re Gault, 387 U.S. 1, (1967).

11. David Matza, *Delinquency and Drift* (New York: John Wiley and Sons, Inc., 1964).
12. Howard James, *Children in Trouble* (Boston: The Christian Science Publishing Society, 1969), p. 18. Reprinted by permission from *The Christian Science Monitor*, © 1968 by the Christian Science Publishing Society. All rights reserved.
13. *The Challenge of Crime in a Free Society: A Report by the President's Commission on Law Enforcement and the Administration of Justice* (Washington, D.C.: United States Government Printing Office, February, 1967) p. 81.
14. James, *Children in Trouble* p. 18.
15. Ibid., p. 3.
16. Ibid.
17. John I. Blavin and Loren Karacki, "Manpower and Training in Correctional Institutions," in *Staff Report of Joint Commission on Correctional Manpower and Training* (1522 K Street, N.W., Washington, D.C., December, 1969), pp. 27–34.
18. Ibid., p. 33.
19. James, *Children in Trouble* pp. 9–15.
20. Shortly after Sally's transfer, an appellate court ruling made it more difficult to transfer young Maine inmates to adult facilities. At the present time, it is still legally possible for Maine officials to transfer "incorrigible" youngsters to adult institutions. However, they must now prove that a youngster actually is "incorrigible" and when attempting to do so, they must observe all of his "due process" rights. See *Shone* v. *Maine* 406 F. 2d 844 (1st Cir. 1969).
21. Habeus Corpus is a writ that requires an individual to be brought before the judge for the purpose of reviewing the legality of his imprisonment. This writ was necessary in the *Gault* case because Arizona law did not permit appellate review of juvenile cases.
22. In Re Gault, 387 U.S. 1, (1967).
23. Kent v. United States, 86 S. Ct. 1045 (1966), 383 U.S. 541, 382 U.S. 803, 381 U.S. 902, 85 S. Ct. 1450, 119 U.S. App. D.C. 378, 343 F. 2d 247.
24. President's Commission, Juvenile Delinquency.
25. In his provocative book, *In the Country of the Young,* perhaps John W. Aldridge accurately analyzes the pseudo concerns of many self-styled American liberals: "By degrees we have fallen into the habit of seeing people as statistical phenomena or as the embodiments of the inequities or injustices which first called

them to our attention. And even as we offer them our official sympathies and register our concern for their predicament by writing our congressmen and supporting our favorite charities, we have lost the power to offer them the felt sympathies—or even, for that matter, the felt hostilities we would automatically be able to give if they were real to us as persons. This is the great castrating dilemma of the American middle class liberal. His humanitarian ideals derive little or no support from his human impulses. . . ." John W. Aldridge, *In the Country of the Young* (New York: Harper's Magazine Press, 1970) pp. 25–26.

26. Edwin M. Lemert, "The Juvenile Court—Quest and Realities," in *Becoming Delinquent: Young Offenders and the Correctional Process* eds. Peter G. Garabedian and Don C. Gibbons (Chicago: Aldine Publishing Co., 1970) pp. 135–167.
27. Ibid., pp. 158–161.
28. Stapleton and Teitelbaum, *In Defense.*
29. Ibid., p. 108.
30. For an analysis of the contributions of legal aid associations see Richard M. Minkoff, "Volunteer Legal Assistance for Corrections," *The Journal of Correctional Education* Vol XXLL, No. 1 (Winter 1970) pp. 24–32.
31. Fred D. Fant, "Impact of the *Gault* Decision on Probation Practices in Juvenile Courts," *Federal Probation* 9 September, 1969) p. 15.
32. Fant, *Federal Probation* p. 15.
33. James, *Children in Trouble* pp. 15–17.
34. Norman Lefstein, Vaughan Stapleton, and Lee Teitelbaum, "In Search of Juvenile Justice—*Gault* and Its Implications," *Law and Social Review* Vol. 3, No. 4 (May, 1969), pp. 491–537.
35. See Lawrence P. Tiffany, Donald McIntyre, Jr., and Daniel L. Rotenberg, *Detection of Crime: Stopping and Questioning, Search and Seizure* (Boston: Little, Brown and Co., 1967).
36. Harwin v. U.S., No. 22, 317 (1971).
37. U.S. v. Howard, No. 23, 830 (1971).

7

Correctional Law

As a result of the *Gault* decision, the same legal rights that are guaranteed to adults must also, at least theoretically, be guaranteed to juveniles. However, as was indicated previously, in the American system of criminal justice, juveniles are often regarded as separate entities, with fewer rights than adults. Also, the appellate courts, in "abandoning the hands off doctrine," have been primarily concerned with adult felons and not with juveniles. Therefore, because of the number of adult cases, and because juveniles are, in fact, treated differently under the law, this chapter will deal only with the legal rights of the adult offender.

The rationale behind the abandonment of hands-off doctrine, will be explained through the discussion of the rights of the correctional client as he goes through the sentencing, probation, incarceration, and parole processes.

SENTENCING

Several other interesting decisions that relate to postconviction proceedings have been handed down within recent years. For example, the *United States* v. *Coffey* case dealt with the question of whether or not an attorney should be present when a probation officer is interviewing a convicted offender for the purpose of obtaining information to be used in the pre-sentence investigation report. The United States Supreme Court has clearly indicated that an attorney should be present during all of the important phases of the judicial process. Thus, the presence of legal counsel is required during custodial interrogation,[1] the actual trial,[2] and even at the final sentencing.[3] However, in the *Coffey* case, the Court of Appeals for the Tenth Circuit was not in conflict with any of these mandates when it ruled that legal counsel is not required to be present after the offender is convicted and is conferring with a probation officer prior to his actual sentence.[4] While this decision is not binding for the rest of the country, it appears to be a logical precedent. After a person has been convicted, the goal of rehabilitation can best be served if the probation officer is allowed to discuss matters with the offender freely without interference by an attorney. In the absence of such interference, he should be able to compile a thorough pre-sentence report that will help the judge in deciding upon the type of sentence that will prove most beneficial to all concerned.

As indicated in chapter three, the progressive judge gives considerable weight to the pre-sentence investigation report in determining the type of sentence that will best serve the interests of both the state and the offender.[5] The legal basis for the pre-sentence investigation was established in 1949, when the United States Supreme Court handed down its decision in the *Williams* v. *New York* case. Williams had been convicted of murder and the jury recommended a sentence of life imprisonment. Basing his decision on material in the pre-sentence investigation report, the judge sentenced the offender to death. Williams claimed that because he was not allowed to confront and cross-examine those individuals who gave information to the official who compiled the report, or to refute any of the material therein, the due process of law had been violated. The Supreme Court rejected Williams' contentions, indicating that the only way to obtain adequate information, arrive at fair judgments, and "individualize punishments" was to rely on the expertise and discretion of probation officers and judges.[6] (It is rather ironic that the pre-sentence investigation that is usually advocated as a rehabilitative tool that reduces the severity of the law finds its legal basis in a case whose decision precluded any rehabilitative efforts.)

It is generally maintained that when sentencing, the trial judge should make the treatment fit the offender or, in other words, give due consideration to his rehabilitation potential. Emphasizing this point in a 1972 case, the Court of Appeals for the Sixth Circuit required the lower court to reconsider a five-year sentence that had been given to a conscientious objector who had refused to report for the civilian employment required of him in lieu of serving in the military. Appellate courts have seldom been concerned with the duration of sentences; however, the lower court, in this case, had an unofficial but automatic policy of sentencing all offenders in this category to five years in prison, even though the law only required that they be given sentences of up to five years. Because the lower court had an arbitrary policy of not considering lesser sentences than five years, it obviously was not individualizing sentencing as recommended by the Supreme Court.[7] In other words, the appeals court was instructing the lower court that the circumstances surrounding each case were different, and that the judge should evaluate the unique qualities of each case before sentencing the individual.[8]

Unfortunately, sometimes the information supplied in the pre-sentence investigation report may influence the judge to the extent that he will punish the defendant for alleged offenses with which he has not officially been charged. Thus, the appellate courts have been on guard against judges who apply unduly severe sentences to individuals whose criminal activity, in the opinion of the judges, extends beyond the offenses associated with the specific cases being tried.[9] Of course, the courts have been given a great deal of discretion in deciding, on the basis of the pre-sentence report, what type of sentence an individual should receive. In fact, if the report indicates that the offender represents a severe threat to society, he will most likely be given the maximum sentence allowed by the law for the particular offense of which he has been convicted. Because the fate of the offender is determined, to a large degree, by information in the pre-sentence report, alert appellate courts have insisted that such evidence be substantiated.

As indicated in the *Williams* case, this does not mean that the lower courts must adhere to the strict rules of evidence demanded in the actual trial, but material in the report should be taken from reliable sources and be well documented.[10]

The 1971 *United States* v. *Weston* case is a good example of an appellate court's insistence on a well documented pre-sentence report. The case involved a woman who was convicted of "concealing and transporting illegally imported heroin." Such a conviction carried a minimum sentence of five years and a maximum of 20 years in prison. The trial judge initially gave some indication that a five-year sentence would be appropriate, but later changed his mind, after evaluating the pre-sentence report, and handed down a 20-year sentence. The report described the offender as a confirmed criminal who was one of the leading suppliers of heroin in that area. However, the Ninth Circuit Court of Appeals ruled that the sentence was improper because much of the information in the pre-sentence report was obtained from an unnamed informant whose reliability was uncertain; therefore, the evidence was unsubstantiated.[11]

Legal controversy continues to revolve around the question of disclosure, or whether or not the offender should have the right to examine the pre-sentence investigation report and attempt to refute any of the material contained therein. Such a right could involve direct challenges to those individuals who supplied the information upon which the report is based. Some authorities contend that allowing disclosure defeats the purpose of the pre-sentence investigation because relatives and personal associates usually will be unwilling to divulge pertinent information about the offender if they cannot be assured of confidentiality, or if they are faced with the possibility of being called on as witnesses in a trial situation. Opponents of disclosure also maintain that by permitting an individual to contest various aspects of the pre-sentence investigation report, and by requiring that legal proof of the accuracy of relevant material be established, not only is the usefulness of the instrument destroyed, but an impossible responsibility is also placed on an already overburdened court system.[12]

Despite the admitted benefits of pre-sentence investigations, the appellate courts, as well as the majority of legal scholars, fear that the danger of inaccurate reporting must be checked. Thus, they demand close legal scrutiny of the pre-sentence investigation reports effects on sentencing. The United States Supreme Court has never ruled directly on the question of disclosure, and many state and federal courts have left the matter to the discretion of the trial judges. Other states require at least partial mandatory disclosure, and such prestigious organizations as the American Law Institute, the President's Commission on Law Enforcement and the Administration of Justice, and the American Bar Association advocate that the offender should be given the opportunity to examine and challenge any derogatory material that may prejudice the judge in his sentencing.[13]

In some states, the judge is required to edit the report and to extract and make available to the defense that information that may have a bearing on the sentencing.[14] As long as the information in question does not affect the severity of the sentence, in almost all of the states the courts may refuse to disclose confidential sources and material that is relevant to the diagnosis of the offender, but, in the judgment of the court, may be inappropriate for him to examine.[15] Such intermediate policies, which require partial disclosure only, are perhaps best; for requiring complete disclosure seldom proves beneficial to the offender and could result in a series of irrelevant subsequent trials that challenge numerous statements appearing in the report. However, the importance of guarding against material appearing in the report that is unsubstantial and detrimental to the offender should not be overlooked.

LEGAL SAFEGUARDS AND CONTROLS IN PROBATION

Ideally, when deciding whether an offender is to be placed on probation or dealt with in some alternate manner, judges and probation officers should consider his rehabilitation potential as well as the possible danger that he represents to the community, and then reach a decision that is consistent with the best interests of both. However, in most states there are either statutory provisions or traditions that sometimes limit the freedom of the courts in granting probation, even when it appears to be the most advisable alternative. In 35 states, statutes place restrictions on who can be granted probation. For example, other considerations aside, an offender who has committed a certain type of crime or perhaps has a previous criminal record, may be ineligible for probation consideration. Also, without any statutory basis, some courts have policies which prohibit the granting of probation to certain types of offenders.[16] Realizing that each case is in some way unique and that there may be peculiar circumstances involved that the formal law has not taken into consideration, the President's Commission on Law Enforcement and the Administration of Justice has recommended the allowance of more flexibility and greater discretion on the part of judges.[17] At present, many judges, when they feel that it would serve no beneficial purpose to incarcerate certain offenders who have committed nonprobationary crimes, will charge them with lesser or related offenses, thereby enabling themselves to grant probation. It seems unfortunate that many judges who have the best interests of the individual at heart find it necessary to engage in this extralegal type of plea bargaining in order to accomplish their goals.

The decision to grant or deny probation is not always influenced by the goals of either rehabilitation or societal protection. While most courts do not necessarily refuse probation to those who are convicted after pleading innocent, it is a common practice to grant probation or reduce charges in return for a guilty plea.[18] It is argued that if such policies were not extensive, then there would be little incentive to plead guilty. As a result, the time and expense involved in maintaining such a judicial system, in which most defendants plead innocent, would be even more prohibitive than it is at the present time. In other words, in order to function, our courts must rely on the practice of rewarding people to plead guilty. Although the appellate courts have not looked favorably on those lower court judges who have standing policies of refusing probation to those individuals who are convicted after an innocent plea, (regardless of their rehabilitation potential), this type of plea bargaining continues without significant higher court intervention.[19]

Such practices, as well as seemingly endless battles between contending attorneys and the related case backlogs that clog our court systems, are not conducive to rational judicial decision making. Perhaps a few offenders are frightened into returning to a law-abiding existence by their experiences within the system. Typically, however, such experiences contribute little to the rehabilitative goal. In fact, the defendant is often confused by talk of writs, petitions, witnesses, delay tactics, legal jargon in general, and extralegal "deals." All of this hardly provides an example of either true justice or the ethical standards that the defendent is expected to abide by.

Viewing our courts from a different perspective, it is also obvious that they are not adequately protecting society from dangerous criminals. One fourth of those individuals known to have been criminally involved in the deaths of the 561 policemen who were murdered during the 1960s were either on probation or parole when they committed their offenses.[20] Figures such as these serve to indicate dramatically the failures in judicial decision making.

It is possible that officials do not have the necessary legal machinery at their disposal and should not be blamed for deficiencies in the system; however, without singling out certain groups to be faulted, it must be emphasized that if our court systems are ever to live up to the ideals of true justice, they must be given the resources that will enable them to abandon questionable practices. They must be able to sentence offenders in accordance with the interests of reform and societal protection only.

Statutes usually allow trial courts or boards of probation to exercise their own judgment in establishing the regulations by which the probationer must abide. The conditions of probation usually range from the vague ("avoid injurious or vicious habits") to the specific ("remain within a specified area"), and may be quite extensive as long as they are not "unduly restrictive."[21] Appellate courts have, on occasion, authorized lower courts, as conditions of probation, to require probationers to pay for family support, court costs, medical expenses of the victim, and even for probation supervision.[22] On the other hand, an appellate court intervened when an offender was ordered to pay restitution in excess of the amount stolen.[23] Other conditions that were judged to be invalid because they were "unreasonable" include a case in which the defendant was required to obtain psychiatric help at his own expense when no expert had testified in court regarding his mental condition. Another appellate court overruled a judge who had, as a condition of probation, prevented a college athlete from participating in varsity basketball.[24]

It has been established that an individual who is accused of committing a felony has the right to secure or be provided with legal counsel. However, there has been some controversy regarding what stage of the legal proceedings this right becomes effective. Important decisions handed down by the United States Supreme Court have, to a large degree, settled this issue. The Supreme Court has guaranteed the accused access to an attorney during the trial period,[25] during "custodial interrogation,"[26] and even at the time of sentencing.[27] These mandates could only be interpreted to mean that an individual should have the assistance of an attorney at any stage in the judicial proceedings where his constitutionally guaranteed rights might be in jeopardy.

However, at that time, a question still remained with regard to whether or not the offender's guarantee of legal counsel extended beyond the sentencing process. Did the law require officials to obtain the assistance of an attorney for the offender at subsequent proceedings such as probation revocation hearings? As was previously discussed, in many jurisdictions, when the judge decides to grant probation, he officially sentences the offender to prison, but instead of actually requiring him to serve his sentence, he is placed on a probationary status in the community. In other words, the judge imposes the prison sentence but suspends its execution. In some instances, it is also possible for the judge to suspend the sentence, place the offender on probation, and at a later date impose and execute the sentence during a probation revocation hearing. Concerning the former type of policy, it has been argued that because the revocation of probation simply involves the execution of the original sentence, legal counsel is not required.[28] Thus, some authorities have contended that when the offender is given all the necessary legal safeguards during the original sentencing, he is, thereafter, within reason, subject to the care and control of the court and correctional authorities only.

In 1967, the United States Supreme Court, in *Mempa* v. *Rhay,* ruled contrary to this position. They upheld the lower court's right to defer sentences—to sentence an individual to prison but place him on probation instead and, at a later date, revoke his probation. They also reasoned, however, that because legal complications and controversies may arise during revocation hearings, the offender must be provided with an attorney during such proceedings.[29] There have been mixed interpretations of this ruling by other appellate courts. One court, for example, relying on *Mempa* v. *Rhay,* indicated that an offender is entitled to legal counsel only if the sentence is imposed, and not simply executed at the revocation hearing.[30] Others have not agreed with this strict interpretation of the *Mempa* decision, and have asserted that a defense attorney should be available at all revocation hearings, regardless of the circumstances.[31]

Most courts and probation departments require their officials to notify individuals and arrange hearings for them before they revoke probation. It is likely that almost all modern appellate courts would consider such practices to be mandatory. However, in 1935, the Supreme Court maintained that it does not violate the due process of law to revoke a person's probation without notification or hearing.[32] Nevertheless, within recent years, when state supreme courts have expressed their views on these points, they have determined that the offender must receive official notification that the revocation of his probation is being considered, and he must also be afforded the opportunity to present his side of the case at an official hearing.[33]

In determining whether or not an individual should have his probation revoked, the judge is usually allowed a great deal of discretion. Accusations against the offender do not have to be proven "beyond a reasonable doubt," as was the case in the original trial, and circumstantial evidence may be taken into consideration. However, common justice dictates that the offender should be allowed to present evidence in his own behalf and cross-examine witnesses. The court is hardly providing an example of fair treatment to the probationer if it does anything less. It must be remembered that the probationer has already been duly tried and convicted; he cannot expect to be given another full-scale trial and have the court adhere to all the rules of evidence to which it was originally obligated. If such requirements were made mandatory, lower courts would most likely be reluctant to grant probation in the first place.[34]

THE INCARCERATED OFFENDER

Perhaps the appellate courts have traditionally adhered to the "hands-off doctrine" more when confronted with petitions from inmates of correctional institutions than when dealing with those from offenders who have not been actually incarcerated. The rationale behind such a policy has usually been two-fold. It has been claimed that since correctional institutions are under the control of the executive branch of government, if the judiciary were to interfere with the internal administrative affairs of institutional personnel, they would be violating the long held principle of separation of powers.[35] Secondly, supporters of the "hands-off doctrine" have asserted that court intervention would seriously hamper prison officials in their attempts to maintain discipline, administer treatment programs, and achieve desirable correctional goals. In other words, because judges are usually not experts in penology, they have no right to instruct specialists in the area on how to conduct their business.[36]

The validity of the above arguments are, to say the least, questionable. The appellate courts have always concerned themselves with the actions of numerous administrative agencies that are technically under the control of the executive branch of government. Likewise, responsible appellate review of penal practices should seldom infringe on the legitimate freedom or creativity of prison administrators. The actions of welfare, public school, and draft board officials have traditionally been subject to the scrutiny of the courts, and there have been few disastrous results.[37] Judges may have little expertise in corrections, but this should in no way restrict them in determining whether or not an individual's constitutionally guaranteed rights have been violated.

The press has kept the public well informed regarding the more dramatic cases that have involved higher court intervention in prison affairs. Several years ago, nationwide attention was focused on the atrocious penal conditions existing at the Cummins Prison Farm in Arkansas. Significantly, the Eighth Circuit Court of Appeals, in 1967, ruled that the whipping of prisoners, as practiced at Cummins, represented "cruel and unusual punishment," and was in violation of the Eighth Amendment.[38] In a subsequent case, the same court determined that the state of Arkansas was constitutionally obligated to protect inmates from each other.[39] The court reached this conclusion after being provided with evidence that indicated that seventeen stabbings, four of which were fatal, had occurred within an eighteen-month time period at Cummins. Another well publicized case involved a California prisoner who was confined for twelve days, the first eight of which he was kept totally naked, in a solitary "strip cell" without heat, ventilation, or light, and with no furnishings other than a toilet. The District Court of Appeals ruled that such treatment amounted to cruel and unusual punishment.[40] Likewise, the "physical abuse, torture, running of gauntlets, and similar cruelty" that was inflicted on Attica State Prison inmates immediately after their disastrous riot was quelled, was also officially determined to be cruel and unusual punishment.[41]

Court action prohibiting cruel and unusual punishment has been well publicized; however, the average citizen is not well informed about cases that involve penal practices that have limited inmates' access to the courts and freedom of speech and religion.

Access To The Courts

The most basic and essential legal right that a person has is the First Amendment guarantee of access to the courts. Any other rights would, in reality, be meaningless if he could not have his complaints regarding the alleged violation of such rights considered in a court of law. The first steps toward abandonment of the "hands-off doctrine" were taken in a case that concerned a prisoner's rights to access of the courts. In *Ex Parte Hull,* the United States Supreme Court ruled that prison officials must allow inmates to correspond with the courts, and that such communications are not subject to censorship or confiscation.[42] Furthermore, before a case has been adjudicated, correctional officials are prohibited from punishing prisoners for statements made in any legal petitions, even if they involve obviously fabricated and outrageous claims.

However, despite the principles established by the Supreme Court in *Ex Parte Hull,* the prisoner's rights to correspond with the courts is not always an unlimited one. Many courts have permitted censorship of "nonlegal" material addressed to lower courts, and some have gone as far as allowing institutional employees to determine whether or not particular correspondence relates to the legality of the prisoner's detention and treatment.[43] Most prison officials have no legal training, and many have vested interests in preventing some material from reaching the courts. Therefore, the practice of allowing them to make such determinations is questionable.[44]

Prisoners may encounter additional difficulties when attempting to have their complaints considered by appellate courts. For example, some courts have maintained that officials can justifiably limit the amount of legal material that inmates may purchase,[45] and they may be prevented from keeping law books in their cells.[46] Obviously, without adequate legal information, it is difficult to prepare a petition for higher court evaluation. Nevertheless, appellate courts usually take the prisoner's lack of resources into consideration, and they seldom require that they adhere to all the technicalities. In fact, some courts have assisted the incarcerated offender in formulating his claims in a legally acceptable manner.[47]

Limiting an individual's access to legal materials is not, in most instances, done for the purpose of placing him at any disadvantage, but to forestall what have been termed "fishing expeditions." Without any real fear of court opposition, institutional

The recent increase in inmate interest in legal literature has been largely attributable to the emphasis that courts have placed on safeguarding the Constitutionally guaranteed rights of felons. Here an inmate discusses some legal issues with the corrections officer who supervises the law library at Clinton Correctional Facility, Dannemora, New York.

officials may attempt to halt legal "fishing expeditions," or, in other words, they are not obligated to allow inmates to peruse law books or other legal materials with no specific intentions other than to chance upon some grounds for appeal.[48]

The importance of the "jailhouse lawyer" in the prison community should not be underestimated. This is the type of individual who, in many instances, exploits, economically and otherwise, other less intelligent inmates. In return for favors of various kinds, the "jailhouse lawyer" provides real or pseudolegal assistance for his less knowledgeable peers. When administrators limit access to legal materials, they are quite often motivated only by a desire to deprive such prisoners of the tools of exploitation, and not of their due process rights.[49] Nevertheless, the United States Supreme Court asserted, in *Johnson v. Avery,* that inmates cannot be barred from assisting each other in preparing petitions for postconviction relief if the state does not provide such assistance. In that particular case, the Court's primary concern revolved around the inability of illiterate prisoners to adequately formulate their grievances. In simplified terms, the opinion of the Court was that "jailhouse lawyers" are better than no lawyers at all.[50]

Once a prisoner has secured the services of an attorney, he must be allowed to confer with him, and administrators are required to make the necessary arrangements that will enable them to meet and discuss legal matters. However, professional legal assistance is often difficult to obtain when incarcerated. Supplying an inmate with an attorney if he desires one, may represent wise and just policy; but if he is not given this privilege, his rights under the Sixth Amendment are not necessarily violated. Under the law, the accused in a criminal prosecution must be provided with legal counsel. However, if he is convicted and sentenced, the authorities are no longer obligated to obtain legal assistance for him.[51] Perhaps if the courts were not flooded with inmate petitions, they would be less hesitant to make legal counsel and complete legal libraries automatically available to prisoners.

Freedom Of Speech

The First Amendment to the United States Constitution guarantees citizens the right to communicate with others. For the convicted felon, however, this right has sometimes been severely curtailed. As indicated in the previous section, prisoners definitely must be allowed to communicate with courts and attorneys in regard to legal matters. Also, recent appellate court decisions show a tendency to authorize inmates to freely correspond with both public officials and the press. Some courts, at least, seem to be motivated by a desire to make the public sensitive to prison conditions. Nevertheless, prison administrators still have the legal authority to limit the contact that inmates have with free society. Such authority is subject to the application of the "clear and present danger" test which requires administrators to be prepared to demonstrate exactly how and why such contact would either be a threat to security or interfere with necessary administrative practices.[52]

In most institutions, officials ask the inmate to select several people outside of the institution with whom he would like to correspond. Traditionally, it has been left up to the prison administrators to decide whether or not the inmate will be allowed to write to, or in any way communicate with, those persons. When the courts have reviewed such practices, they have usually decided that administrators should be entrusted with the responsibility of deleting anyone from the inmate's mailing list who may be a detrimental influence or who, in turn, may potentially be harmed by his relationship with the inmate. Such practices, however, have been questioned by some courts. In *Palmigiano* v. *Travisono,* for example, a district court ruled that prison officials should not have absolute authority in deciding issues of this kind, and that "total censorship" cannot be justified in terms of the goals of deterrence, rehabilitation, or security.[53] Another district court, in *Morales* v. *Schmidt,* determined that officials could not justifiably prevent an inmate from sending a love letter to his wife's sister. In the opinion of the court, there must be "a compelling state interest" at stake before any of a prisoner's "fundamental" rights can be denied.[54]

The problems associated with determining visiting privileges are similar to those involving mailing lists. As long as they are "reasonable" requests and take the inmate's welfare and public safety into consideration, officials are usually allowed to exercise their discretion in determining who is allowed to visit the prisoner, as well as the length and frequency of their visits.[55] It is, of course, in the best interests of society, and presumably the inmate himself, to thwart any communication that would support a continuing illegal business in the outside world or any which would allow the inmate the opportunity to receive contraband or escape plans.

To a lesser degree, it seems advisable to prohibit correspondence with various individuals who, because of their known criminal involvement, may prove to be detrimental influences on the inmate.[56]

Another reason for limiting the amount of letters that an inmate may send or receive and the number of visitors that he may have relates directly to the staff shortages that occur in most institutions. In the majority of cases, there are not enough institutional employees who would have the time to censor the large quantities of mail that would exist if there were no restrictions placed on the number of letters being sent or received. Likewise, it would take more staff members than are now available in most facilities to supervise more extensive or frequent visitations. Despite such administrative problems, the dangers associated with lenient mailing and visiting policies are perhaps not as real as many prison officials suspect. The smuggling of contraband and, if there actually are such attempts, escape plans can usually be detected by carefully checking visitors before they are allowed to see the prisoners. Also, administrators could guard against the traffic in contraband by requiring inmates to open their mail only when officials are present. The officials could examine the contents of envelopes and packages, but not actually read the letters. For rehabilitative purposes, it is advisable to allow inmates who are soon to be released relatively free communication with outside sources such as potential employers.[57]

Related to an individual's right to express his ideas is the corresponding right to become aware of the views of others. In at least two cases, appellate courts have definitely extended this right to prisoners. In *Rowland* v. *Sigler* and *Fortune Society* v. *McGinnis,* the courts demanded that prison officials allow inmates to read certain publications that were allegedly inflammatory. The former case involved a Black Muslim publication entitled *Mohammed Speaks,* and the latter concerned a newsletter published by ex-convicts. While the courts, in these cases, did not prohibit the censorship of all inflammatory publications, they did indicate that officials must offer proof, not mere speculation, that certain materials are socially harmful before they can prevent inmates from having access to them.[58]

A number of companies have published articles and books that were written by individuals while they were confined in correctional institutions. However, when prison administrators have prevented inmates from engaging in such outside business activities, they have traditionally gained the support of the appellate courts. The Supreme Court has never ruled contrary to its *Stroud v. Swopes* decision, in which it declined to intervene when prison administrators refused to allow an inmate to make arrangements with an outside concern for publishing a book.[59]

It is difficult to justify prohibitions against inmate involvement in outside business interests. It has been asserted by some that the outside business activities of prison inmates are likely to be illegitimate ones, and that the money that the inmates receive may be used to bribe guards or buy favors from other inmates. As Barry Fox indicates, these dangers can be eradicated by administrative scrutiny of the inmate's business activities and by requiring, as is the practice in most institutions, that moneys earned from outside sources be used either to support the inmate's family or to be held in deposit for him until he is released.[60] Admittedly, the average correctional institution does not have enough staff members to conduct investigations of the various types of complicated business enterprises that inmates may want to become involved in. Nevertheless, blanket prohibitions against outside business activities are too restrictive. For example, to prevent a gifted inmate from seeking a publisher for his literary efforts, seems counterproductive in terms of rehabilitation.

Speech between inmates has also been subject to some restrictions. As previously indicated, in some specific instances, inmates have the right to confer with each other regarding legal matters.[61] However, when speech between prisoners is of such a nature as to arouse emotions and, thereby, is threatening to the safety of the staff or inmate populations, officials are within their right if they take steps to deny such speech.[62]

If the inmate is allowed to freely express his ideas, he then, at least, has a firm basis for establishing his individuality. Furthermore, the inmates' ideas, as well as those of the prison officials, must be heard beyond the confines of the prison if the public is to become knowledgeable regarding prison conditions. If complaints are heard and given just consideration as they develop, the danger of their becoming the basis for smoldering resentment and revolutionary action is reduced. To safeguard the right to free speech and other rights, prison officials should be, and at least theoretically are, legally required to show that each prison regulation limiting the freedom of the inmate does so for a justifiable reason that balances the needs of the individual inmate with those of the larger society.[63]

FREEDOM OF RELIGION

Freedom to believe in a particular religious faith is, of course, absolute within the prison or any other setting. However, the inmate's freedom to practice his religion is, on occasion, subject to some controls. For example, one court determined that prison officials were justified in preventing certain inmates from attending religious services that were available to the general prison population. The court accepted the official contention that troublesome inmates sometimes must be segregated from their peers if prison discipline is to be maintained.[64] Also, in many institutions, members of particular religious faiths may be given certain privileges such as the freedom to observe work-free holy days. However, if an inmate switches his allegiance to another religion for, in the opinion of the staff, the purpose of obtaining nonreligious benefits, officials will most likely refuse to recognize his "conversion." Thus far, the appellate courts have not dealt with administrative policies of this nature.

Perhaps because, in the minds of many, religion is associated with rehabilitation, the courts have historically been sympathetic to the religious needs of prisoners, but questions concerning the rights of inmates who are Black Muslim are often viewed from a different perspective than are those of more traditional American religions. The Black Muslim religion, which allegedly teaches racial supremacy, has a ministry partially comprised of numerous exconvicts and convicts, and its requirements for the adherence to unusual dietary practices, poses unique problems for both correctional officials and the courts.

In a California case, *In Re Ferguson,* the court rejected the inmate claim that the official prohibition of Muslim services and the possession of certain religious articles amounted to racial discrimination. The court agreed with institutional officials that such practices were so disruptive that they threatened prison discipline and security.[65] This particular case, however, represents one of the few exceptions to a trend in court decisions. In general, the appellate courts have viewed the Black Muslim faith as a legitimate religion.[66] In reference to the Muslim controversy, some courts have held that when religious privileges are granted to some groups, similar privileges must be accorded to all others, if they demand them.[67] Other courts have maintained that to deprive Black Muslims of the right to participate in their own religious activities amounts to a denial of equal protection under the law.[68]

Much has been said about the dangers involved in allowing "racist" and volatile organizations to proselytize within institutional walls. However, it has never been conclusively established that any well known religious group, including the Black Muslims, deserves to be categorized in such a manner.[69] Likewise, while some contend that certain religiously oriented associations represent threats to prison discipline and security, "mere speculation" regarding such concerns "is insufficient." As was indicated by the *Brown* v. *McGinnis* decision, the danger that inmate behavior might become disruptive must be real and substantiated before prison administrators can prohibit any religious activities.[70] Nevertheless, if it can be demonstrated that certain religious groups have abused their right to religious freedom in the past, or that security precautions would have to be forfeited in order to allow certain religious activities, or that the expense of such activities would be prohibitive, then religious freedom may justifiably be curbed.[71]

Other interesting legal questions regarding religious rights may have to be decided in the near future. For example, if it can be shown that a significant number of inmates in an institution are Black Muslims, will the courts conclude that the state must employ a full time chaplain representing that religion and also require prison administrators to conform to the dietary needs of this portion of the inmate population?[72]

INTERNAL DISCIPLINE

The "cruel and unusual punishment" cases that were discussed previously represent clear-cut examples of correctional officials violating the rights of their charges. However, it is most difficult to state with any certainty what traditional methods of maintaining order and discipline within American correctional institutions are no longer viewed as legally acceptable. Various courts have handed down differing and conflicting decrees.[73] Professor Larry Kraft has examined a number of court cases that relate to prison disciplinary practices. On the basis of the decisions rendered in these cases, he suggests the following procedural guidelines (all of which are not presently legally binding) that the prison administrator of the future would be wise to consider.

1. The prisoner should be made fully aware of the types of behavior that are officially prohibited so that he is prepared to guide his behavior accordingly.
2. Only official staff members should be allowed to impose "disciplinary sanctions or charge inmates with rule violations." Inmates should never be given the responsibility of determining what disciplinary action should be taken against other inmates.
3. The inmate's caseworker should verbally notify the inmate of the charges against him, and explain them to him. A written notification of the charges should follow and include: "(1) an explanation of the procedure and the inmate's rights, (2) the specific act of misconduct alleged, (3) a complete summary of the results of the supervisor's investigation, and (4) the time and place of the hearing."
4. If he so desires, the inmate should be allowed to select a staff member to assist him in defending himself.
5. The hearing or disciplinary board, before which the inmate who is accused of violating institutional regulations appears, should not include any officer or official who is making the accusations or investigating them. Objectivity is a necessity.
6. A permanent record of the disciplinary hearing, including in-

formation on how and why the particular decision was reached, should be maintained.
7. A "reviewing officer," with "the authority to reduce or suspend action," should be assigned the task of re-examining the case after a certain time period has elapsed.
8. Some form of external review board, made up of nonprison personnel should serve as a quasi-appellate court to which the inmates could take their complaints.[74]

The ombudsman system, which is common to Scandinavian countries and is now well established in the state of Minnesota, may provide the ideal type of external review board. The ombudsman is an individual, or committee, with the sole duty of evaluating and acting on inmate grievances. Such individuals may, of necessity, be employed by state departments of corrections. However, they are not affiliated with particular institutions and, therefore, should remain relatively free of vested interests.

While the courts are increasingly concerned with safeguarding the procedural "due process" rights of the incarcerated offender, it is frequently impossible for the latter to obtain professional legal assistance. It will be remembered that the states are not obligated to provide legal counsel for prisoners. However, several legal aid societies, such as the legal section of VISTA, and some law schools have developed programs that are proving beneficial to the convicted offenders both inside and outside of institutions. Volunteer students from law schools, sometimes for academic credit and under the direction of faculty members, are becoming active in the legal affairs of prisoners. Among those who are committed to such assistance are the law schools of the University of South Carolina, Emory University, George Washington University, American University, Boston University, the University of Minnesota, the University of Wisconsin, Kansas University, and the University of Chicago. Where the law allows, such as in Massachusetts, senior law students may actually represent prisoners in court. Where this is not possible, students perform the initial background investigations and research, and their professors actually handle the cases in the final stages. While offering no panaceas, both volunteer legal aid societies and universities can effectively bring about positive changes in the field of corrections.[75]

The reader may question the advisability of attaching a great deal of importance to preventing any infringement on the rights of the incarcerated felon. After all, he has had his "day in court," so to speak. Obviously, it can be counterproductive to devote extended time and effort to the detection of any legal technicality that will enable the prisoner to be freed or the administrator to be punished. However, in the interest of justice, emphasis should be given to safeguarding the basic constitutional rights of the individual. This entails, at a minimum, granting the inmate access to an outside source that is qualified to determine: (1) if he has been justifiably incarcerated in the first place, and (2) if the control that is exerted over his life is more restrictive than is necessary.

After offering his procedural guidelines, Kraft aptly cautions: "Again, it must be remembered that the prison situation is unlike any found in the free community. Since our concepts of 'judicial,' 'administrative,' and 'fact finding' review are based on the latter, care should be taken not to adopt without modification these traditional review procedures. Rather, what is needed is a hybrid procedure that gives to some external agency, preferably the court, access to all of the inmates."[76]

LEGAL RIGHTS AND PAROLE PRACTICES

A number of courts have dealt with questions pertaining to whether or not the offender retains his "due process" rights when he appears before a parole board or parole revocation board. Does, for example, the individual have the right to an official notice of the charges against him, to legal counsel, and to confront and cross-examine witnesses when he is called before the board that determines if he will be granted parole or that has the power to revoke his already obtained parole status?

Most of the courts that have considered these questions still regard the discretionary power of parole-granting boards to be nearly absolute. Only when a board violates actual statutes that are designed to afford the offender certain rights or when the action of a board appears to be "fundamentally unfair" are the higher courts likely to rule in favor of the inmate.[77] It has been observed repeatedly that parole hearings are not of an adversary nature as was true of the original trials. Ideally, parole boards are tools in the rehabilitative machinery that help the individual in his progress toward reform. It is generally assumed that prison and parole officials are in the best positions to know whether or not placing an offender back in the community will serve the interests of rehabilitation and societal protection. They alone are familiar with his progress in prison and with social and psychological information relating to his background and potential. Therefore, it is usually reasoned that judicial intervention should be avoided in all but extreme circumstances. In fact, in most states, authorities are not even legally required to hold a hearing before they decide whether or not parole will be granted.[78] Therefore, many questions relating to the offender's due process rights at such hearings may be quite meaningless.

While parole authorities still retain much of their traditional discretionary power, adversary type parole hearings, with all the legal safeguards such as the guarantee of legal counsel, may become realities in the near future. A number of states already allow the offender to be represented by an attorney at parole hearings, and at least one appellate court has affirmed this right for the offender during cases involving "factual disputes."[79]

Most likely, other appellate courts will eventually follow the example set by the New York State Court of Appeals and demand that the individual's procedural due process rights be observed during revocation hearings before they make the assurance of such rights mandatory at hearings that are conducted to determine whether or not parole is to be granted in the first place.[80] Obviously there are more "private interests" to be lost by a person who is already living in the community, even if he is obligated to abide by parole regulations, than by one who is confined in a prison.[81]

Several higher court justices have mentioned that the cost,

both in economic and manpower terms, of allowing the convicted felon to maintain and exercise his "due process" rights would be prohibitive, and would result in our already overburdened judicial system's becoming virtually inoperative. This factor has never been offered as the sole reason for the court's refusal to intervene in parole proceedings. However, if economic and manpower problems are alleviated in the future, justices will then, in all probability, be more willing to extend due process rights to the individual at parole eligibility hearings.

Some authorities refer to the *Mempa* v. *Rhay* case and reason that, like probation, parole is merely a deferred sentence. Therefore, they conclude that the individual should be accorded the right to counsel and all the other procedural due process rights that were guaranteed him during the original sentencing process when he appears before a parole board. Thus far, the courts have rejected such reasoning. In *Menechino* v. *Oswald,* the court asserted that, while probation may be a deferred sentence, by the time an individual reaches prison, his sentence has been finalized and he, therefore, has lost some of the rights that were his prior to and during sentencing.[82] At the sentencing proceedings, the offender may be in need of legal assistance in order to adequately comprehend such matters as the waiver of legal rights, appeal procedures, questions relating to the withdrawal of guilty pleas, and the rules of evidence. However, by the time he has the opportunity to appear at a parole hearing, such matters are usually not relevant. Therefore, parole-granting hearings are generally regarded by the appellate courts as nonadvisary fact finding sessions in which the offender does not have to be given all of the traditional due process rights.

It remains to be determined definitely whether an individual has a guaranteed right to assistance from an attorney when appearing at his parole revocation hearing. Conflicting mandates from various appellate courts have done much to confuse this issue. For example, in *United States ex rel. Bez* v. *Connecticut,* the court, relying primarily on *Mempa* v. *Rhay,* granted parolees the right to limited representation by attorneys during revocation hearings.[83] In contrast, the *Ellhamer* v. *Wilson* decision asserted that such representation did not have to be allowed.[84] Likewise, the few appellate courts that have permitted parolees to be represented by attorneys at parole revocation hearings have often differed regarding the pros and cons of mandatorily appointing attorneys to represent those parolees who cannot afford their own legal counsel.[85]

It has also been claimed that, in denying parole, many boards have been "arbitrary and capricious" and have denied some individuals "equal protection under the law."[86] The courts have usually responded by maintaining that in order to accomplish the goal of rehabilitation, criminals must sometimes be treated differently from each other and such differential treatment is, at least theoretically, based on psychological and sociological factors, and is in the best interests of the individual. Nevertheless, if it can be shown that parole hearings are discriminatory or otherwise unfair, there is little doubt that courts will assert their authority and bring about significant changes in parole hearing procedures.[87] The lack of standardization in parole regulations is already a growing concern among legal and penal authorities.[88]

As indicated above, there have been several conflicting appellate court rulings that relate to the authority of parole and parole revocation boards and the rights of parolees. In summary, however, it is generally true that parole is not considered a legal right, but a privilege, and that parole procedures are usually not subject to judicial review unless they violate state or federal statutes or are "fundamentally unfair" in nature.[89]

In *Morrissey* v. *Brewer,* the United States Supreme Court did much to advance the rights of the parolee who is charged with violating the conditions of his parole. As a result of this decision, authorities are now required to conduct at least a "minimal inquiry" to determine whether or not there are reasonable grounds to revoke parole, and they must do so near the location of the alleged violation as soon after the individual is apprehended as possible. The individual (or individuals) who makes the final decision regarding the reasonableness of the charges that are lodged against the parolee must be an outside observer who, up until that time, did not play an active part in the case. Such a person, while he must maintain his objectivity, however, does not have to be an attorney and may even be another parole officer.[90]

To understand the more exact requirements of *Morrissey*, we will rely on the expertise of John W. Palmer, whose perceptive analysis of the case revealed the following "procedure" which "must be followed in a parole revocation hearing to conform with the requirements of due process:

1. There must be written notice of the claimed violations of parole.
2. The evidence against the parolee must be disclosed to him.
3. The parolee must be given the opportunity to be heard in person and to present witnesses and documentary evidence.
4. The parolee has the right to confront and cross-examine adverse witnesses, unless the parole authority specifically finds good cause for not allowing confrontation such as a risk of harm to the informant if his identity were disclosed.
5. The hearing body, such as a traditional parole board, must be neutral and detached, but need not be judicial officers or lawyers.
6. The parole authority must compose a written statement as to the evidence it relied on and the reasons for revoking the parole."[91]

Court action in some other parole related areas may indicate a trend toward the development of more judicial control over correctional officials. For example, a California court ruled that parole authorities have no right to prevent a parolee from speaking to a public gathering, no matter what the subject of his talk might be, unless there is a "clear and present danger" that his speech will lead to a violation of the law.[92] Furthermore, it is uncertain as to how "clear and present danger" could be detected prior to a speech, since the court indicated that officials have no way of knowing what an individual would say until he says it. Therefore, it would seem that in the state of California, to prevent a person who is on parole from delivering any speech, is to engage in the prohibited practice of "prior restraint" and is, thus, considered unreasonable.

Of course, there are other cases balancing such examples of

court intervention in correctional matters, in which the courts have affirmed the discretionary powers of correctional officials. Into such a category falls another California court ruling that permitted the revocation of an individual's parole, even though it was clearly demonstrated that the evidence that formed the basis for the parole revocation was illegally seized. In other words, the court indicated that even if material, because of the way it is gathered, would be excluded in a court of law, it can still be used as "legitimate" evidence to justify sending a parolee back to prison. The court's rationale involves the belief that in order to further the goals of both rehabilitation and societal protection, officials are obligated to take all available information into consideration so long as it is accurate.[93]

SUMMARY

Support for and adherance to the "hands-off" doctrine has diminished tremendously within the last decade. Most appellate courts are no longer hesitant to intervene in the sentencing, probation, incarceration, and parole processes. Such willingness to participate in correctional affairs exists, not only when correctional officials have been "arbitrary" or "grossly negligent," but also, in less blatant cases, when the courts have determined that the correctional client is in danger of being deprived of his legal rights.

There are, however, many inadequacies in the correctional system that have not been remedied by court action. The majority of states are, for example, hampered by restrictions, either in the form of statutes that determine what types of offenders are to be considered for probation, or by standing policies that have the same result. Judges are sometimes prevented, by statutes that prohibit the granting of probation to those convicted of committing certain offenses, from allowing offenders to remain in the community, even though they represent no threat to public safety and would be harmed by the prison environment. Some judges contend that such statutes force them to resort to the legally questionable practice of charging individuals with less serious offenses than they actually committed, so as to be able to grant them probation. Other judges bend the law for less noble reasons and grant probation without consideration for rehabilitation or societal protection, but in return for guilty pleas. While the practice of rewarding individuals by granting them probation in return for pleading guilty has been defended as a means of preventing the judicial process from being rendered inoperative, such policies have been justifiably attacked by several appellate courts.

Trial courts or probation boards are usually allowed a great deal of discretion in determining the regulations by which probationers must abide. When called before a probation revocation board, however, the offender should be assisted by an outside source. Contrary interpretations notwithstanding, the *Mempa* v. *Rhay* decision indicated that, because of the possible legal technicalities involved, the offender should have access to an attorney at his probation revocation hearing. Also, in almost all of the states, the probationer must receive official notification that the revocation of his probation is being considered, and he must be given the opportunity at the hearing to defend himself against all the charges made against him. Of course, he will not have all the legal safeguards and rules of evidence that protected him during his original trial.

Within recent years, higher courts have voiced a new concern for the welfare of the incarcerated offender. The press has kept the public well informed about some of the more dramatic "cruel and unusual punishment" cases that appellate courts have dealt with. Other, less dramatic cases, however, have also had their impact on correctional practices. For example, the courts have accorded the inmate the most basic of all legal rights, namely, access to the courts. The inmate, at least theoretically, has the right to correspond with court officials without fear of censorship or confiscation. Because of appellate court action, prisoners are also now more likely to enjoy greater freedom of speech and religion than they have ever known in the past.

Traditional methods of maintaining order within correctional institutions have been called into question by the courts;

however, rulings have been so conflictual that it is difficult to propose exact standards to guide prison administrators in maintaining discipline. Most recommendations include granting the inmate basic legal rights when he appears before prison disciplinary boards or courts.

At the present time, the discretionary powers of both parole granting boards and parole revocation authorities are quite extensive. The appellate courts are likely to confirm the parolee's rights if they are protected by statute or if the parole authorities are judged to be fundamentally unfair. While the parolee does not retain all his traditional due process rights when he appears before a revocation hearing, the *Morrissey* v. *Brewer* decision has assured him of fair proceedings.

ENDNOTES

1. See Escobedo v. Illinois, 378 U.S. 478 (1964).
2. See Gideon v. Wainwright, 372 U.S. 335 (1963).
3. United States v. Behrens, 375 U.S. 875, 373 U.S. 902, 83 S. Ct. 1290, 375 U.S. 162, 84 S. Ct. 295 (1963).
4. United States v. Coffey, 415 F. 2d 119 (1969).
5. Pre-sentence investigations, as the name implies, are generally initiated only after conviction. However, in some federal cases they have been conducted at various stages in the judicial process. Since such a practice involves looking into the personal affairs of individuals who are not actually convicted of crimes, it is, to say the least, constitutionally questionable.
6. Williams v. New York, 337 U.S. 241 (1949).
7. United States v. Daniels, 492 F. 2d 1273 (1970).
8. For further analysis of sentencing discretion, particularly as it relates to *U.S.* v. *Daniels,* see Eugene N. Barkin, "Looking at the Law," *Federal Probation* (December, 1971).
9. See State v. Kunz, C.A. N.J. 462 F 2d 1025 (1969).
10. When a higher court sets a sentence aside, can the trial court, after re-evaluation, sentence the offender more severely than it originally did? Appellate court opinion on this issue has been mixed;

however, the United States Supreme Court, in 1969, ruled that a more severe sentence may be allowed if it can be justified by reliable information in the record regarding the deviant conduct of the offender since the original trial. North Carolina v. Pearce, 395 U.S. 711 (1969). Also see United States v. Gross, 8th Cir, St. (1969), and Barnes v. United States, D.C. Cir. Ct. (1969). In these two cases the appellate courts emphasized the need for well documented evidence of additional deviant involvement on the part of the offender. Without the required evidence, the lower court cannot increase the original punishment.

11. United States v. Weston, 448 F. 2d 626 (1971).
12. See dissenting opinion in State v. Kunz.
13. *The Challenge of Crime in a Free Society: A Report by the President's Commission on Law Enforcement and Administration of Justice* (Washington, D.C.: Government Printing Office, 1967) p. 145.
14. See State v. Kunz.
15. Ibid.
16. See Frank W. Miller, Robert O. Dawson, George E. Dix, and Raymond I. Parnas, *The Correctional Process* (New York: The Foundation Press, Inc., 1971), pp. 912–913.
17. Ibid.
18. Ibid., pp. 934–935.
19. For an example of higher court intervention into such practices, see United States v. Wiley, 267 7th Cor. Ct. 453 (1959).
20. Miller, Dawson, Dix, and Parnas, *The Correctional Process* p. 112.
21. Ibid., p. 947.
22. See Dickson v. State, 323 S.W. 2d 432 (Ark. 1959) and People v. Becker, 349 N.W. 2d 833 (Mich. 1957).
23. United States v. Taylor, 305 F 2d 183 (1962).
24. In Re Bushman, 83 Cal. Rptr. 375 (1970) and People v. Higgins, 22 Mich. App. 479 (1970).
25. Gideon v. Wainwright, 372 U.S. 335 (1963).
26. Escobedo v. Illinois, 378 U.S. 478 (1964).
27. United States v. Behrens, 375 U.S. 162 (1963).
28. See Miller, Dawson, Dix, and Parnas, *The Correctional Process* pp. 964–972.
29. Mempa v. Rhay, 389 U.S. 128, 88 S. Ct. 254 (1967).
30. Shaw v. Henderson, 430 F. 2d 1116 (1970).
31. Hewett v. North Carolina, 415 F. 2d 1316 (1969); Ashworth v. United States, 391 F. 2d 245 (1968).

32. Escoe v. Zerbst, 295 U.S. 490 (1935).
33. See Lester v. Foster 207 Ga. 596 (1951) and Blaine v. Beckstead, 10 Utah 347 (1959).
34. See Miller, Dawson, Dix, and Parnas, *The Correctional Process* pp. 958–972.
35. For a thoughtful criticism of this rationale, see Barry M. Fox, "The First Amendment Rights of Prisoners," *The Journal of Criminal Law, Criminology and Police Science* Vol. 63, No. 2 June, 1972, pp. 162–163.
36. For a criticism of this position, see Richard P. Vogelman, "Prison Restrictions—Prisoner Rights," *The Journal of Criminal Law, Criminology, and Police Science* Vol. 59, No. 3 (1968) pp. 386–387. The serious student of correctional law should also familiarize himself with the "doctrine of federal abstention." Those who support the "doctrine" maintain that the federal courts should abstain from hearing a case for a "reasonable" period of time during which the state courts may hear the case.
37. *The Journal of Criminal Law, Criminology, and Police Science* Vol. 63, p. 164.
38. Jackson v. Bishop, 268 8th Cir. Ct. 804 (1967).
39. Holt v. Sarver, 300 8th Cir. Ct. (1969).
40. Jordan v. Fitzharris, 257 N.D. Cal. 674 (1966).
41. Gonzales v. Rockefeller, 2d Cir. Ct. (1971).
42. Ex Parte Hull, 312 U.S. 546 (1941). For a more recent confirmation of the inmate's right to freely correspond with an attorney, see Brabson v. Wilkins, 280 N.Y.S. 2d 561 (1967).
43. Lee v. Tahash, 352 F 2d 970 (1965).
44. See *The Journal of Criminal Law, Criminology, and Police Science* Vol. 63, p. 172.
45. Roberts v. Papersack, 265 D. Md. 415 (1966).
46. If the materials that the inmate desires to keep in his cell pertain directly to a petition that he is developing, he should be allowed to keep them.
47. For an excellent explanation of how the United States Supreme Court handles petitions for indigents, see Anthony Lewis, *Gideon's Trumpet* (New York: Vintage Books, 1964).
48. See Roberts v. Papersack, 265 D. Md. 415 (1966).
49. See Justice White's dissenting opinion in Johnson v. Avery, 898 S. Ct. 747 (1969).
50. Johnson v. Avery, 898 S. Ct. 747 (1969).
51. As previously noted, there are exceptions to this general principle. At sentencing and during probation revocation hearings, the

offender is entitled to the assistance of an attorney. Thus far, however, the courts have not extended this right to the convicted offender under any circumstances.
52. Palmigiano v. Travisono, 317 F. Supp. 776 D.R.I. (1970).
53. Ibid.
54. Morales v. Schmidt, 340, E.D. Wis., 544 (1972).
55. Abamine v. Murphy, 108 2d 294 (1951), and Rowland v. Wolff, 336, D. Neb. 257 (1971).
56. The *Journal of Criminal Law, Criminology, and Police Science* Vol. 59, pp. 386–396.
57. For an example of a higher court's refusing to curb the discretionary power that correctional officials have in determining who will be on mailing and visiting lists, see Numer v. Miller, 165 9th Cir. Ct. 986 (1948).
58. Rowland v. Sigler, 327, D. Neb. 821 (1971), and Fortune Society v. McGinnis, 319, N.D. Cal., 901 (1971).
59. Stroud v. Swope, 342 U.S. 829 (1951).
60. The *Journal of Criminal Law, Criminology, and Police Science* Vol. 63, p. 174.
61. Johnson v. Avery, 898 S. Ct. 747 (1969).
62. See Fulwood v. Clemmer, 206, D.D.C., 370 (1962).
63. For further discussion regarding these points, see *The Journal of Criminal Law, Criminology, and Police Science* Vol. 59, pp. 386–396.
64. McBride v. McCorkle, 44, N.J. 468 (1957). Also see U.S. ex rel. Cliggett v. Pate, 229 F. Supp. 818 (1964).
65. In Re Ferguson, 55 Cal. 2d 663 (1961).
66. See Brown v. Peyton, 437 F. 2d 1228 (1971).
67. Fulwood v. Clemmer, 206, D.D.C., 370 (1961), and Sewell v. Pegelow, 291 4th Cir. Ct. 196 (1961).
68. State ex rel. Tate v. Cubbage, 210, Del. 555 (1965).
69. Many authorities point out that generally Black Muslims conform to a rigidly moralistic life style and that the religion itself has been instrumental in reforming many former criminals.
70. Brown v. McGinnis, 10 N.Y. 2d 531, 225 N.Y.S. 2 479.
71. Long v. Parker, 390 F 2d 816 (1968).
72. The *Journal of Criminal Law, Criminology, and Police Science* Vol. 63, pp. 170–171.
73. Nolan v. Schafati, 306, D. Mass. 1 (1969). Sostre v. Rockefeller, 312, S.D.N.Y., 863 (1970).
74. 47 N.D. L. Rev. (Fall 1970).

75. See Richard M. Minkoff, "Volunteer Legal Assistance for Corrections," *The Journal of Correctional Education,* Vol. XXLL, No. 1 (Winter 1970), pp. 24–32.
76. 47 N.D. L. Rev. (Fall 1970) p. 73.
77. Briguglio v. N.Y. State Bd. of Parole, 24 N.Y. 21, 298 N.Y.S. 2d 704.
78. See Miller, Dawson, Dix, and Parnas, *The Correctional Process* p. 1091. Also see Tarlton v. Clark 441 F. 2d 384 (1971).
79. Warren v. Michigan Parole Board, 179, Mich. App., 664 (1970).
80. Combs v. Lavallee, 286 N.Y.S. 2d 600 (1968).
81. See Miller, Dawson, Dix, and Parnas, *The Correctional Process* pp. 1090–1091.
82. Menechino v. Oswald, 430 F 2d 403 (1970).
83. U.S. ex rel. Bey v. Connecticut, 443 F. 2d 1079 (1971).
84. Ellhamer v. Wilson, 445 F. 2d 856 (1971).
85. See Earnest v. Willingham, 406 F. 2d 681 (1969).
86. Tyler v. State Dept. of Public Welfare, 19 Wis. 166 (1963).
87. Alvarez v. Turner, 422 F. 2d 212 (1970).
88. See Miller, Dawson, Dix, and Parnas, *The Correctional Process* pp. 1132–1134.
89. Ibid., p. 1122.
90. Morrissey v. Brewer, U.S. 40 U.S.L.W. 50 16 (1972).
91. John W. Palmer, *Constitutional Rights of Prisoners* (Cincinnati: The W. H. Anderson Co., 1973).
92. Hyland v. Procunier, 311 N.D. Cal. 749 (1970).
93. In Re Martinez, 83 Cal. 382 (1970).

8

Probation and Other Community Based Corrections Programs

With the problems of prison organization and structure that have been discussed, the conclusion might be reached that while prisons keep some offenders out of the community, they do so at the expense of severely restricting the likelihood of rehabilitating the offender. Many professionals in corrections have come to this conclusion. For example, the President's Commission report *The Challenge of Crime in a Free Society,* states:[1]

> Institutions tend to isolate offenders from society, both physically and psychologically, cutting them off from schools, jobs, families, and other supportive influences and increasing the probability that the label of criminal will be indelibly impressed upon them.

The Commission's statement implies that a rehabilitation setting must be one that does *not* isolate offenders from the community. On the contrary, the Commission's statement would imply the need for a correctional setting to be a relatively "normal" environment in which the offender could relate to schools, jobs, family, and other important aspects of our social world in as "normal" a way as possible.

Considering the type of people associated with and the behavior engaged in while incarcerated, it is likely that an offender's institutional experiences do not prepare him for a noncriminal, noninstitutional life. Speaking on this subject, William Nagel, a noted penologist, states:[2]

> ... the inmate community, being distinctly antisocial, works against the goals of the larger society and thereby against rehabilitation efforts. The status that inmates acquire is gauged by the intensity and consistency of their anti-authority reactions to the prison situation, and therefore the behavior of the convicts is determined by convicts themselves. Through assimilation and acculturation, prisoners take on the delinquent values, norms, customs, and general culture of the penitentiary. The prison represents—in fact is—the ultimate in social rejection, and its inmates develop increased anti-social values in order to "reject the rejectors."

Nagel's voice denouncing the impact of prisons is not peculiar. The idea of removing an individual from society with the hope that when he is returned to society he will be a more law-abiding person has come under attack. These concerns about the negative impact of correctional institutions upon the offender have lead to a feeling that offenders must be treated in the community, not in some isolated, debilitating environment.[3] Such community placement would be designed to force the offender to confront the problems and pressures of living in society, perhaps the same pressures that caused his criminality. A rehabilitative trend today is toward "community based corrections," which for this discussion will refer to correctional activities that exist in a community environment, and through which the offender actively participates in the normal life of the community.

PROTECTION OF THE PUBLIC AND COMMUNITY BASED CORRECTIONS

Both community based corrections and correctional institutions are given the responsibility of protecting the public from those who have been convicted of crimes. Social isolation of offenders does protect the public—while they are isolated, but protection of the public is a much more complicated issue than this. If incarceration increases the likelihood of criminality upon release or at least does not reduce it, can it be argued that the public is being protected? The arguments that institutions fail to protect the public in the long run usually cite high recidivism figures, and point out that the average prison stay for an adult is approximately two years,[4] and incarceration for juveniles is much shorter. Therefore, institutions fail not only to protect society by keeping the offender isolated, but they return him from his isolation as a more dangerous person.

In line with this argument, if community based correctional programs can do a more effective job in creating more law-abiding people out of offenders, then the protection of the public is better served. Thus, while the offenders who are placed in a community program might have a greater opportunity to commit another offense against the public, in the long run, their threat to society will be diminished. The attempts to keep offenders in the community are not new. Probation was started in the mid-1800s, but now there are new proposals for its expansion. Most experts suggest that a majority of the offenders in correctional institutions (both juvenile and adult) could be in community programs without seriously jeopardizing the public.

Most arguments "for" community based corrections are based on arguments "against" prisons, suggesting that corrections is responding, not to the positive impact of community problems, but to the negative aspects of institutions. Until the positive impact of community based programs is demonstrated, judgment should not be made, even though they may be appealing in a philosophical way.

PROBATION

As was indicated in previous chapters, while probation is usually treated as a sentence handed down by the judge, it is more accurate to regard it as a suspended sentence. The probationed offender is placed under the supervision of an officer of the court, whose duty it is to counsel, supervise, and, in some cases, to return the offender to court and ask that his suspended sentence be imposed.

As was indicated earlier, prisons tend to encourage an inmate "to do his own time," i.e., don't cause trouble. Probation offers a much less structured situation. The offender may be closely supervised by his probation officer or he might be expected to make it on his own, with little assistance. In either case, the offender is interacting with the community and consequently his chances of becoming integrated into the community are greater.

The integration of the offender into the community should utilize the resources of both the probation officer and the community. The probation officer is the key; his counseling skills have been traditionally viewed as his most significant contribution to the probationer. Because of the increase in caseload size and the awareness that counseling alone is not enough, the emerging role of the probation officer emphasizes not so much the caseworker-counselor role, but a "broker" role. The "broker" role is analogous to the stockbroker who is able to make a wide variety of investments. The probation officer acting as broker for his client would not so much attempt to help the probationer himself, but to put him into contact with agencies or individuals that could deal with his particular problems. For example, few probation officers have the counseling talents to work well with the wide variety of offenders on their caseload. A caseload may include alcohol problems, drug problems, educational deficiencies both academic and vocational, mental retardation problems, and a multitude of other problems.

Although any one probation officer is not capable of dealing with this variety of problems, the collection of agencies and individuals in the community can. According to the broker concept, it becomes at least a part of the probation officer's role to become aware of services available in his area and to put his client in touch with these services. If certain services are not available, it then becomes part of the officer's responsibility to assist in the development of the needed services.

Probation has been a community based form of corrections whose focus has been casework—usually involving some form of individual counseling. In effect, because the focus has been on counseling, one of the potentially significant factors in probation has not been extensively developed—namely, the extensive use of community resources such as vocational and educational training, volunteers, treatment of special problem offenders such as alcoholics, drug users, sex offenders, and others. In order to put this in perspective, a brief overview of the development of probation is necessary.

The Development Of Probation

As we indicated in chapter three, John Augustus is usually given credit for inaugurating probation in the United States. Augustus did several things which have become characteristic of the present day probation system. First, he developed a concept determining the types of people who were good risks. Those indicted for their first offense, and those who gave promise of adopting acceptable behavior were included. Second, Augustus introduced to probation the pre-sentence investigation, by not taking responsibility for an offender without an investigation into his background. Previous character, age, and social influences were among the factors considered in evaluating the suitability of the offender for probation.[5]

Perhaps those aspects of John Augustus' procedures most characteristic of present day probation are the reports he kept on each offender, his attempt to get them employment or more education, and his impartial reports to the court. These are the essence of contemporary probation officers' functions and serve as a model of both the casework and the broker approach to probation.

It should be understood that probation under Augustus was an extralegal measure. It was not illegal but, at the same time, it was not sanctioned by law. In fact, it was not until 1878 that Massachusetts passed a statute "providing for the appointment of a paid probation officer for the courts of criminal jurisdiction in the city of Boston."[6] This statute provided that a probation officer attend court, investigate the accused or convicted offenders, make recommendations to the court as to whether or not the person is suitable for probation, and assist and encourage probationers to prevent their recommitting an offense.[7]

While Massachusetts made it mandatory that each police district and each municipal court appoint a probation officer in 1891, other states did not jump on the bandwagon.[8] In fact, the development of probation follows closely the development of the juvenile court. It was not until 1899 that Illinois passed the first juvenile court act. Dissatisfaction with the manner in which children were dealt with in our justice system gave impetus to the development of special juvenile courts. As was pointed out in chapter one, the juvenile court redefined the role of the state from the administrator of punishment to that of a parent whose desire was not to punish per se, but to do what was in the best interest of the juvenile. The formal development of the protective and treatment orientation in the juvenile court movement helped to bring about the extension of probation. Since correctional institutions were frequently regarded as not being in the best interest of the juvenile, probation was relatively quickly adopted as an alternative means for helping juvenile offenders. By 1925, probation was available to juveniles in every state. Probation was not available in every state for adults until 1956.[9]

The President's Commission on Law Enforcement and the Administration of Justice found that while probation has been formally adopted in each state this can be very misleading because of the wide variability in terms of its availability. As late as 1966, in only 31 states were there probation services available for juveniles in every county, and in one state only two counties had probation services.[10] Even fewer probation services are available to adults. Several states have no probation services available at all to misdemeanants. This frequently means that a judge can either turn the offender loose with no supervision or incarcerate. Although probation has come a long way since the days of John Augustus, it has not come far enough.

Probation Officer's Work Load

As described earlier, a probation officer has a number of duties. Foremost among these duties is the supervision of a caseload of probationers sentenced by the court. However, the pre-sentence investigations are also important. It is recommended that a probation officer's caseload should be 50 work units.[11] In calculating these units, one case under supervision is counted as one unit; a pre-sentence investigation (P.S.I.) is counted as five units because of the amount of time required to adequately complete such an investigation. If 50 work units is the standard, how closely do actual caseloads approximate this standard?

Figure 8.1 presents one view of caseload size by presenting the percentage of juveniles, misdemeanants, and felons supervised by officers with caseloads of 50 or less, 51–70 cases, 71–100 cases, and over 100 cases. It must be noted that Figure 8.1 is somewhat misleading because it does not give the number of pre-sentence investigations the officers have, only their supervisory caseloads.

In looking at this figure, it becomes obvious that even in juvenile probation, with its treatment model, the majority of juveniles are supervised by officers with caseloads exceeding 70. Caseloads are even larger at the adult level, having 76 percent of misdemeanant cases on probation, and 67 percent of the felony cases on caseloads of over 100. Therefore, if we assume that probation officers have the capability of helping their clients, it becomes apparent that the size of the caseload prohibits close and consequently significant contacts with the offender.

Add pre-sentence investigations to the caseload of most probation officers and the job becomes even more overburdening. A national time study revealed that probation officers were spending as much time on one pre-sentence report as on 13 regular supervision cases.[12] Daniel Glaser suggests that one reason for this is that officers are rewarded more for investigative work because it produces "a tangible product, the pre-sentence report."[13] Super-

Probation Officers with 0-50 cases are responsible for:

11.76 percent of all juvenile cases.
.86 percent of all misdemeanant cases.
3.10 percent of all felony cases.

Probation Officers with 51-70 cases are responsible for:

31.15 percent of all juvenile cases.
8.12 percent of all misdemeanant cases.
9.16 percent of all felony cases.

Probation Officers with 71-100 cases are responsible for:

46.41 percent of all juvenile cases.
14.68 percent of all misdemeanant cases.
20.69 percent of all felony cases.

COMMUNITY BASED CORRECTION PROGRAMS 265

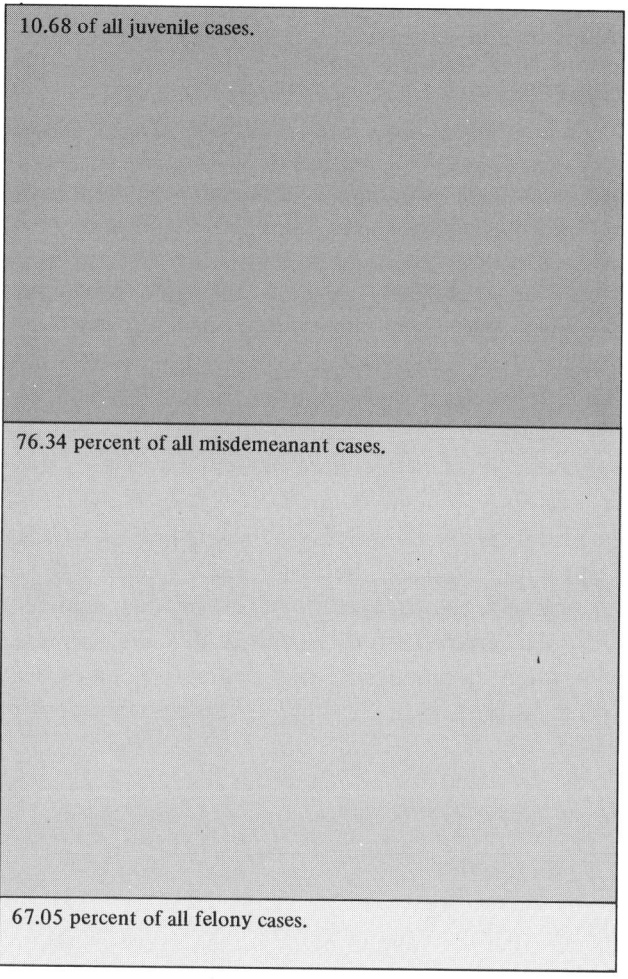

Source: National Corrections Survey. The President's Commission on Law Enforcement and Administration of Justice, *Task Force Report: Corrections,* Washington: U.S. Government Printing Office, 1967) pp. 98-99.

Figure 8.1 Caseloads of Probation Officers

visors use these reports as a means of evaluating the officer, which encourages officers to spend an unusual amount of time on this task. Glaser sums up his analysis of why probation officers with both caseload and pre-sentence investigations emphasize the investigations by stating that:[14]

> Understandably, therefore, when an officer must both advise the judge on sentencing and try to check on and assist those already on probation, the former activity has deadlines and gets priority, while the latter tends to be secondary.

Explicitly, probation officers in all except some of the larger metropolitan areas are expected to perform both casework supervision and pre-sentence investigations. Implicitly, the job becomes much broader than this. Besides these specific responsibilities, they frequently serve as resource persons to colleges and universities for training students in probation; they provide impetus to develop resources for the needs of their clients as well. Observations of probation officers' behavior leads one to the conclusion that working with the caseload is of low priority. Time studies in the California Youth Authority confirm this. These studies found that even when caseload size was reduced, it had no effect on supervision because the extra time available was spent on office activities.[15]

Effectiveness of Probation

Effectiveness is defined here as the degree of attainment of the goals of probation. The traditional view of effectiveness of correctional services uses the recidivism rate as its basis for evaluation. This measure tends, however, to be vague. Recidivism may be violation of a rule of probation (such as associating with someone prohibited in the conditions of probation) or commiting a new offense. Most would agree that while both are recidivism in the sense that they may lead to a revocation of probation, there is a qualitative difference between the two. The commission of a new offense should not, therefore, be treated as equivalent to violation of a noncriminal rule of probation. Another issue is whether or not to treat all new offenses as equivalent. For example, is an offender on probation for burglary who commits a shoplifting offense as serious a recidivist as one who commits a rape? In evaluating the effectiveness of probation, it will first be compared to other types of dispositions such as fines and incarceration, then to caseload size.

Probation versus Other Dispositions With the increasing belief that institutions debilitate the incarcerated offender instead of rehabilitating him, judges have looked increasingly to probation. A consequence of this increased use of probation is that offenders who would previously have been incarcerated are being placed on probation. As a result, caseloads are becoming composed of more serious offenders, placing a greater burden on the probation officer to supervise his clients.

Generally speaking, probation is just as effective as an institutional sentence when comparing recidivism rates. Following 5,274 adult male offenders in Wisconsin, Babst and Mannering found that the success rate of those placed on probation was about the same as for those imprisoned when current offense, past criminal record, and marital status were held constant.[16] When only first offenders were examined, it was found that probationers were significantly less likely to be recidivists. Several other studies support the notion that basically probation is at least as effective as imprisonment, but there are no conclusive findings that probation is necessarily better for any particular type of offender.[17]

Although probation has normally been compared to imprisonment in terms of effectiveness, there also has been a study comparing probation to fines and discharges. This study supported fines and discharges as being more effective than either probation or imprisonment for first offenders and recidivists of all age groups.[18] This study is only suggestive because it is possible that judges gave fines and discharges to less serious offenders, even though offense and previous record were held constant. With the minimal amount of supervision offenders are given on probation, it should not be surprising that fines and discharges are at least as effective as probation and, as the Hammond study shows, perhaps more effective.

Attempts to compare the relative effectiveness of probation with alternative dispositions, as discussed above, suffer from a number of methodological problems. For example, in comparing those placed on probation with those receiving fines or imprisonment, there are differences in the kinds of offenders receiving these sentences. Furthermore, there are variations within probation, and between institutions in terms of "treatment" provided to the offender. These factors are not considered in the research; therefore, one must be cautious in deciding that there are no differences in the effectiveness of the sentencing options, or that one option is better than another.

Caseload Size and Effectiveness   Theoretically, the greater the amount of supervision and counseling, the greater will be the effectiveness of probation. Also, the smaller the caseload, the greater will be the supervision and, consequently, effectiveness. The logic is clear. Offenders on small caseloads are less likely to be recidivists than those on large caseloads. Does this logic hold true?

Perhaps the most extensive study was performed by Lohman et al.[19] In their study, offenders were randomly placed on intensive, ideal, normal, and minimum supervision caseloads. Intensive caseloads carried 25 offenders and averaged 6.71 contacts per month. At the other end of the range, the minimum supervision load had 125 offenders and averaged .48 contacts a month or about one contact every two months. Basically, they found that there were no real differences in terms of new major violations between those on the different caseloads.

Other studies randomly placing offenders on varying sizes of caseloads have found inconsistent results. The Test of Probation Services (TOPS) project in the Los Angeles County Probation Department reduced the regular caseload of 75 supervision cases and 8 investigations per month to 50 supervision cases and 6 investigations per month.[20] Because just reducing workloads frequently does not change job performance, the probation officers in the experiment received special training in casework dynamics, caseload management, and recording techniques. As a consequence of this training, it was hoped that the officers would utilize the reduced workload to work with their clients more closely. Stuart Adams, in summing up the results of this study, states:[21]

> Several objective measures were used to ascertain effects, and in almost every area of client performance and management behavior, the reduced caseloads showed themselves superior. There was a reduction in average length of detention at time of admission, reduction in the time a case remained active, reduction in unnecessary court hearings, and greater use of informal services by the experimentals.

Following the TOPS project, the Los Angeles County Probation Department started the Intensive Supervision Caseload Project for hard to place girls.[22] Specially selected officers were assigned a caseload of 15 of these girls as opposed to the normal caseload of 50. When the success of this group was compared to a group matching them on many characteristics, it was found that the small caseload girls were less frequently referred back to court, and were less frequently referred to the Youth Authority for diagnosis and possible incarceration.[23]

One of the more suggestive, although less successful, experiments was the San Francisco Project.[24] The experiment was designed to test the relative effectiveness of minimum, regular, ideal, and intensive caseloads. Minimum caseloads were the largest and involved the offender's reporting to the probation officer by mail as opposed to the more traditional personal contact and counseling or assistance that was provided only upon request by the offender. Regular caseloads consisted of 85 persons and were 100 units of workload, with each supervision case being 1 unit and each investigation unit equalling 4 units. The ideal caseload was a 50 unit workload, and the intensive load, 25 units.

In order not to bias the study, new probations were assigned randomly to the different caseloads. When the violation rate (both technical violation of the rules of probation and commission of a new offense) were compared, the regular caseloads had a violation rate of 22 percent, ideal caseloads had a 24 percent violation rate, and the intensive caseloads had a violation rate of 38 percent. One might conclude from this data that the smaller the caseload the greater the recidivism, as measured by violation rates. Such a conclusion would not necessarily be warranted. For example, the intensive caseload had a 38 percent violation rate; however, this contained a high percentage of technical violations, which were perhaps due to greater supervision by the probation officer and his greater awareness of the activities of his client.

Concerns about reducing caseload size are frequently oversimplified, as the San Francisco Project indicates. To reduce probation caseloads will not necessarily make probation a more effective rehabilitation strategy. Consideration must be given to the probation officer and to training him for dealing with small caseloads. Officers who are accustomed to providing minimal supervision because of excessive caseloads will not change their behavior just by reducing their caseload. It seems that what does happen is that the officer's supervision of each person on his caseload remains about the same so that, in effect, he supervises less. It has always been assumed that probation officers will increase their supervision of each case as their caseload becomes smaller. Training such as in the TOPS project not only provides new tools but perhaps more importantly defines the responsibilities of an officer with a relatively small, intensive caseload.

Another factor of extreme importance for probation is that many offenders do not need much, if any, supervision. It is known that under the excessively large caseloads they receive minimal supervision, and yet many of these cases have not fallen into new serious trouble. As noted in chapter one, most youths commit acts of delinquency; however, only a few of those youths are caught. Since most of the youths committing delinquent acts seem to grow out of that behavior regardless of whether or not they are caught, it becomes obvious that many such youths do not require intensive supervision. It is widely suggested that probation caseload size should vary according to the needs of the offender. Those in need of intense supervision should be on small caseloads, while those thought to need little, if any, supervision should be on very large caseloads. This appears to be a logical suggestion; however, there is very little information available as to which type of offenders work out best under the varying conditions of probationary supervision.

Another factor which also may be of importance is the type of treatment while on probation. Treatment strategies may focus upon vocational rehabilitation of the offender, group treatment, individual counseling, and any of several other strategies for helping the offender. The idea is that one type of treatment may be more effective for certain offenders than other types of treatment. Studies have not found that any one treatment strategy is necessarily more effective than others.[25] Although not clearly supported by research, if we assume behavior can be affected by treatment, it seems plausible that different kinds of people will be affected by different kinds of treatment.

It is not the purpose of this discussion to review all of the different strategies employed to categorize people for correctional purposes; such a discussion would carry us far afield from the focus of this discussion. It should be noted that not all offenders are alike and that their differences may be, and probably are, important in the effects of treatment on them. More investigation is needed into the development of types of offenders funneled into the correctional system.

Size of caseload, types of treatment, and types of offenders have been pointed out as significant factors for consideration in creating a more rational system of probation treatment. It may be that caseloads of over 100 are not improper for many types of offenders, whose best treatment is to be left alone. Some probationers may be more amenable to treatment if they are placed in smaller caseloads. Likewise, certain methods (such as group counseling) may be effective with some and not with others. In other cases, the offender may be provided with individual counseling. Consideration of the interaction of these factors for caseload assignment must be accompanied by extensive testing. Without testing the effectiveness of these ideas, it will be impossible to develop a rational system of offender assignment to caseload by their size and type of treatment.

Cost of Probation

Probation and its effectiveness have been discussed, but one very important aspect of probation that has been ignored up to this point is its cost. The President's Commission reports:[26]

> The overall daily cost for a juvenile in an institution is 10 times more than the cost of juvenile probation or aftercare. For adults, state institutional cost is about 6 times that of parole and about 14 times that of probation.

Such tremendous cost differences are exaggerated by the oversized caseloads in probation, but we also must not forget that institutional programs are not usually well developed either.

Another economic advantage in addition to the direct savings of probation is that probation allows the offender to maintain a job, thereby contributing to his own support, his family's support, and to the tax base. Thus, probation has a double cost benefit. It keeps the offender and his family off welfare, and the cost of institutionalization is avoided. Considering these economic advantages, it is easy to understand why it has become a more popular disposition.

Community Protection and Probation

Judges are not only given the responsibility of protecting the rights of the offender, but they must also protect the community from offenders. Frequently we are guilty of emphasizing the offender and overlooking the community. Probation is always a gamble. The judge is taking a gamble by placing the offender in the community with the amount of freedom that probation allows. If the offender commits a new offense while on probation, it creates the risk that the community will not only reject the politically oriented judge but also reject community based treatment. Consequently, judges are reluctant to release offenders on probation if they present too great a risk to the community. Offenders whose past records and social positions leave them marginally between a probation placement and an institution placement are frequently placed in an institution. It has been found, for example, in the California Community Treatment Project,[27] that more than 30 percent of those juveniles presently institutionalized can be placed on probation without great risk to the community, and for the money it costs to keep them in an institution, they could be supervised on very small caseloads. For adults the percentage may be less, but still a sizable percentage could be placed on probation without creating undue risk to the community.

CAN PROBATION BE EFFECTIVE?

Probation officers are usually from the middle class and have college degrees. The offender is usually from the lower class, does not have a degree (or even a high school diploma), and is black. Probation is frequently based on casework techniques, wherein the offender and officer form a meaningful relationship. Within this counseling relationship the offender, hopefully, becomes motivated to conformity to both the rules of probation and of society.

Those who have the most profound impact on who we are as people and what our behavior is are in close relationship to us (e.g., family members or peer group members). What might be the impact of the middle class, college graduate upon the lower class individual? The offender and the officer see the world from considerably different perspectives. The credibility of the officer is threatened by his inability to bridge the gap between himself and his client. Their languages and perspectives are different. This is not to suggest that the offender and the officer do not want the same things out of life such as a good job, success, and money—they probably do. However, the likelihood of their realizing these goals is slight and the manner of achieving them may be different. These problems would seem to diminish the chance of a typical probation officer's having a significant reformative impact upon the offender.

Thus, the middle class officer must overcome a social barrier that may exist between himself and the offender. Barriers such as these are not easily overcome in light of large caseloads with minimal contact, and frequently the emphasis is on "getting by" in terms of caseload work and emphasizing the paper work associated with investigations.

Even with these limitations, probation is receiving more and more emphasis. This emphasis is due to several advantages that probation has over imprisonment. First, it permits the offender to confront the normal day-to-day problems that would eventually confront him only after his release from prison. This point is really an indictment of the abnormality of imprisonment. It also makes the basic assumption that the causal forces of criminality and delinquency lie in the community. Growing out of this assumption, it is felt that if the offender is to be rehabilitated he must be reintegrated into the community, not isolated through imprisonment. Probation provides a "normal" social context for this reintegration, while still providing some control over the offender. Daniel Glaser summarizes this point and suggests another when he says concerning probation:[28]

> ... with minimal disturbance it permits control of any anti-criminal activities and commitments in which the offender is involved. If he or she is employed and has good family relationships and helpful non-criminal friendships or group memberships, probation permits continued residence in the community and preservation of these ties, as well as the continuation of self-support and support for dependents.

Probation is not the only form of community based corrections, although it is the most common one. Because of the minimal control over the offender in probation, alternatives have been developed providing greater control, as well as alternative types of treatment for the offender.

OTHER COMMUNITY BASED PROGRAMS

Halfway-In Houses

The set of programs described in this section have been developed in response to the need for alternatives between the freedom of probation and the security of incarceration. Traditionally, judges have had the options of dismissing the case, placing the offender on probation, or sentencing him to incarceration. To fill the wide gap between probation and incarceration, foster homes, group homes, halfway houses and other community programs have been and are being developed. The benefit of these alternatives is that they provide more guidance and structure than probation, but more contact with society than incarceration.

These community programs vary considerably and thus will be described separately. It is also important to note that within each of these types of programs there is considerable variation

Foster Homes and Group Homes

Foster homes and group homes are juvenile-serving programs that provide a homelike environment. A juvenile might be removed from his own home or other living arrangement and placed in the home of a private citizen. Usually, these private citizens are approved and licensed to be foster parents by the welfare department or other licensing agency, and they receive a fee for their services. Group homes on the other hand are licensed community facilities that provide room and board for from six to ten juveniles. Frequently, group homes are located in large older homes purchased and renovated to serve the needs of a group of youngsters.

Both of these alternatives provide the judge with the opportunity to remove the juvenile from his home which may be thought to be the genesis of the juvenile's problem. At the same time that the judge removes the juvenile from his home, he can see that the juvenile is an active member in either the juvenile's home community or another community. Being active in the community means that the juvenile goes to the regular schools, participates in local community activities such as dances and is perhaps employed.

Group homes do provide more structure for the individual and more therapy than foster homes. Foster homes infrequently provide therapy beyond that of living in a normal home. On the other hand, group homes provide a setting in which professional counselors are available and group or individual counseling may take place. Thus, with these two alternatives available, juvenile judges are given greater latitude in their sentencing decisions.

One group that is not widely discussed but frequently incarcerated is the dependent neglected child. A dependent neglected child usually comes to the attention of the court because of the youth's own misbehavior, although the behavior is usually of a minor nature and, from the court's point of view, this misbehavior is an outgrowth of an inadequate home. The judge, confronted with a child whose parents are ignoring or perhaps mistreating him, does not frequently have any option at all but to institutionalize the child, unless there are foster or group homes available. Probation normally leaves the child in his present home and thus is frequently not an alternative for the judge although it can be used in conjunction with a foster home placement.

Group homes and foster home placements are not new inventions and, in fact, have been used for many years. The reason for the renewed interest is the recent turning away from incarceration. It has been said of these programs:

> Such placements keep the offender in the community where he must eventually work out his future. They carry less

stigma and less sense of criminal identity, and they are far less expensive than incarceration.[29]

OTHER ALTERNATIVES TO INCARCERATION

It is not easy to label many of the experimental programs that serve as alternatives to incarceration. Perhaps the label of "halfway-in house" is as appropriate as any. Some programs are for juveniles only, others for adults only, and still others for both. Most such facilities have maintained a unisex program, although there are rare attempts to put both men and women together in such centers. In place of attempting to define classes of programs a description of some of these programs may be more helpful.

The Provo Experiment One of the early experiments in community based treatment alternatives was the Provo or Pinehills study.[30] The Provo program provided that those participating in the program were to actively participate in community activities such as local schools and local employment. Offenders continued to live at home, although each afternoon after school or work, all boys returned to Pinehills where they participated in group meetings. In the evenings they returned to their homes. On Saturdays, the program participants worked full time for the city, and were paid 50 cents an hour.

The Pinehills project provided an opportunity for youngsters who were in trouble with the law to participate in a rehabilitation program, without the usual disruption of their lives. This program dealt with boys within their home community and, in fact, the juveniles were given some of the responsibility for program operations and deciding when a boy was ready to leave Pinehills. The boys evaluated each other and assessed when they were ready to leave the institution.

The research evaluating this project was well designed. Offenders were to be randomly sentenced to a training school, probation, or Pinehills; however, the randomness was not completely maintained throughout the study. The findings to date support

Pinehills as being more effective than the training school and just as effective as probation. The probation success rate is suspect because the proportion of probationers successfully completing probation rose sharply during the study, suggesting that since they were part of a study the probation department decreased its revocations.[31]

PORT Program The Probationed Offenders Rehabilitation Training (PORT) program in Rochester, Minnesota is one of the more innovative programs in the country. Started in 1969, the PORT program is peculiar in that it provides for both adults and juveniles in the same facility. Even more peculiar, adults and juveniles are often roommates. One purpose of the mixing of juveniles and adults is to place upon the adult the responsibility of socializing and aiding in the rehabilitation of the juvenile, and in so doing to help himself.[32]

The program centers around life within the community, although the facility itself is located on the grounds of a hospital. The offenders are placed in PORT based upon their potential for reformation and their threat to the community. If the offender does not present a serious threat to the community, and yet needs more supervision than is provided by probation, PORT provides the in-between option. Upon his acceptance into PORT, the offender signs a contract with PORT and the probation officer stating his intent to live up to the expectations of the program.

The program provides group sessions in which offenders learn to relate to each other and help each other by supplying peer reinforcement to nondelinquent, noncriminal behavior.

The effectiveness of this program has not been well documented.[33] Regardless of PORT's effectiveness, it provides an example of the potential for community involvement with and acceptance of a community correctional setting. This point will be discussed in more detail later, but acceptance of community corrections is a serious problem. People frequently do not want criminals in their neighborhood. PORT in Rochester, Minnesota has gained a community acceptance that is rarely found in community based corrections.

POST INSTITUTIONAL COMMUNITY PROGRAMS

A wide variety of programs has been developed and is being developed to reintegrate the institutionalized offender into the community. Educational release programs, work release programs, and halfway-out houses are a few of the types of programs being developed to ease the strain of release from a "closed" institution.

Educational Release

There are numerous programs outside of adult institutions in which offenders are released from the institution in order to attend classes at vocational schools and colleges. These educational release programs frequently start with the inmate's living in the correctional institution and going outside to school. Some programs enable the offender to progress from this stage to living outside the institution in a residential living center and attending school.

Educational release has been expanding considerably in the last several years, and in 1965 it was brought to the federal prisons. While many prison systems have developed some form of education release, many such systems are plagued by the rural settings of many institutions. Educational release requires that institutions be in close proximity to educational facilities. Since many institutions have been built great distances from population centers, they do not offer opportunities for educational release programs.

Education release has several advantages for the institution as well as the offender. It permits the offender to test himself in the community, while at the same time he benefits from the supervision supplied by the institution or halfway house. Finally, education releases allow for educational programs that most correctional institutions would be incapable of providing, thereby allowing the offender to improve his employment opportunities and perhaps enhance his self-concept.

Work Release

A program similar to educational release, but with a longer tradition, is work release. Work release allows prisoners to hold a job in the community. This practice dates to 1913 in Wisconsin, when the Huber Act was passed, permitting work release in the local jails. Local jails have been able to utilize work release to a greater extent than larger prisons because of their proximity to job markets and because they incarcerate less serious offenders. Work release is also peculiarly appropriate for local jail settings because it does not require additional facilities such as classrooms or vocational training workshops. Furthermore, jails usually house short term prisoners, which makes the jail an inappropriate location for programs requiring long term involvement. Thus, while jails do not usually have the appropriate facilities or the appropriate offenders to develop many rehabilitation programs, it is possible for them to effectively use work release type programs.

Jails and correctional institutions developing work release do have problems. Many people resent inmates taking jobs that "law-abiding" people could hold. The communities are also fearful that work released inmates may commit crimes while released, especially crimes of violence.

Pre-Release Centers

Pre-release centers may be referred to as "halfway-out houses." They are usually centers where offenders are placed from three months to a year prior to their release. Their basic purpose is to provide a place for the offender to live while he makes arrangements for his release on parole. The arrangements usually involve obtaining employment, arranging for a place to live, and adjusting to the trauma of community life. Pre-release centers are an acknowledgement of the peculiarities of prison life, and are an attempt to facilitate the transition back into the community.

THE COMMUNITIES' RESPONSIBILITY IN COMMUNITY BASED CORRECTIONS

One very significant factor in community based corrections that has been ignored is the community. In order for the offender, juvenile or adult, to learn to live in the community in a conforming manner, he must be able to participate in and develop a stake in the community. Communities send their offenders away because their behavior is not acceptable to them; however, for community based corrections to operate, this must be reversed. Communities must not only desire to retain offenders that they previously sent away, but they must open up opportunities for those returning from an insitution, whether it be on work release, education release, or placement in a pre-release center.

In effect, the crucial ingredient in community based corrections is the community. Its willingness to permit group homes, pre-release centers, and other forms of community based corrections will perhaps determine the extent of such programs in the future. Two techniques have been used to place particular programs into a community. One of these techniques is to start the program without publicizing it so that the community does not have time to develop the resistance necessary to stop it. An alternative strategy is to "sell" the concept of a program to the community so that the community plays a role in the planning for the program, and thus develops a commitment to the program. This latter technique is the most popular because it insures the provision of services to the clients of the program and it avoids the necessity of spending the first several months of the program's operation overcoming community resistance. The techniques for introducing community based correction programs will be discussed in chapter ten.

SUMMARY

Community based corrections, while not a new conception, is receiving greater attention. This chapter has provided a brief overview of some of the basic forms that community corrections is taking; but, equally as important as the types of programs, is the process through which these community located programs are formed and offenders diverted to them. It is with this in mind that chapter ten examines two strategies of implementing community based corrections.

ENDNOTES

1. President's Commission on Law Enforcement and Administration of Justice, *Task Force Report: Corrections* (Washington, D.C.: U.S. Government Printing Office, 1967), p. 165.
2. William G. Nagel, "With Friends Like These, Who Needs Enemies?" *Crime and Delinquency* (July, 1974), p. 231.
3. National Advisory Commission on Criminal Justice Standards and Goals, *Corrections* (Washington, D.C.: U.S. Government Printing Office, 1973), p. 221.
4. President's Commission: *Corrections* p. 179.
5. United Nations, "The Origin of Probation in the United States," Robert M. Carter and Leslie T. Wilkins, eds., *Probation and Parole: Selected Readings* (New York: John Wiley and Sons, Inc., 1970), pp. 11–14.
6. Ibid., p. 12.
7. Ibid., p. 13.

8. Ibid., p. 14.
9. President's Commission: *Corrections* p. 179.
10. Ibid.
11. Ibid.
12. Daniel Glaser, "Correction of Adult Offenders in the Community," in *Prisoners in America,* Lloyd E. Ohlin, Ed., © 1973 by The American Assembly, Columbia University. By permission of Prentice-Hall, Inc., Englewood Cliffs, N.J.
13. Ibid.
14. Ibid.
15. Ibid.
16. D. V. Babst and J. W. Mannering, "Probation vs. Imprisonment for Similar Types of Offenders—A Comparison by Subsequent Violations," *Journal of Research in Crime and Delinquency* 2 (1965).
17. For an excellent discussion of this see Roger Hood and Richard Sparks, *Key Issues in Criminology* (New York: McGraw-Hill Book Company, 1970), pp. 171–192.
18. W. H. Hammond and E. Chayen, *Persistent Criminals* (London: England: Home Office Research Unit Report No. 3, 1963).
19. John D. Lohman, A. Wahl, and R. M. Carter, The San Francisco Project, Research Report No. 11: The Intensive Supervision Caseload, (Berkeley, California: School of Criminology, U. of California, 1967).
20. Stuart Adams, "Some Findings from Correctional Caseload Research," in Carter and Wilkins, op. cit., pp. 364–378.
21. Ibid., p. 368.
22. Ibid., p. 368–69.
23. Ibid., p. 369.
24. Ibid., p. 373.
25. See for example Lamar T. Empey and Steven G. Lubeck, *The Silverlake Experiment* (Chicago, Illinois: Aldine Publishing Company, 1971); Gene Kassebaum, David Ward and Daniel Wilner, *Prison Treatment and Parole Survival* (New York: John Wiley and Sons, Inc., 1971); H. Ashley Weeks, *Youthful Offenders at Highfields* (Ann Arbor: University of Michigan Press, 1963).
26. President's Commission: *Corrections* op. cit.
27. Ibid., p. 194.
28. Glaser, op. cit., p. 98.
29. President's Commissions: *Corrections* op. cit., p. 40.
30. Lamar T. Empey and Jerome Rabor, "The Provo Experiment in

Delinquency Rehabilitation," *American Sociological Review* (October 1961), pp. 679–695.
31. LaMar T. Empey and Maynard L. Ericson, *The Provo Experiment Evaluating Community Control of Delinquency* (Lexington, Mass.: D.C. Heath and Co., 1972).
32. See Nevin D. Hunter, Robert Pockrass, and Luanne Hostermann, *Probationed Offenders and Rehabilitation Training: An Evaluation of Community Based Corrections* (Mankato, Minn.: Urban Studies Institute, Mankato State College).
33. See LaMar T. Empey and Steven G. Lubeck, *The Silverlake Experiment* (Chicago: Aldine Publishing Co., 1971).

9

Parole

In a recent and excellent book concerning deviance, the authors made a statement which is not uncharacteristic of the way that many people view, or fail to view, the parole process. In essence, Rubington and Weinberg made the fundamental error of viewing the correctional process as if parole doesn't exist. Their error is contained in a description of the correctional system in which many deviants are likely to find themselves. They indicated that, "the careers that many deviants pursue take them through the correctional cycle from *beginning to end*. Thus, they are arrested, detained, tried, sentenced, and sent away to prison."[1] The terminal nature of this statement would lead one to believe that prison serves as a life long residence for its inhabitants and ignores the fact that 95 to 99 percent of all people sent to prison return to "the streets," many of whom return on parole status.

Despite the rather limited view of Rubington and Weinberg concerning the correctional cycle, others view parole as, "the single most critical element in our system of crime and punishment."[2] In view of the wide disparity between these two perspectives of the same process, one might reasonably ask how the two perspectives can coexist? While these two perspectives have been

Chapter nine was written by Professor Frederick Hussey of Pennsylvania State University.

presented merely for illustrative purposes, and thus, the answer to this rhetorical question is not of central concern, the solution to this puzzling question may be found in the developmental history of parole. In essence, parole started[3] as a reasonably well defined social policy in the middle 1800s, deteriorated to a state of ambiguity and controversy in the 1930s, and may now be returning to a position where the goals of parole and the means used to achieve them are relatively clear.

The purpose of this chapter is not to provide a cook book on how to become a parole officer, nor will it necessarily focus on the kinds of things a parole officer does in the daily performance of his job. The goals here are much more modest than these; rather, they are to present a feeling for what parole is and how it got to be what it is; to present the basic goals of parole and an understanding of the various ways that people have viewed parole; to cast parole in a systems perspective, as opposed to the unique, "stand alone" view that is often presented; to present an understanding of the ways that parole agencies and parole agents function; and finally, to be presumptuous enough to challenge the linear approach to man and to suggest viewing the client of parole as an individual like all individuals. It not only is appropriate, but imperative, that we apply what we know from disciplines such as sociology and psychology to the processing of all parolees.

CONCEPTIONS OF PAROLE

Parole is not a unitary, invariant procedure about which everyone can agree. For instance, it is relatively popular to view parole as simply a mechanism invoked to bridge the gap between the closely ordered walls of a correctional institution and a terrifically complex society. A second conceptual level entails viewing parole as the interaction of a parolee and a parole agent, both cast within the framework of a complex organization and environment. Yet a third conceptual level consists of viewing parole as one of many social policies which can be analyzed in terms of:

(1) the kinds of benefits involved, (2) the distribution of certain rights to those affected by the policy, and (3) the processes of being assigned to a particular status within the boundaries of the policy under discussion. Each of these three perspectives will be dealt with in this chapter. The first perspective can be seen as aligned with those who see probation and parole as similar procedures in the field of corrections, designed to serve both the offender and society. It is said that both contemplate the treatment of the offender in the community by a "uniformly organized system of constructive rehabilitation."[4] Although there is general consensus that parole is to serve both the treatment and surveillance function, there is a disturbing amount of inconsistency in various definitions or conceptions of parole. This variability can be seen in the following examples:

> Parole is a penological measure designed to facilitate the transition of the offender from the highly controlled life of the penal institution to the freedom of community life.[5]
>
> Parole is a procedure for the release of an individual from an institution or prison to the community by a paroling authority and to its supervision through supporting parole services.[6]
>
> The dual purpose of parole is the protection of society on the one hand and the rebahilitation of the offender on the other. These goals are inseparable.[7]
>
> The objective of probation and parole supervision is the rehabilitation of the offender for the protection of society. Supervision is primarily the rendering of a personal service of guidance and assistance by the probation officer to the person under supervision through which the latter is helped to develop capabilities and resources sufficient to live comfortably, happily, and justly with himself, his family and his neighbors.[8]

It is clear in these sample perspectives of the parole process, that there is a varying amount of emphasis put on the restraint versus the rehabilitative function. Not only does this inconsistency create problems in defining the parole process, but it provides a dilemma for parole agents in terms of the focus of their efforts. There does seem to be some consensus, however, that parole is primarily social casework, but with legal overtones. According to Dressler, "probation and parole . . . should stand midway between the tear gas and tear duct schools of thought in penology. They must be recognized as casework functions with a law enforcement orientation and responsibility."[9]

Seen in a broad context, parole is supposed to (1) enhance the rehabilitation of the offender, and (2) in addition to rehabilitating the parolee, to protect the public. Because parole is the last step in the criminal justice or correctional process, it is perhaps surprising that parole shares the same goals with pre-trial diversionary programs, probation, and to some degree the incarceration process. Each of these components attempts in some way to rehabilitate the offender and protect the public. If, while on parole, the parolee violates the rules governing his behavior or commits a new offense, parole may be revoked and the offender returned to prison.

The Systems Perspective

Outlined above were the three possible ways of examining parole and the parole process: as a bridge between prison and society, as an interaction process between client and agent, and as a social policy involving resources, rights, and status. These three relatively unique and distinct perspectives reflect both traditional and innovative orientations of parole and the parole process.

Adopting one of these perspectives to the exclusion of others, as so frequently has been done, is dysfunctional in the sense that it promotes a fragmented approach to understanding a very complex process. We need to be able to conceptualize parole as a subunit within a complex of subunits that are acting and interacting together to achieve a more or less consistent and shared goal. Thinking of parole in this way has been labeled a "systems perspective," a perspective which encourages a broad and comprehensive understanding of agencies, organizations, policies, or efforts that man is involved with.

Unfortunately, it is not easy to define a system because of the confusion that can exist between the elements of a system and their relationships to subsystems. For instance, you are a person/system, made up of many components including the respiratory, circulatory, nervous, gastrointestinal, and other subsystems. However, if you are a member of a fraternity or sorority, then you are perhaps an element of a larger subsystem, the subsystem of student organizations within the university or college system. The point is that all things are systems within system and systems beyond system.

By adopting a systems perspective of parole, we are more likely to understand the interrelationships of the views of parole as a bridge between the institutional wall and the community; of the view that would stress the offender within a complex structure of organizations; and the view that parole is a social policy that effects people in identifiable ways. It is important to view parole in the wider web of relationships in which it functions in order to more accurately comprehend its main goals and pressures. We could characterize the parole system as illustrated in Figure 9.1.

This diagram portrays the five principal characteristics of the parole action subsystem. It illustrates that the *input* for the parole subsystem, or the raw material coming into the subsystem to be processed, consists of (and is completely dependent upon) the *output* of the prison system. It is very important to stress that the parole subsystem receives as its "raw material," the end product of a prior system, and consequently a major parameter for success/failure is the pre-conditioning, or lack of it, in the prison. In defining the parole officer's role, it is necessary to stress that parole officers must deal with a unit that has already been worked on or processed—a parolee is *not* naive, unbiased, or unknowing. The effects of incarceration on each parolee, to the extent that they are unknown or negative, present formidable barriers to the potential successful interaction of the parolee and parole officer, and to successful reintegration to the community as well.

The box labeled "parole officer" (meaning parole agency as well) in Figure 9.1 has the goal of establishing the interaction

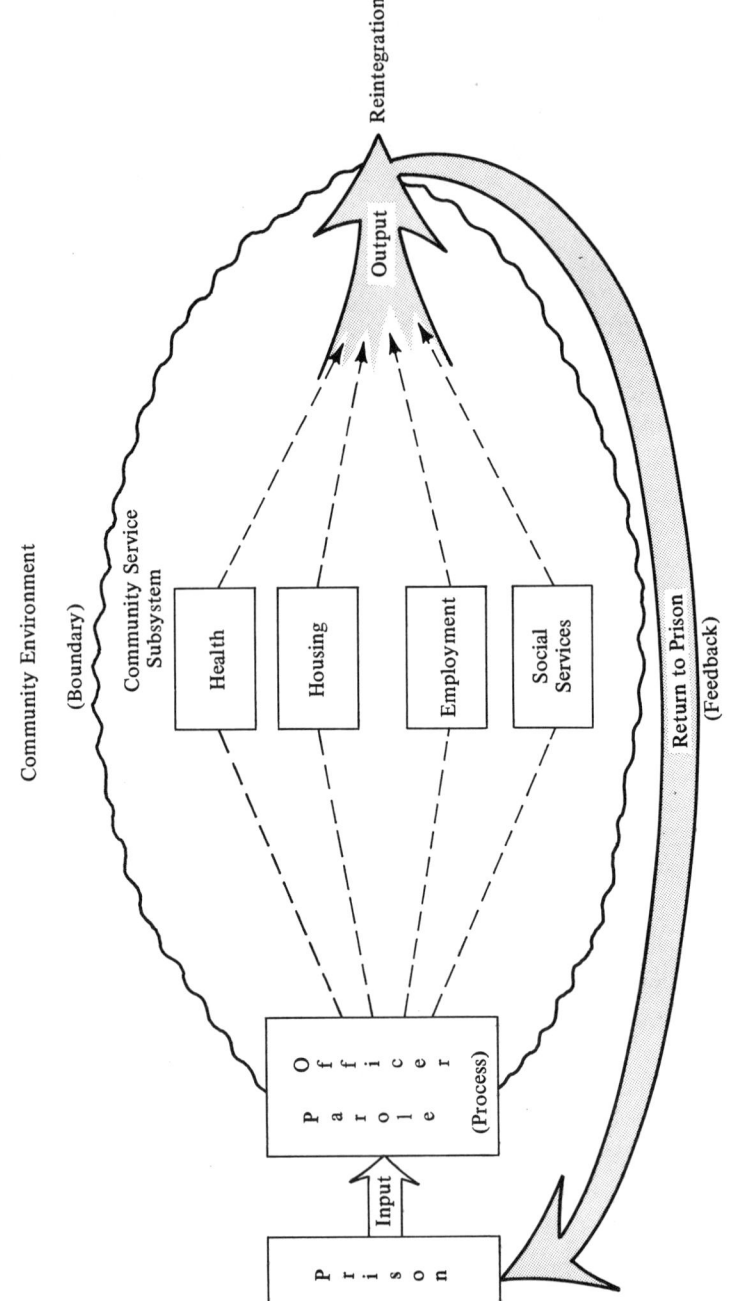

Figure 9.1 Principal Characteristics of the Parole Action Subsystem.

between parolee and parole officer that will lead to successful reintegration. In pursuing the goal of reintegration, the officer will often establish linkages with the broader community such as with employers, friends, social service agencies, health agencies, churches, schools, and others. It is often assumed within the parole subsystem that the correctional subsystem provides inputs which have been rehabilitated, punished, or deterred. They in turn define their task to be: (1) reintegration into the community as the final stage of the rehabilitation process, and (2) the provision of continued surveillance and evaluation as a final step in the social protection process. To the degree that parole focuses on the second of the goals, the assumption that the correctional process has rehabilitated or deterred is violated.

What happens within the box is referred to as process, or the transformations that are to be performed on the input of raw material—in our case, offenders from correctional institutions. Parole ostensibly consists of aiding the offender by transforming him into a viable, independently functioning member of society *and/or* transforming or reconverting him to the status of offender, should the surveillance performed by a parole agent indicate that this is warranted. It is easy to see that unlike a shoe factory process where leather, thread, cardboard, rubber, and synthetics are processed and transformed into shoes, the parole process seems to reflect competing orientations. On one hand, the task of the agent is to impart feelings of self-confidence and the skills necessary to function in society, but on the other hand, the task of the officer may be to allege real or imagined deviance and to reduce the parolee again to the status of offender. Many people feel that these two processes are fundamentally antithetical. The output stage of the parole subsystem consists of either expelling the parolee to the environment or free world, or returning him to the prison as a prisoner. However, in light of the above comments on dual goals, it can be seen that these two states are intimately related to another characteristic element of systems, the feedback process. Feedback is essentially the process of conveying to the central actors information on how well they are doing. As there are two goals for the parole process, so feedback in the parole system would probably also have two manifestations—to the community or return to prison. These two types of feedback would reflect the success not only of the parole system but of the entire correctional process. In the first case, reintegration to the community, the feedback message would seem to be that the corrections system had succeeded in providing the parole system with appropriate inputs, *and* that the parole system had provided successful linkages with the community. The second manifestation of feedback, return to prison, however, could tend to signal failure at some point—either the prison system provided inappropriate inputs to the parole system, or the parole system failed to provide for the successful reintegration of the offender.

Unfortunately, feedback in both the parole and prison system is often summarized in the form of recidivism statistics or revocation rates to the exclusion of other criteria. Rather than recidivism rates, the system perhaps ought to look at the diverse areas such as jobs, family, education, and personal stability. Ideally, such feedback would be utilized in evaluating the system and changing certain parts of it as a result of the evaluation.

Finally, the term environment has been used to define all that is external to the central focus of the system or subsystem that is being analyzed. Although it is fairly easy, on the surface, to define the environment of the parole subsystem, one of the problems that is inherent in various traditional perspectives of parole and other criminal justice components is a tendency to fail to comprehend the interactions within the environment that are necessary. For instance, while the Division or Bureau of Employment Security may traditionally be defined as external to the parole system, there are undoubtedly many times when interaction between the subsystems is necessary for the parole process to succeed. The tendency to define certain agencies as part of the "environment" causes many problems not only for the parole subsystem but for many other human services as well. While these agencies are correctly perceived as part of the environment of the parole system, the goals of the parole system cannot be achieved without the establishment of appropriate linkages with these agencies. It is precisely for this reason that parole must be seen in the context of the larger correctional process, of which it is but a subsystem.

The Components of the Parole Subsystem

In the previous discussion it was indicated that parole can be seen as one component of the larger criminal justice system. Just as the criminal justice system can be described as composed of subunits or subsystems, the parole subsystem can be described as a collection of components, which constitute subsystems in their own right. In making the decision to release an inmate from the institution to the responsibility of the parole agency, there is an identifiable, temporal sequence that is followed and relevant actors of the parole system that correlate with each event in the sequence can be identified. In preparing an inmate's case for his appearance before the parole board, which will make the decision as to whether or not the inmate will be released, an institutional parole officer readies all the necessary records and information. The institutional parole officer located at an institution may spend his time making sure that there is a job and a home that will accept the offender if the parole board decides that release is in order.

The parole board is the duly constituted authority that makes the decision whether to release an inmate at some point after he has attained eligibility, or to keep him incarcerated. Parole boards are usually comprised of lay people who are political appointees, but there are now a few parole boards comprised of professionals such as doctors, lawyers, sociologists, and others with training in the behavioral sciences. The National Advisory Commission on Criminal Justice Standards and Goals indicates that knowledge of law, behavioral sciences, and corrections are three basic fields that ought to be represented on a parole board.[10]

What information do parole boards utilize in making their decisions to release inmates? This is an important question not only from the perspective of enhancing general understanding of the criminal justice system, but also from the perspective that inmates want to know how parole decisions are made. While this is, indeed, a very important question, there is a real lack of research dealing with the process.

It is not surprising to find that the rhetoric of parole board

Parole Boards. The National Advisory Commission on Criminal Justice Standards and Goals indicates that knowledge of law, behavioral sciences, and corrections are three basic fields that should be represented on parole boards.

decisions does not correlate well with the findings of the limited amount of research that has been done. It has been contended, for instance, that juveniles will be paroled when (1) they come to grips with who they are, (2) they are able to maintain stable and productive relationships with others, and (3) when they have shown improved social functioning and have made constructive use of the resources of a training school.[11] In the area of adult federal parole, in 1955, Richardson indicated that the following are taken into account: reports of the prosecuting attorney and pre-sentence reports; social history; institutional rehabilitation reports, including psychiatric analyses; the inmate's participation in educational programs; conduct during confinement; maturation; respect for authority; work reports; and attitude. In addition to all of these considerations, other factors include the nature of the offense; aggravating and mitigating factors; previous criminal record; escapes; detainers; military record; employment history; family ties; determination to make good; parole plan; and the attitude of the community toward his return.[12] It may be possible to consider each of these factors in making a parole decision, but the relative importance or the degree to which a particular variable contributes to the decision cannot be determined from this list. While it seems very unlikely that fair or equal consideration could be given to each factor in a consistent manner, Reed indicates that the Federal Board weighs all relevant information before entering an order to grant or deny parole.[13]

Although some would assert that each factor receives due consideration, it is easy to understand that to give equal weight to all of these factors is nearly impossible. One of the most comprehensive studies of parole decision making indicates that parole boards consider the following sets of factors. The first set includes those factors which are considered for the purpose of determining the probability of recidivism if the inmate were released. These considerations include psychological change, participation in institutional programs, institutional adjustment, criminal record, prior experience with probation or parole supervision, and the nature of the parole plan, including home and work factors. A second set of factors considered are those which justify granting parole despite serious reservations about whether the inmate will recidivate. Such factors include the seriousness of the likely violation, length of time served, imminency of mandatory release date, and whether or not informant services have been provided by the inmate in question. The last set of factors considered are those that justify parole denial despite the judgment that if released, the inmate would not be likely to recidivate. Falling within this category are considerations of assaultive tendencies, serving of only minimal time on a sentence, institutional discipline considerations, and the avoidance of criticism of parole.[14]

Although the Dawson study is perhaps one of the most comprehensive early studies of the parole release decision, the methodology used to arrive at conclusions was essentially participant observation. A more recent study focused on the statistical analysis of case records of juveniles.[15] The methods adopted have the advantage of statistically determining which factors are considered, and thus, the possible bias of a participant observer is avoided. In spite of the claims of those who would assert that just about everything is given just consideration, Hussey found that one factor was pivotal in parole decisions—race. Contrary to what one would expect from juvenile court ideology, Hussey found that a separate and fairly unique set of factors was looked at in making the release decision within each racial group.

While this discussion is necessarily brief, it is clear that more research is needed concerning the very important question of what factors are actually considered by parole boards in making their decisions. The results of such research would have at least two related implications. At the least, it could provide meaningful information to those who are incarcerated, and secondly, the research would go right to the heart of the issue of the equalitarian dispensation of justice.

The Parole Officer

Although knowledge of the behaviors of parole boards is important and necessary, it is in a sense academic to the man on the firing line, the parole officer who must manage the parolee while he is committed to the care and custody of the agency. The parole officer is cast into the difficult position of all first line managers—he must be responsive to the needs and demands of the client, while at the same time, being responsive to the needs and demands of the organization. In a previous section, we portrayed the dual goals of the parole system, and nowhere is the conflict more apparent than when we address the job of the line parole agent. It is up to him to implement policy, to interpret the needs of clients, and make the decision as to whether a parolee may continue to reside in the community or should be returned to prison as a parole violator.

The parole officer is, in fact, in the difficult position of having to make judgments about the continuing eligibility of the parolees assigned to him; but what do we know of the definition of his job and the ways agents interact with parolees? In describing his job, we must remember that the officer finds himself in a situation where there are three possible competing conceptions of his role: that of the agency, of the agent himself, and of the parolee. In spite of this definitive problem, it is generally asserted that the agent's functions include doing social investigation (this would probably not be true in the case of an agent who serves only a parole and not a probation function); supervising the parolee (which includes modifying his attitudes and behaviors); stressing obedience to the law and to the conditions of parole, and rendering assistance as well as surveillance; effectively using community resources; and interacting with the public at large for the purpose of public relations.[16] While this is only a partial list (a more complete list would include such things as visiting parolees at home or work and developing or securing jobs), it does not indicate the preferences of parole officers.

A study by Wahl and Glaser found that 40 percent of the 444 probation officers surveyed would prefer to specialize in pre-sentence investigation, 39 percent in probation supervision, and only 10 percent in parole supervision.[17] In terms of priorities assigned to the different tasks, 69 percent gave investigations top priority, and 11 to 12 percent indicated that offering the client supervision received top priority in their work.

Although probation and parole agents are supposed to perform a variety of duties, and they express a preference for activities that are more easily counted (investigations), they are nevertheless saddled with the basic "treatment vs. control" dichotomy alluded to earlier. Attempts to understand the various types of parole supervision have tended to invoke these relatively distinct dimensions of activity in developing a typology of parole officer style. Glaser, extending the work of Ohlin, Piven, and Pappenfort,[18] asserted that there were essentially four types of agents: punitive or paternal agents who guard middle class morality through threats and coercion; protective agents who vascillate between the protection of the offender and the protection of society; the welfare worker whose ultimate goal is the improvement of the welfare of the client; and the passive agent who sees the job as a reward for services granted elsewhere.[19] Although each of these categories may reflect certain systematic differences on such dimensions as age, education, and length of service, the utility of such a scheme is questionable, unless it can be associated with differential case outcomes (and to this point, we know little about the efficacy of various styles). Not only has this typology received little or no systematic evaluative research, but other writers wonder whether it has any validity in the eyes of the parolee. Irwin has argued that differences in behavioral style are either not discerned by parolees, or are unimportant to them.[20] What is of importance to the parolee is the intensity of supervision, the tolerance of the agent in accepting "deviant" behavior, and the rightness or fundamental fairness of the agent.[21] It should be apparent that even though we can discern various behavioral styles among agents, we must focus on the interaction between agents and clients and determine what is meaningful to the client in order to understand what may be of real importance. In order to gain a meaningful understanding of the parole system, it is necessary to include in our examination the perspective of the client. For without understanding the clients perspective, we are well prepared academically and ideologically to deal with a world that doesn't exist. In a word, we must have an interactionist perspective rather than a linear perspective.

The Client

Based on the previous discussion, it is logical now to discuss the "client" or the benefactor of service. It is fashionable to speak of parolees as clients, as if to imply that there is a certain professional omniscience on the part of the agent in this dyadic relationship. It will be asserted below that an agent who internalizes such a perspective may be incapacitated by it more than we may presently know, or care to acknowledge.

The parole relationship is essentially an authority relationship. That is, the agent has a legally based legitimate role to play in guiding the parolee in his attempts at community reintegration, and he can control the parolee's behavior with the threat of reincarceration. Arguments can be made in favor of the role of authority as well as against it. While some claim that authority forms the basis for the casework relationship,[22] others assert that help or treatment can only be rendered to those who seek it out voluntarily, rather than having it built in as a condition of gaining "freedom." Whatever the true effects of authority in the agent-client relationship, the authority possessed by the agent undoubtedly acts to limit his perspective. For instance, if the agent conceptualized the parole relationship as a terminal stage in a system that has already acted to process the client, he might begin to realize that threats of reincarceration may actually fulfill a need of the released inmate, rather than frighten him into conformity. In this section, we want to comment briefly on the degree to which incarceration can induce dependency, and secondly, to illustrate the congruence between the prison setting and basic human motives.

One of the topics that has received little attention in the parole literature is the nature of total institutions and the effect they have on inmates. In order to fully comprehend the problems faced by a parole officer, we must view the client as the input of the correctional subsystem. We can perhaps best benefit by describing the nature of the incarceration experience and how confinement may satisfy many of man's basic needs and motives.

In the literature on human motivation, we find frequent reference to four motives that are basic to all human beings: security, affiliation, competence and esteem, and achievement.[23] Security refers to physical and psychological well being of the person and will be preserved at whatever cost is necessary. The need for security is reflected in such things as pensions, hospitalization and life insurance plans, or entering the military service as a basic way of caring for oneself. It seems, furthermore, that people may choose to lie, cheat, or commit crimes to preserve their well being.

The *affiliation motive* is expressed in a desire to establish and maintain interpersonal contacts. Anxiety, perhaps arising from the threat of physical harm or interpersonal rejection, may be the basis for affiliation, as it is for the drive of self-evaluation. Festinger feels that a need for self-evaluation and a desire to have our beliefs confirmed or denied by like minded individuals leads to affiliative tendencies.[24] Anxiety has consistently been associated with affiliation. One of the more interesting research findings concerning the relationship between anxiety and affiliation is that people who are in similar plights are preferred as companions over other people.[25]

In terms of *competence and esteem,* adults, in particular, behave as if to confirm their own feelings of competence. Those who have successfully overcome obstacles in the past strive to confirm their feelings of competence by continuing to strive to overcome obstacles in the present and future. Those who have not encountered much success may be less ready to take on difficult tasks, since they seek to avoid the pain of confirming their own relatively low estimates of themselves. In the world of work, if the job doesn't allow the job holder to demonstrate competence, he may turn to other interests such as recreation, crime, or industrial sabotage.

Related to the desire for esteem or competence is the more general desire *to achieve* something of value. The choice of what constitutes achievement for a given individual depends in part on the probability of being able to accomplish a desired goal. McClelland points out that early training in mastery promotes high need achievement, provided it does not reflect generalized restrictiveness, authoritarianism, or rejection.[26] Presumably, those situations which are restrictive, authoritarian, or rejecting will lead to low need to achieve.

These four motives are said to be pervasive in our society and are perhaps functional and necessary for a society which attempts to meet the needs of the people through the market mechanism. But what of the people who do not participate in the market—those in prisons, for instance? It would be naive to assume that they are motivated by an entirely different need system. Assuming the validity of these four basic motives, and given the experiences of those who undergo long periods of incarceration, how might we expect these needs to affect recently paroled men? In answering this question, it does not seem bold to suggest that a prison meets, perhaps in a strange way, many of these basic motives. Furthermore, as was mentioned previously, a parole officer must be attuned to the recent experiences of his charges if he is to know and appreciate their perspective of the world.

Think of it. What better place is there to feel secure than in a prison? Although some prisons may be marked by violence and other forms of predatory activity, there are definitely psychological and physical signs of safety present in prisons. If we can assert for a moment that many prisoners have had difficulty in dealing with a complex society where boundaries were unclear, perhaps eating and housing were uncertain, and various limits were ambiguous, then the high walls which define the perimeter of many prisons, the regular food, exercise, and a place to sleep, and the fixity of physical objects—all must be a dramatic change. In prison, the necessity to make decisions is severely mitigated for long periods of time and the security of daily living is continually reinforced. Even when deviation from the norm takes place, such as a fight, there is a well established and stable mechanism for dealing with it, and the outcome is often predictable.

Not only must prison provide a certain sense of security, but it, paradoxically, must also create a certain amount of anxiety. In addition to "rejecting their rejectors" and second guessing treatment and custody staff, anxiety may be induced from an uncertainty concerning one's status in prison society. If anxiety gives rise to affiliation with individuals of a like mind, prison must indeed provide a unique opportunity to do this. In addition to sharing a common status and perhaps a common occupational preference (crime), all inmates have undergone the status degradation ceremonies of the criminal justice process and, therefore, have a common rallying point.

The needs for competence, and to a degree self-esteem, seem to be met quite well by the prison in the sense that the environment not only doesn't change, but there are built in components (such as education or vocational training) which may provide the opportunity for a man to experience competence and esteem without the risks that were associated with "free world" school or work. For instance, it may be impossible to "flunk out" of the prison classroom. The need for competence is related to the need for exploration and mastery of the environment. In the same way that the physical structure of prison provides security, the physical structure enhances the chances for competently exploring and mastering a limited segment of the world. In prison, one knows that the mess hall will be in the same place from day to day, that the exercise yard location doesn't change, that outside groups will visit the prison on certain specified nights; and eventually, the social role that the individual offender is to play in the "institutional life" becomes clear. It is learning and comprehending this small social system that must give rise to a sense of competence and esteem.

Finally, prison can also satisfy whatever level of need for achievement that exists. If, as was hinted above, the individual's prior life experiences have resulted in a low level need for achievement, then the minimal level of prison expectations fit well with accepting low achievement levels. Conversely, high achievement can be attained through publishing a prison newspaper, getting a high school equivalency diploma, chairing a prison action group, or through numerous other activities.

It is felt that the prison experience, particularly for those who have endured it more than once, may induce more dependency that we presently know. It may have been a combination of these needs and other characteristics of prison life that led a parolee to observe:

> Sure I miss the place. I had a lot of good friends there. I actually hated to leave. I knew I wouldn't see most of these guys again. And I had a lot of good things going there. I had my house fixed up. I had my job, I was getting used to the food, was going to school. And I had some goofy friends, we used to do a lot of wild things together. Except for broads, I didn't mind the joint at all.[27]

Irwin sums it up as follows: "Many ex-prisoners . . . actually long for the prison setting. The memory of the undesirable aspects of prison fades, and life among their friends, the familiar activities, the freedom from the worries they are now facing become more and more appealing."[28] If more parole officers were to analyze the client in terms of his immediate past experiences and needs, it might lead to a greater emphasis on service and less on surveillance. The parole officers must take a meaningful look at the parolee's life, begin to think in ways that can help a man whose perspective and experiences may be far different. In this way, he may realize that the improper use of authority, the threat to revoke parole, or the exercise of more subtle coercion can result in just the opposite effect than that intended.

THE HISTORICAL PERSPECTIVE

We have reviewed the present condition of the parole system and, in chapter three the origins of parole were discussed. We cannot hope to understand a current social policy without looking back in time to find and analyze its roots. Unless we do this, we cannot understand why parolees today are given only gate money (around $50) and a prison-made suit, or why certain conditions are imposed on the parolee, to the exclusion of certain other conditions. A re-examination of the history of parole will reveal that it has undergone several rather substantial shifts in its development, and that it may be returning to a position that reflects an orientation characteristic of its very early days.

In the historical analysis that follows, we will highlight some of the material that was presented in chapter three and discuss some additional key points that are particularly relevant to the development of modern parole practices.

Any review of the historical antecedents of a social policy which is as diverse as parole runs the risk of being confused and confusing. In order to avoid this potential liability, our analysis of parole will focus on *resources* developed for the parolee; the procedures for *allocating* inmates to parole status; and the *rights distributed* to parolees as part of parole policy. It will be seen that parole has endured many changes during the course of its development and that some of the early orientations in parole may be readopted in the future.

ALEXANDER MACONOCHIE

Maconochie's contributions to penal theory go far beyond his efforts in the area of "parole." He was one of the first to offer a revolutionary plan of penal reform which embodied a philosophical justification for reformation as well as practical measures by which reformation could be achieved. Maconochie's principles or techniques for securing the reformation of the offender included:

1. Sentences which were not for a period of time but were for a specific quantity of labor.
2. Marks were used as rewards and were gained through improvement in conduct, frugality of living, and development of habits of industry.
3. Inmates earned everything they received in prison.
4. Inmates worked in small groups late in their incarceration and each member of the group was answerable for the conduct of the others.
5. In the final stages, an inmate was given a hut and garden but still had to earn marks. This stage was somewhat comparable to present day parole.

In terms of the resources developed for a parolee, the hut, garden, and other material benefits far exceed any resources developed for parolees since that time. It was assumed that as the "parolee" accepted responsibility for his own property, he would learn the life enhancing resource of respecting the property of others. Parolee status was earned by the inmate through his own instrumental activities in the pursuit of earning marks. Rights were earned by inmates only after parole status was earned. Specifically, the parolee had a right to a hut, piggery, and other material goods.[29]

CROFTON'S IRISH SYSTEM

As previously indicated, Maconochie's penal system was adopted and extended by Sir Walter Crofton when he became the Chairman of Directors of the Irish Prisons in 1854.[30] Crofton made full use of the English Penal Servitude Act of 1843, which established three stages in penal treatment. During the first stage, convicts spent eight to twelve months in confinement at hard labor. The amount of time spent in this stage, the prisoner's diet, and other conditions were regulated by the accrual of marks. After this stage, an inmate was transferred to another prison where he worked with other convicts, and the final stage was spent in an intermediate prison to which inmates were promoted as a reward for exemplary conduct.[31] The Crofton system held reformation as its goal and a ticket-of-leave, comparable to present day parole, was granted only to those prisoners who gave visible evidence of achievement and change of attitude. Several conditions were attached to the ticket-of-leave and they closely resemble the parole conditions prevalent in many states today.

When we compare Crofton's system to that developed by Maconochie, we can see a demise in the resources made available to the parolee. Furthermore, requiring certain portions of a sentence to be served prior to eligibility for a ticket-of-leave, as opposed to granting tickets-of-leave based on the attainment of marks, may have limited a prisoner's hope (which serves as a symbolic resource). Just as there is slippage in the resources developed in the Irish and English systems, there is also a less clear pathway for the attainment of parolee status. In the Maconochie system, parolee status was attained based on one's own efforts, while in Ireland clear signs of reformation were expected, and in England, parole was granted only after a certain passage of time. In addition to the demise in these areas, few if any rights or positive rewards were granted during this period. In fact, rather than rights being distributed, constraints in the form of parole conditions were invoked. We also note in these two systems an increased emphasis on community protection rather than treatment of the offender.

ELMIRA REFORMATORY

The first attempts at a parole system in the United States took place at the Elmira reformatory in New York. The parole system at Elmira provided a guardian or volunteer who provided supervision services to released inmates. An indeterminate sentence, with release depending on behavior and capacity, was coupled with careful selection of inmates for parole. In order to be paroled from Elmira, an inmate had to gain the confidence of the managers and superintendent, had to have a good conduct record for twelve months, and was required to present suitable plans for permanent employment. Parolees were required to report to their guardian on the first of every month. Elmira, in turn, kept track of all parolees through contact with the guardian for a period of six months.

As we can see, the trend toward discretion in the system and decreasing resources continued with Elmira. In terms of being allocated to parole status, the process continued to increase in complexity. The allocation process was based on good behavior, gaining the confidence of administrators, and the development of employment plans. The instrumental role played by the offender himself in the Maconochie system seems totally forgotten in the Elmira system. Elmira parolees were responsible to prison administrators, potential employers, and future guardians. Perhaps the only right distributed to the offender was the right to parole itself.

The Early Federal System

A federal parole system was developed in 1910, and any offender whose sentence was equal to or greater than a year, and who had served one third of the sentence, was eligible for parole. Boards of parole were established at each institution and were comprised of the Superintendent of Prisons from the Department of Justice and the institution's physician and warden. Each grant of parole required approval of the Attorney General, but this practice was discontinued after the establishment of a single federal board in 1930. Parolees were supervised by probation officers of the federal courts who were to "perform such duties with respect to parole as the Attorney General shall request."[32]

Early parole in this country failed to fulfill the high expectations held out for it. The first quarter of the 20th century was a period of conflict for the system. Parole was marked by a lack of uniformity in definition and administration, was riddled with accusations that it provided leniency, or was used in some cases for political patronage. As the result of this confused state of affairs, President Roosevelt called the First National Parole Congress in 1939.

The results of this 1939 Conference can be summarized by focusing on resource development, the allocation of parole status, and rights distribution. The Proceedings of the 1939 Conference indicate that the parole resources developed were focused on the community and not on the offender, whose resources were to be administered primarily within prison walls. When an offender received parole, however, he was given enough money to get him home and a grant of clothes that were to facilitate his re-entry into the community. We find the 1939 Conference placing more emphasis on parole boards as the appropriate arbitors of status conveyance. They were to make extensive use of medical, social, criminal, institutional, and psychiatric information in reaching decisions. Clearly, the grant of parole no longer depended only on the behaviors of a man, but it was influenced by the opinion of those who subjected the inmate to various separate expert analyses. In terms of rights, it is clear that in 1939, parole was the right of the community and was to be used as a protective device in the interests of the community. This orientation reflects an attachment to the idea of closely scrutinizing the actions of parolees and returning them to jail when appropriate.

RECENT DEVELOPMENTS AND A PERSPECTIVE ON THE FUTURE

The organization, purpose, and methods of present day parole are very similar to those of 1939. There is, however, a distinct trend toward developing a more meaningful, treatment centered role for parole in the lives of those who are finishing their time in the streets. Recent federal legislation suggests many innovative moves, only some of which can be mentioned here.[33] Changes in the nature and purpose of parole conditions are perhaps the most meaningful changes that are of interest to the parolee. For instance, the proposed legislation holds that there should be a reasonable relationship between the conditions of parole, and previous conduct, and present situation; the conditions should provide minimum deprivation of liberty, freedom of conscience, and freedom of association; conditions should be sufficiently specific to serve as a guide to supervision and conduct; the conditions should be such that compliance is possible given the emotional, physical, and economic resources of the offender.

This proposed bill, and others like it, call for assisting the offender's re-entry into society, and may give him the right to appeal conditions of parole. The bill also calls for telling an inmate why a particular decision was made regarding his parole (something that inmates have frequently wanted to know). Furthermore, the inmate could assume that he would be paroled when eligible rather than assuming that he would not be. The rights distributed to parolees are substantial and too many in number to mention here. Suffice it to say, however, that a very significant departure with tradition would occur.

While this proposed legislation contains many positive and innovative steps to recommend it, it seems to call for returning to a condition that may have contributed significantly to Maconochie's success—the inmate's knowledge of what he must do to be released and an increase in his optimism about release. In Maconochie's time, release depended on the offender's industry in accruing marks; the new legislation would in part provide the same cognitive component by requiring the parole board to share conclusions regarding each factor considered in the decision, by providing access to information, and by requiring explanations concerning decisions. Finally, it could appear that those in the parole system will more adamantly strive to be an advocate of the inmate rather than to act as his keeper.

The Start of a New Life. The future is, at best, uncertain for new releasees and parolees from correctional institutions.

SUMMARY

In an effort to give the reader a comprehensive introduction to parole and to portray its development, to present information that will enable one to have a solid cognitive understanding of the area (without teaching "how to do it" or to present the day-to-day functioning of parole officers), we have identified some of the problem areas that confront those who choose to work in the parole setting.

The organization and administration of parole services faces the same problems as many other bureaucratic human service agencies. Parole is overburdened with paper work and large caseloads, suffers from serving two distinct and often competing purposes, and attempts to deal with clients who do not enter the relationship voluntarily. Given the debilitating and often destructive effects of incarceration, a well administered parole agency can assist the offender in returning to the streets. In order to assist offenders in reintegrating into a society that has become alien and even hostile, parole agents will have to continue to identify their primary task as service and help, rather than surveillance and coercion.

A more sincere attempt to understand the perspective of the parolee and a thorough knowledge of community agencies and services is needed to aid the offender in adapting from the closely guarded walls of the institution to the relative freedom of the streets. Both the parolee and parole officer face tremendous responsibilities in their joint, reintegrative project.

ENDNOTES

1. Rubington, E. and Weinberg, *Deviance: The Interactionist Perspective* (2nd) (New York: The Macmillan Co., 1973), p. 213, (Emphasis added). © 1973 by The Macmillan Company.

2. *Civil Liberties* No. 286, April 1972, pp. 1, 6.
3. To speak of a "start" for parole is perhaps presumptuous, but for the present discussion, we are asserting that the foundations for parole were apparent in Maconochie's penal colony on Norfolk Island in the 1840s.
4. *Standards for the Selection of Probation and Parole Personnel* New York: National Council on Crime and Delinquency, 1968.
5. Vedder, C. and Kay, B., *Penology: A Realistic Approach* (Springfield: Charles C Thomas, 1969).
6. NCCD, *op. cit.*
7. *Parole in Principle and Practice* (New York: National Probation and Parole Association, 1957), p. 66.
8. United State Probation Officers' Manual, cited in *A Survey of Supervision Practices of Probation Officers in the U.S. District Courts* (Federal Probation Training Center, Chicago, 1964).
9. Dressler, D., *Probation and Parole* (New York: Columbia University Press, 1951), p. 11.
10. *National Advisory Commission on Criminal Justice Standards and Goals: Corrections* (Government Printing Office, Washington, D.C., 1973).
11. Eliot, A. E., "Parole Readiness: An Institutional Dilemma," *Federal Probation 28,* 1, 1964, pp. 26–30.
12. Richardson, S., "Policies and Procedures of the United States Board of Parole," *Federal Probation 19,* 4, 1955, pp. 14–19.
13. Reed, G. J., "Federal Parole and the Indeterminate Sentence," *Federal Probation 18,* 1, 1959, pp. 12–14.
14. Dawson, R. O., "The Decision to Grant or Deny Parole: A Study of Parole Criteria in Law and Practice," *Washington Law Quarterly,* 3, 1966, pp. 243–303.
15. Hussey, F. A., *The Decision to Parole: A Study of the Parole Decision Process with Juveniles* unpublished Ph.D. dissertation, Brandeis University, 1975.
16. NCCD Standards, *op. cit.*
17. Wahl, A. and Glaser, D., "A Pilot Time Study of the Federal Probation Officers' Job," *Federal Probation 27,* 3, 1963, pp. 20–24.
18. See Ohlin, L. E., Piven, H., and Pappenfort, D. M., "Major Dilemmas of the Social Worker in Probation and Parole," *National Probation and Parole Association Journal* 2, 3, 1956, pp. 211–225.
19. Glaser, D., *The Effectiveness of a Prison and Parole System* (Indianapolis: Bobbs-Merrill, 1964).

20. Irwin, J., *The Felon* (New York: Prentice-Hall, Inc., 1970), p. 165.
21. Ibid., p. 167.
22. See, Elliot Studt, "Worker-Client Authority Relationships," *Social Work* Vol. IV, No. 1, (January, 1959).
23. Dunnette, M. D. and Kirchner, W. K., *Psychology Applied to Industry* (New York: Appleton-Century-Crofts, 1965).
24. Festinger, L., "A Theory of Social Comparison Processes," *Human Relations* 7, 1954, pp. 117–140.
25. Schachter, S., *The Psychology of Affiliation* (Stanford: Stanford University Press, 1959).
26. McCleland, D., *The Achieving Society* (Princeton: Van Nostrand, 1961).
27. Irwin, *op. cit.,* p. 134.
28. Ibid.
29. Barry, J. V., "Alexander Maconochie," in Manheim, *Pioneers in Criminology* (London: Stevens and Sons, Ltd., 1960).
30. Giardini, G. J., *The Parole Process* (Springfield, Ill.: Charles C Thomas, 1959).
31. Sandborn, F. B., "How Far is the Irish Prison System Applicable to American Prisons," in E. C. Wines (ed.) *Transcriptions of the National Congress on Penitiary and Reformatory Discipline of 1870* (Albany, Weed Parsons, and Company, 1871).
32. 46 Stat. 503 (1930) 18 U.S.C. #27 (1934).
33. See, H.R. 13118, 92nd Congress, 2nd Session.

10

The Future
of Corrections

Chapter eight raised the question of what the role of the community is or should be in the acceptance and development of community based corrections. Such a consideration clearly points out that while corrections is only a part of the criminal justice system, the criminal justice system is only a part of a social system which also includes components such as welfare, education, communities, churches, and many others. In the first chapter this was in part pointed out by the discussion focusing on the funneling of offenders into the correctional system. As this chapter investigates some trends in corrections, it will become apparent that a number of these components of the social system are becoming more important as the capability of corrections to change the law violator to law abider has come under serious question. In fact, it is the contention of this chapter that corrections will be looked to less and less for the direct delivery of services to the offender, and that corrections will look to the talents of others to aid in the rehabilitation process.

In many respects, the trends in corrections probably lie almost as strongly in the process of change as in the particular form to which the process is leading. Thus, while some concern will be expressed about the changes thought to occur, more emphasis will be spent on competing strategies designed to bring about the desired change. Some prefer a revolutionary type of change, while others focus on the evolutionary process. Which of these competing orientations will hold sway, if either one, could make a tremendous difference in the likelihood of any change occurring. Before looking at two strategies for change, consideration will be given to the general mood for change within the field.

THE IMPETUS FOR CHANGE

One source of pressure for change came from the National Advisory Commission on Criminal Justice Standards and Goals, in 1973. In looking at the future of institutions it indicates:[1]

> From the standpoint of rehabilitation and reintegration, the major adult institutions operated by the States represent the least promising component of corrections. This report takes the position that more offenders should be diverted from such adult institutions, that much of their present populations should be transferred to community based programs, and that the construction of new major institutions should be postponed until such diversion and transfers have been achieved and the need for additional institutions is clearly established.

Regarding juvenile institutions, this same commission states:[2]

> Use of State institutions for juveniles and youths should be discouraged. The emerging trend in treatment of young offenders is diversion from the criminal justice system. When diversion is not possible, the focus should be on community programs.

These statements were made, not by a commission composed of a narrow segment of people in criminal justice, but of correctional administrators, judges, police, scholars, and others. Thus they represent a relatively broad range of perspectives in criminal justice.

DIVERSION

Diversion refers to "halting or suspending formal criminal or juvenile justice proceedings against a person who has violated a statute, in favor of processing through a noncriminal disposition or means."[3] By this definition, diversion is not the same as the prosecutor's decision not to prosecute in order to reduce the court load, or his decision to negotiate a guilty plea for the same reason. While the impact of diversion may be to reduce the load on the system, that is not the main purpose of diversion.

Diversion may come in a multitude of forms and at a number of stages in the justice process. The availability of treatment alternatives outside of the criminal justice system, as well as the increasing belief of the corrupting influence of criminal justice upon the offender, have both lead to increased use of diversion. While the bulk of diversion has focused on juveniles, there have been programs mainly for adults such as the Accelerated Rehabilitative Disposition (ARD) program. A look at this program and several varieties of those for juveniles may provide the best means of communicating what diversionary programs are all about.

Adult Diversion from Court

The Pennsylvania Rules of Criminal Procedure Committee, in 1971, adopted Rules 175–185, permitting an offender to be diverted from court and from the court record, to a probationary status for a period of up to two years. The district attorney selected those cases for this Accelerated Rehabilitative Disposition (ARD) that he felt were not in need of placement in a correctional institution, and would benefit from a probationary status perhaps accompanied by special treatment such as vocational rehabilitation.

The advantages of ARD are that it reduces court load by diverting offenders before they get to court, the offender is kept from having a court record, and the offender may be referred more quickly to treatment not directly available through court sentencing. The reduction of court load by diversion of less serious offenders permits the court to focus on more serious problems requiring legal disposition.

Prevention of an offender from developing a court record is desirable according to the proponents of the program because it protects him from having to indicate that he has ever been convicted of an offense. This is most directly oriented to employer's forms asking an applicant if he has ever been convicted of an offense. Since ARD recipients have never been "convicted," they can honestly indicate that they have not been. Employers frequently will not hire those who have been convicted of a criminal offense; therefore, ARD gives the offender greater job opportunities than someone who has been convicted in court.

Diversionary programs like ARD are also used to refer offenders to treatment. For example, one district attorney indicated that sex offenders such as voyeurs do not benefit by going to court because the court process itself does nothing to help reform the offenders of this type. Consequently, this district attorney attempted to get the nonviolent sex offender into ARD where he could be given treatment. Some diversionary programs similar to ARD attempt to focus on offenders who have certain problems such as vocational deficiencies. Offenders identified as having no vocational skill and whose offenses appeared to be an outgrowth of this weakness are provided with intensive vocational guidance and training. Their "diversion" is designed to protect them from the negative labelling attributed to a court record by employers, and to prepare them for higher quality employment.

The impact of these diversionary programs, beyond reducing court load, is not clear. Programs such as these do raise some negative concerns. One question about programs that "divert" offenders into treatment is whether they provide due process safeguards to the offender. For example, while programs such as these are usually only for those not claiming innocence, it might be that an offender may agree to ARD, even though the procedural safeguards provided by the court would find that the evidence against him had been obtained illegally. In this case pre-court diversionary programs may cover up errors in legal procedure, resulting in *legally* innocent offenders being "treated." The argument against this is that the offender has a right to an attorney and is not required to be diverted. Participation is voluntary.

Another concern is that if offenders are protected from having a court record, those who should know about an individual's criminal history will not be able to find out about it. For example, if an individual applied for work in law enforcement and had been on ARD, the law enforcement agency would not be able to find out about his offense if the records were actually expunged. This means that the agency may be required to use arrest data, if available, and infer guilt, which violates our conception that an individual is "innocent until proven guilty."

JUVENILE DIVERSION FROM COURT

Juvenile diversion has been much more extensively developed than that for adults. Schools, police, and other community groups have become involved in the diversion of youth from court. The most widely discussed diversionary system is the Youth Service Bureau. In 1967, the President's Commission on Law Enforcement and Administration of Justice suggested:[4]

> Communities should establish neighborhood youth-serving agencies—Youth Service Bureaus—located if possible in comprehensive neighborhood community centers and receiving juveniles (delinquent and nondelinquent) referred by the police, the juvenile court, parents, schools, and other sources.
> These agencies would act as central coordinators of all community services for young people and would also pro-

vide services lacking in the community or neighborhood, especially ones designed for less seriously delinquent juveniles.

In effect, the Youth Service Bureau was designed to be a general community organization that would: 1) provide brokerage services, 2) develop new services when needed, and 3) modify the system that is adding to or creating the problems of youth.[5]

It is not clear how successful those Youth Service Bureaus that have been developed are in terms of diverting and rehabilitating. There has been disappointment expressed because of their slow development across the country.[6] In 1972, only 150 bureaus were able to be identified[7]—a far cry from the goal of the President's Commission in 1967.

The National Advisory Commission, in 1973, noted that Youth Service Bureaus attached to agencies such as the police, probation, or courts are surviving better than those operating independently.[8] An example of an attached program is the Richmond Police Department's Juvenile Diversion Program in Richmond, California.[9] In this particular project, the police are "providing direct helping and counseling services to youth involved in predelinquent and certain delinquent activities.[10]

Diversion's Impact on Corrections

The diversion of offenders (both juveniles and adults) out of the justice system, and consequently out of the correctional system, has a tremendous impact on the caseload of the correctional system. Diversionary programs are becoming more extensive, paralleling the developing belief in the negative influence of correctional institutions and the adjudication process. If this continues, and there are indications that it will, the proportion of offenders arrested "making it" to corrections should decrease, but with rising crime rates and possibly more offenders being arrested, the number of offenders reaching corrections will probably continue to rise.

Perhaps the greatest trend that diversion portends for the correctional system is in terms of the type of offender entering corrections. As programs such as ARD and community based corrections divert offenders from institutions, the problems of the administrator of correctional institutions will increase. Both adult and juvenile institutions will house more concentrated populations of "hardened" offenders. Such populations would be less prone to reformation, and security would become even more important. As indicated in chapter six, however, correctional administrators have consistently complained about overcrowding. Reductions in the size of institutional populations could give them opportunities to develop innovative programs for small manageable groups.

REFORM IN CORRECTIONS— WILL IT OCCUR?

It has been pointed out that there is increasing pressure for reform in corrections. This pressure usually comes from commissions and reform groups and individuals who are actively involved in corrections. However, reform may or may not be able to occur as a consequence of the feelings of these few. In order for reform to actually take place, there may be a need for a wider base of support.

The question being raised is whether or not the reform movement in corrections can take place as a consequence of administrative decisions or if it requires the development of a broad base of support prior to the reform. One view, referred to here as the administrative perspective, sees change as almost necessarily occurring directly as the result of administrative decisions. In effect, the orientation is that if change is needed, those in a position to do so should use their power to make the changes. A part of this perspective is that people will adjust to and learn to accept changes once they are instituted, yet these same people may prevent reform if allowed to participate in its development. Juxtaposed to this so-called administrative perspective is what will be referred to as the democratic perspective. This style of reform accepts the principle that change must be brought about with the input and participation of private citizens, local government groups, law enforcement officials, and others. According to the democratic perspective, if the movement is able to develop support from such a broad base, then the chances of success are much greater. This is of special importance when the reform involves the community to the degree necessary in community based corrections.

While the goal of the administrative versus the democratic perspective for change may be the same, the process of change is considerably different, and the result may also be significantly different. The manner of change is thought to be so important for the future of corrections that examples of the two styles described above will be discussed in some detail. Massachusetts and Minnesota have both been undergoing reform, and planning its development. Their experiences and orientation will be described, not with the implication that all the other factors are equal in the two cases, but with the intent only of conveying a feeling for the differences in strategy of implementation used.

The Minnesota Community Based Corrections Act

Before describing the particulars of Minnesota's attempt to inspire the development of community corrections, it is necessary to briefly describe Minnesota. Minnesota has a relatively small population base of only three million people. It has one basic population center, consisting of Minneapolis-St. Paul and a very racially homogeneous population. There are many other important features of Minnesota which make it *not* typical of much more urbanized states such as New York, New Jersey, Pennsylvania, and Massachusetts. Whether these factors increase or decrease the likelihood of success of the proposed system of change, is not clear; however, it is important to consider the possibility that techniques of change may not be as transferable as could be assumed.

Minnesota's basic philosophy of change is perhaps best described as stimulated, evolutionary change. When David Fogel became Commissioner of Corrections in 1971, he and his staff worked on a strategy for reducing the need for correctional institutions. Meetings were held across the state to communicate to the public why changes were needed, what form these changes should take, and to get their reaction and ideas. While the impact of the meetings is not known, the intent was to show the people that correctional administrators were interested in their ideas and concern, and to sway them in support of the Commissioner and his program for change.

Passage of Community Corrections Act Fogel's term of office lasted a little over a year before he moved on to another position in Illinois. Shortly after his departure, Kenneth Schoen was appointed Commissioner. Under Schoen, a bill was passed by the State Legislature attempting to provide the impetus for communities to develop their own correctional strategies. The purpose of this bill is best expressed in the bill itself.

> For the purpose of more effectively protecting society and to promote efficiency and economy in the delivery of correctional services, the commissioner of corrections is hereby authorized to make grants to assist counties in the establishment and operation of community based corrections programs including, but not limited to preventative or diversionary correctional programs, probation, parole, community corrections centers, and facilities for the detention or confinement, care and treatment of persons convicted of crime or adjudicated delinquent.[11]

There are several key points concerning this bill and its purposes. First, the fact that a legislative act was passed is interesting. It indicates legislative commitment to corrections, and to community based corrections. A second factor of significance in this statement of purpose is that community corrections will be more effective and economical than previous forms of corrections. Finally, the purpose of the bill is to decentralize corrections. In Minnesota, as in many other states, corrections has been given over to large state bureaucracies. This particular bill sets up the possibility of reversing the centralization trend in favor of greater community involvement in the correctional process.

It is not necessary to go into great detail regarding the specifics of the bill; however, some discussion may be helpful in evaluating the Minnesota experiment. The law proposes that any county or, in some situations, groups of counties, may develop a corrections authority, and it is the responsibility of this corrections authority to prepare a comprehensive plan for the administration and delivery of correctional programs and services. Counties opting to do this (they are not required to do so) are provided with consulting services by the Department of Corrections.

In effect, the Department of Corrections will pay counties to develop correctional services that will reduce their necessary expenditures by reducing the commitments to the Department. In order to determine the allotment for each county, all counties were ranked on the basis of four criteria: 1) per capita income, 2) per capita taxable value, 3) per capita expenditures per 1,000 population for correctional purposes, and 4) percent of county population 6 to 30 years of age. The formula provides that counties with lower per capita income, lower per capita taxable value, high per capita expenditure on corrections, and high ranking in crime prone age range (ages 6–30), will receive more money for their population size than other counties.

An example may serve to point out how it works. Table 10.1 provides the ranking on each factor of County A and County B. It can be seen that County A receives a summed ranking score of 50, while County B's total was 200. In terms of the money each county will receive, each total is to be divided into the median total score (rank all total scores and take the middle occuring score). In this case, let us assume that the median total score is 100. When we divide 100 by 50 we get 2, and 100 divided by 200 is 0.5. This score is multiplied by a figure set by the legislature—for

TABLE 10–1

	County A	County B
per capita income ranking	8	62
per capita taxable value	14	43
per capita expenditure	18	48
percent age 6–30	10	47
	50	200

purposes of our calculations this figure will be $10. When we multiply, we get 2 × 10 = $20 for County A, and 0.5 × 10 = $5 for County B. These figures are then multiplied by the population of the respective counties. Consequently, County A would receive $20 per person in their county, while County B would receive only $5 per resident. It should be clear that the poorer counties, those with higher expenditures on corrections, and those with high proportions in the criminogenic years are given the benefit of greater returns per individual.

There are several other aspects of the Community Corrections Act which should be mentioned. First, the programs and facilities must comply with operating standards established by the Commissioner. The Commissioner of Corrections maintains an overseer role to approve and review yearly facilities and programs established under the Act.

Second, counties not opting to come within the Community Corrections Act will receive the same services provided by the state prior to its enactment. Third,

> Each participating county will be charged a sum equal to the per diem cost of confinement of those persons committed to the commission of corrections or the youth conservation commission and confined in a state institution.[12]

In the case that the penalty exceeds five years, then no charge is made to the county, and at no time should the charges from the state exceed the amount of subsidy provided under the Act.

Minnesota has developed a subsidy plan intended to stimulate counties to take care of those violators of the law with which they are capable of dealing. Plans such as these are dependent upon a positive community response, yet they permit counties to maintain the status quo if they so desire. The logic behind this strategy is that people will develop community correctional resources and, consequently, institutional populations will decrease to the point that perhaps only one relatively small maximum security institution will be necessary.

There are some questions left unanswered. Will communities develop alternatives to institutionalization? How long will it take them to develop? Will the programs and facilities developed necessarily be less oppressive than the present state institutions?

ALTERNATIVE SUBSIDY PROGRAMS

The California Youth Authority instituted the California Probation Subsidy Program in 1966. In this program, the Youth Authority pays up to $4,000 to each county for every adult and juvenile offender not committed to a state correctional institution. It is the responsibility of the county to indicate improvement of probationary services through increased number of agents and reduced caseloads.

> In all, the program has resulted in substantial savings to taxpayers. In the six years between 1966 and 1972, California canceled planned construction, closed existing institutions, and abandoned new institutions that had been constructed. Almost $186 million was saved in these ways, while probation subsidy expenditures came to about $60 million. Furthermore, although there has been a general decrease in

commitments to State institutions throughout the United States, the decrease is sharper in those counties in California that participate in the subsidy program.[13]

Reform in Massachusetts

Jerome Miller was brought to Massachusetts by Governor Volpe to reform the Department of Youth Services in 1969. Dr. Miller's appointment was the culmination of several years of controversy. Lloyd Olin et al.,[14] in their excellent description of the reform of juvenile corrections in Massachusetts, state:

> From 1965 to 1968 the DYS was the subject of six major critical studies. The initial investigations were stimulated by reports of brutal and punitive treatment of youth at the Institution for Juvenile Guidance at Bridgewater. The publicity attending these charges led Governor John A. Volpe to request a study and recommendations from technical experts in the Children's Bureau of the U.S. Department of Health, Education, and Welfare.

HEW found in their study:[15]

> ... dominance of custodial goals and practices over those of treatment, the lack of effective centralized supervision and direction of child care, the absence of an adequate diagnostic and classification system, the failure to develop flexible and professional practices, and the ineffectiveness of parole supervision.

With a backdrop of controversy and a call for reform from many sources, Jerome Miller was appointed Commissioner of the Department of Youth Services in 1969. His appointment began with the not so radical notion "to humanize the treatment of offenders and to build therapeutic communities within existing institutional facilities."[16] The reform of the existing facilities, as Miller saw it, would require democratically run institutions in which both juveniles and staff shared decision making. This model was in serious conflict with the traditional operation of these institutions in which the staff maintained all decision-making power.

In attempts to overthrow the traditional running of the institutions, Miller issued some apparently innocuous directives, but directives that questioned the very essence of the traditional command. One of these directives related to the way the youths wore their hair. Traditionally, boys' heads were shaved on admission. Hair length was regulated thereafter and frequently used as punishment. Miller's directive that youth be allowed to wear their hair as they chose called into question the authority of institution staff. Other directives quickly followed. Youths were allowed to wear street clothes rather than institutional clothing, and silent marching from one activity to another was discontinued. Ohlin et al. believed that, "the edicts signified to staff that custodial concerns would increasingly be subordinated to treatment objectives."[17] After attempting to reform the regimented institutional programs, Miller concluded late in 1970 that:

> ... despite the storminess of the preceding year and the feeling of traditional staff that DYS was being turned completely upside down, there had really been little or no fundamental change. He felt the same way a year later, even after some of the therapeutic community oriented cottages began to achieve conspicuous success.[18]

With this realization, Miller's strategy for the type of change needed was revised considerably. It was decided that therapeutic correctional communities would be most successful outside of the institutions, not inside. Consequently, it became obvious that because of an inability to reform the institutions and the probability that treatment outside of the institutions in community based corrections would be more successful, he must de-institutionalize Massachusetts' corrections. To replace the institutions, it was necessary to create a new, decentralized structure. Contrary to the philosophy of Minnesota's correctional reform, Miller did not feel that it was necessary to build the alternative prior to de-industrialization.

The closing of the Lyman School and Shirley Cottage provides an interesting illustration of the philosophy and techniques used by Miller. The University of Massachusetts Conference was organized to permit the closing of Lyman and Shirley by transfering the institutionalized youths into the community as quickly as possible.[19] College students were selected to serve as advocates for the DYS until placements in the community could be worked out. "Arrangements for future placement of youth, e.g., sending the youth home, placing youth in a foster home or in a group home, were worked out in a collaborative manner between the DYS staff, the advocate, and the youth themselves by considering the range of program alternatives and the needs of specific youths."[20]

In the closing of Lyman and Shirley, a caravan of cars went up to the institutions, the college student advocates picked up their assigned youth and the caravan returned to the University of Massachusetts. Although the staff at Lyman had been warned of a possible closing of the institution, they had no warning of the student caravan which emptied their institution in a matter of hours.

This method of closing the Lyman School, and the eventual closing of all the juvenile institutions in Massachusetts, was peculiar in the history of corrections. In view of the negative reaction by the traditionalists, Miller determined that in order to close the institutions, which he felt was necessary, he must do so quickly and quietly before strong opposition developed. Miller's methods indicate a significant difference from the attack that Minnesota is developing.

ADMINISTRATIVE AND DEMOCRATIC REFORM

Administrative reform is exemplified by the activities of Jerome Miller. To understand Miller's ability to radically de-institutionalize juvenile corrections, one must first understand the power of his position. As a governor appointee, he could maintain his position as long as the governor was able to support him. Also, his position allowed him to move juveniles from one institution to another or to release them from an institution at his department's discretion. This ability enabled the Lyman School closing to take place. For example, at one point Miller ordered that committed youth be kept in the institution a *minimum* of three months. However, the staff misinterpreted this to mean a *maximum* of three months and started releasing youths before this time. Although this example points out mis-communication, it also shows the latitude of staff and the commissioner.

While Miller was using the power of his position and the support given him by the governor to bring about reform in juvenile corrections, Minnesota is attempting to sell reform to a more general public. In fact, reform under the Minnesota strategy is actually stimulated by the holding out of money to support local correctional reform. Another aspect of the Minnesota plan is that a committee of local citizens must be formed to develop the local strategy for change. By the Minnesota law, local communities can maintain the status quo—i.e., continue to send both juveniles and adults to institutions without the development of new options. The strategy employed by Miller forces both the Department of Youth Services and local communities to develop options for the youths.

It is too early to evaluate the success of the two techniques, and in many respects it would be unfair to compare their success because of the differences in the two states. Minnesota is basically a white rural state, compared to urbanized, racially mixed Massachusetts. Further, Miller was only de-institutionalizing at the juvenile level while Minnesota's plan incorporates both juveniles and adults. Closing the Massachusetts adult institutions would no doubt have caused a considerably more severe reaction.

The Massachusetts reform movement has been labelled "administrative change" because of its focus on the use of administrative power to create the change. Miller, however, was supported by a number of groups across the state such as the League of Women Voters. On the other extreme, Minnesota is referred to as representing democratic reform because of the extensive involvement of local citizens. Which, if either, of these reform strategies are effective remains to be seen.

CREDIBILITY OF REFORM

Richard Ericson[21] raises some serious questions that must be addressed if reform is to have credibility from both within and outside the justice system. Among these issues that must be confronted are: 1) decriminalization, 2) economic conversion of institutions and people working in them, 3) evaluation of reforms, 4) concerns for public safety, and 5) the role of punishment in criminal justice.

DECRIMINALIZATION

The attempts by society to legislate morality have thus far proven unsuccessful. For example, laws prohibiting narcotic use, prostitution, homosexuality, drunkenness, and gambling are often referred to as "victimless crimes" because they are offenses voluntarily entered into by the parties involved. The victim of gambling is the one who gambles, but because he solicits the offense, it is sometimes difficult to see him as a victim comparable to one whose home has been burglarized.

There are extensive criticisms of these offenses by those advocating their legalization and thus the decriminalization of the behavior. These arguments center around the minimal impact of the law in controlling "victimless crimes," the tremendous amount of resources fruitlessly spent trying to control them, and the amplification of the problem by increased costs because of its illegality. (For example, heroin would not be expensive but for the huge profits demanded by criminal distributors.)

Society must decide whether the criminal justice system is the appropriate mechanism to deal with these offenses, and also whether these offenses are perhaps best ignored. Several states have abolished drunkenness laws and one, Minnesota, has required that detoxification centers be set up throughout the state.

If a number of the "victimless crimes" were to be removed from the criminal offense category, it would significantly affect the correctional system by reducing the numbers and types of offenders in juvenile, misdemeanant, and felony institutions. This issue far transcends the reform within corrections itself, and is really an issue to be resolved by legislative bodies. If "criminalization" creates more problems than it solves, then the credibility of criminal justice is best served by consideration of alternatives such as decriminalization.

Economic Conversion of Institutions and People

Richard Ericson posits another issue that must be dealt with by correctional reform: "What are we going to do with our prisons?"[22] Over the past 150 years, we have invested a sizable amount of money in facilities, people, and their training. In order for proposals that involve the closing of institutions like those discussed in Massachusetts and Minnesota to be successful, Ericson believes that a plan for "economic conversion" is necessary to gain the confidence of those working in the institutions and the general public.[23] As Ericson notes, "It often appears to the outside world that we don't care about the people who run the institutions as much as we care about the offenders housed in the institutions."[24]

This is of interest for reform not only because of the humanitarian concern for those working in the institutions, but also in order to develop a broader base of support for change. Business has long been concerned with overcoming resistance to change and has found that by involving those whose job is to be changed in the process, and by considering their needs, conversion is more successful. Ericson's point is that correctional reform should consider the social impacts of closing institutions upon institutional staff as well as offenders. This may mean providing jobs for those becoming unemployed, or perhaps vocational training to retrain them.

"TODAY'S FAILURES ARE YESTERDAY'S SOLUTIONS"[25]

Community corrections appears to be a more humanitarian and theoretically sound approach to reformation. Convincing the public, however, may require more substantive proof than is presently available. Evaluation research is needed to test some of the alternative strategies proposed for handling offenders in the community and their relative effectiveness on different types of offenders. The correctional strategies that are being rejected today were the innovations of fifty years ago. With little foundation in research, today's new solutions may face a similar fate.

PUBLIC SAFETY

One of the main concerns of corrections is public safety. If reform creates greater risk to the public, then the reform will not be seen as beneficial.[26] When discussions suggest that offenders should be given greater access to the community, or even live in local neighborhoods, it frequently raises fear in the residents that their families might be burglarized, molested, or assaulted. Those proposing reform must convince the public that reforms present no immediate threat to the community. It is incumbent upon corrections to demonstrate its capability to experiment with reform and still protect the public.

THE ROLE OF PUNISHMENT

The impact of punishment has not been adequately confronted. The public frequently cries that offenders are not only not given enough punishment, but are almost coddled. While punishment of offenders does not appeal to humanitarian interests, it is still a factor to be reckoned with in corrections. Little information is available as to either the reformation or deterrent effect of punishment. There are indications that behaviors involving rational considerations are more likely to be deterred,[27] and that as the certainty of punishment increases, the deterrent effect also increases.[28] This is not to suggest that community based corrections is not punishment because any restriction of freedom is punishment. It is only to suggest that, although the concept of punishment has little acceptability among the therapeutic correctional communities today, it should not be ignored.

SUMMARY

Corrections is clearly not isolated from the rest of the criminal justice system, nor from society. Yet corrections is expected to do what others have not been able to do—control and reform deviant members of society. Probation officers, correctional officers, and counselors cannot be relied upon to correct the ills of a social system through intermittent contacts or even several years of incarceration. To the benefit of both the individual and the society, some shaping of human behavior may be possible. The question of how to most effectively bring about the desired behaviors remains unanswered.

ENDNOTES

1. National Advisory Commission on Criminal Justice Standards and Goals, *Corrections* (Washington, D.C.: U.S. Government Printing Office, 1973), p. 349.
2. Ibid., p. 350.

3. Ibid., p. 73.
4. President's Commission on Law Enforcement and Administration of Justice, *The Challenge of Crime in a Free Society* (Washington, D.C.: U.S. Government Printing Office, 1967), p. 83.
5. Sherwood Norman, *The Youth Service Bureau* (Paramus, N.J.: National Council on Crime and Delinquency, 1972), pp. 12–13.
6. National Advisory Commission op. cit. p. 79.
7. Ibid.
8. Ibid.
9. Ibid., p. 82.
10. Ibid.
11. Senate File No. 1353, H.F. 1487, March 21, 1973.
12. Ibid., p. 8.
13. National Advisory Commission, op. cit., p. 315.
14. Lloyd E. Ohlin, Robert B. Coates, and Alden D. Miller, "Radical Correctional Reform: A Case Study of the Massachusetts Youth Correctional System," *Harvard Law Review* Vol. 44, No. 1 (February, 1974), p. 78.
15. Ibid., p. 78.
16. Ibid., p. 80.
17. Ibid., p. 82.
18. Ibid., p. 94.
19. Ibid., pp. 95–96.
20. Ibid., p. 96.
21. Richard Ericson, "Credibility of Correctional Reform," talk presented at Mankato State College (February, 1973).
22. Ibid.
23. Ibid.
24. Ibid.
25. Ibid.
26. Ibid.
27. William Chambliss, "The Impact of Punishment or Compliance with Parking Regulations," in W. Chambliss (ed.) *Crime and Legal Process* (New York: McGraw-Hill, 1969), pp. 388–394.
28. T. Chiricos and G. Waldo, "Punishment and Crime: An Examination of Some Empirical Evidence," *Social Problems* No. 18, pp. 201–217.

Index

Accelerated Rehabilitative
    Disposition (ARD),
    319–320
Administrative reform, 323
Adult offenses
    extensiveness of, 11
Almshouses, 37–38
American Association of Social
    Workers, 150
American Bar Association, 225
American Correctional
    Association, 93
American Law Institute, 225
American reformers, 47
ARD. *See* Accelerated
    Rehabilitative
    Disposition
Argot roles. *See* Inmate, role
    types
Attica
    prison riots in, 172–176,
        183–184, 231
Auburn penitentiary systems,
    53, 55, 60, 72, 78

Augustus, John, 73–74,
    261–262

Bates, Sanford, 88
Beccaria, Cesare, 39, 42, 198
Behavior modification, 66, 92
Bettelheim, Bruno, 116
Black Muslims, 238–239
Blackstone, Sir William, 47
Borstal system, 77
Boston Prison Discipline
    Society, 55
Bridewell, 36
Brighter Day League, 81
Brockway, Zebulon, 69, 77, 79
Brown v. *McGinnis,* 239

Caldwell, Morris G., 130
Caldwell, Robert G., 30, 79,
    81, 199

343

Capital punishment, 28, 34, 40, 58
Casework supervision, 226
Chain gangs, 83
Cherry Hill Prison, 49, 72
Clemmer, Donald, 110, 117
Community based corrections, 187, 257–282, 324
  definition of, 258
  protection of public, 258–259
Corporal punishment
  history of, 29
  forms of, 29
Corrections, defined, 3
Cressey, Donald, 118, 119, 120, 158
Crime causation
  demonistic explanations, 38
  19th century view of, 45
  utilitarian explanation, 41
Crofton, Sir Walter, 65, 69, 70, 72, 93, 306–307
Custody oriented institutions, 159–160

Davis, Allan J., 129
Davis, Dr. Katherine B., 80
Declaration of principles, 93
Delinquent behavior
  extensiveness of, 8
  self-report studies of, 9
Dependent, neglected, 276
Deprivation of security, 103
Deterrence, 67, 68, 152
Diversion, 3, 318, 319–323
  definition of, 319

Ellhamer v. *Wilson,* 244
Elmira reformatory
  parole from, 307–308
English Penal Servitude Act of 1843, 306
English penal system, 28, 66
Enlightenment philosophy, 9, 40, 59
Ericson, Richard, 333–336
European reformers, 47
Ex Parte Hull, 232

Fant, Fred D., 211
Federal parole system, 308
Federal system of corrections, 79, 80, 87, 279
Federal Bureau of Prisons, 88, 94
Felony, 16
First Amendment, 231, 234
First National Prison Congress, 74–76
Flock, Maurice, 166, 176, 177, 182
Fogel, David, 325
Fortune Society v. *McGinnis,* 236
Foster homes, 275–276
Freedom of religion, 238

Gagnon, John, 127
Garabedian, Peter, 112, 124
George Junior Republic, 88
George, William Revben, 88, 94
Giallombardo, Rose, 135, 138
Gill, Howard B., 88, 89, 90, 94

Glaser, Daniel, 112, 123, 263, 274, 299
Goals of corrections
   deterrence, 158
   incapacitation, 158
   reformation, 158
   retribution, 158
Goffman, Ervin, 116, 117
Goldman, Nathan, 11
Group homes, 275–276, 281
Grusky, Oscar, 163
Guard, 177, 179
Guided group interaction programs, 207

Hartung and Flock, typology of individuals, 182
Halfway-in houses, 275
Halfway-out houses, 280–281
Hartung, Frank, 166, 176, 177, 182
Harwin v. *United States,* 213
Haviland, John, 49
Hawes-Cooper Act, 82
Hodder, Mrs. Jesse D., 80
Homosexual assaults, 129
Homosexuality in prison, 126, 129, 129–131, 136–138
Homosexual types in prison. *See* inmate roles
Hopper, Isaac, 71
Howard, James, 47
Howard, John, 40, 41, 59
Huber Act, 280
Hussey, Frederick H., 287, 298

Incarceration, 19, 41. *See also* institutionalization

Incarcerated offender, civil rights of, 230
Indeterminant sentence, 76–78, 81
Indictment, defined, 16
Infamous crime, 213
Information, 16
Inmate guard system, 89
Inmate jargon, 104–115
Inmate role types
   fag, 130
   gorilla, 125, 134
   homeys, 138
   merchant, 103
   peddler, 103
   punk, 129–130
   rat, 109, 124–125, 135
   real man, 108, 134
   right guy, 124
   square john, 124
   toughs, 134
   wolf, 125, 127–129
Inmate self-government, 90
Inmate subcultures
   diffusionist view of, 100, 116–118, 120, 123, 139, 140
   functionalist view of, 100, 103, 105, 109, 111, 113, 117, 120–123, 132, 139
   types of, 118
In Re Ferguson, 239
In Re Gault, 18, 19, 204–207, 210–213, 215, 221
In Re Homes, 206
Irish prison system, 78, 306
Irwin, Richard, 118–120, 186, 300, 304
Institutionalization, 59
   almshouses, 30

Institutionalization—*cont.*
  history of, 30
  houses of correction, 30
  workhouses, 30, 33–34, 37, 40
Institutionalized. *See* prisonization
Institutional parole officer, 295
Intake officer, 15

Johnson, Elmer, 124–125
Johnson v. *Avery*, 234
Joint Commission on Correctional Manpower and Training, 202
Juvenile correction
  failures of, 200–202
  types of, 202–203
Juvenile court
  first court, 262
  history of, 196–200
  philosophy of, 18–19, 195–215
  referral to, 9, 10
Juvenile justice system, 7, 195, 200

Kasselbaum, Gene, 133
Kent v. *United States*, 18, 206
Kinsey, Alfred, 126
Kraft, Larry, 240

Lease system, 171–172
Lemert, Edwin M., 208
Livingston, Edward, 70
Local jails, role of, 71

Lohman, John D., 268

Maconochie, Alexander, 65–69, 93, 305–307, 310
Maconochie's principles, 306
Mark system, 66, 78, 93
Matza, David, 199–200
Maximum security institutions, 167, 173
Mempa v. *Rhay*, 229, 244, 248
Menechino v. *Oswald*, 244
Messenger, Sheldon, 100–101, 112
Middle range punishments, 34
Militancy in prison, 182–187
Miller, Jerome, 329–33
Minnesota Community Based Corrections Act, 324–328
Miranda v. *Arizona*, 212
Misdemeanor, 16, 71, 87
Morales v. *Schmidt*, 235
Morrissey v. *Brewer*, 245–246, 249

Nagel, William, 258
National Advisory Commission on Criminal Justice Standards and Goals, 295, 318
National Prison Association, 93
New Castle County Workhouse, 89
New Left, 184
Newman, Donald, 17
New York Prison Association, 69, 70, 73, 93

Official goals, 152, 155
Ohlin, Lloyd, 177, 182, 299, 329–30
Ombudsman, 241
Operative goals, 152, 155
Organizational effectiveness, 162
Osborne, Thomas Mott, 88, 89, 94

Pains of imprisonment, 105, 108, 112–114, 116, 129, 133–134, 136, 138, 140, 173
Palmer, John W., 246
Palmigiano v. Travisono, 235
Parens patriae, 8, 18, 212
Parole, 73, 78
    components of, 295
    decision making, 296–297
    definitions of, 70, 288–289
    federal system, 80
    feedback, 293
    history of, 69, 305–309
    input into, 291
    Irish system of, 70
    legal rights of, 242
    output into, 291
    recent developments in, 309–311
    revocation of, 294
    systems perspective of, 290–298
    use of, 296
Parole board, 295, 298, 308
Parolee, 298, 300–305
Parole officer, 298–301, 312
Penal codes, 28
Penal confinement, 68
Penitentiary movement, 46–47

Penn's Great Law, 36, 58
Pennsylvania Quakers, 36
Pennsylvania system, 49, 53–55, 57, 60
Penn, William, 36–37
Perrow, Charles, 152, 154
Plea bargaining, 17
Plummer, Mordecai, 88–89, 94
Police
    adults, 14
    juvenile, 9
PORT Program, 278–279
Post Institutional community programs, 279–281
    educational release, 279–280
    pre-release centers, 280–281
    work release, 280
Pound, Roscoe, 199
Poverty, 31–33
Pre-sentence investigation, 222–225, 261, 263, 266
Pre-sentence report, 224, 296
President's Commission on Law Enforcement and the Administration of Justice, 198, 207, 225, 257, 321
Prisons
    administrators, 84
    argot, 117
    code, 119
    conditions, 84, 86
    courts, 89
    effectiveness of, 152, 160
    formal organizations, 156
    industries, 71
    political groups in, 182–187

Prisons—*cont.*
   power groups, 164
   prisoner aid societies, 80
   racial conflict in, 184
   reform, 40, 42, 44, 46, 70, 74, 87
   treatment oriented, 112, 154, 158–159, 187, 204, 262
Prisonization, 99, 117–119, 140
Probation, 19, 73–74, 225–230, 247–248, 259–274, 297, 299
   advantages of, 272
   broker role, 260
   California Community Treatment Project, 273
   caseload size, 268–272
   casework techniques, 273
   community protection, 272–273
   cost of, 272
   duties of officer, 263
   effectiveness of, 266–272
   history of, 261–262
   misdemeanants, 262
   regulations of, 227
   revocation of, 229
   San Francisco project, 269–270
   test of probation (TOPS), 268–270
   versus other dispositions, 267–268
Prosecution, 17
Provo experiment, 277–278
Punishment, 150, 178, 204. *See also* capital punishment

Quakers, 71

Riots, prison, 166–184
Rationalizations, 128
Reformatory movement, 69, 78, 81
Reforms in corrections
   administrative perspective of, 324, 331–332
   decriminalization in, 334–335
   democratic perspective of, 324, 332
   economic conversion in, 334–335
   role of punishment in, 335–336
Rehabilitation, 68, 90–91, 94, 117, 150–151, 154, 161, 187, 226–227, 266, 294, 296–297, 317
Religion
   historical role of, 31
   punishment and, 35
Retribution, 67, 150, 152
Road gangs. *See* chain gangs
Road labor programs, 83
Role types. *See* inmate role types
Rothman, David J., 33–34, 41, 45–46, 48
Rowland v. *Sigler,* 236

Schrag, Clarence, 123
Self-concept, 104–105, 113, 127, 132, 303
Sentencing, 221–225
Settlement laws, 32
Sheriff, fee system for, 87
Simon, James F., 127

Social casework, 290
Social organization of the prison, 100, 164
Social work philosophy, 156
Societal protection, 67, 226
Solitary confinement, 174
Stapleton, Vaughn, 196–197, 209
State use system, 82
Stratton, John, 112
Street, David, 112
Subsidy programs. *See* Minnesota Community Based Corrections Act
Suspended sentence, 19
Sykes, Gresham, 100–104, 108, 112, 123–124, 157, 177–179, 181
System, defined, 3

Tappan, Paul, 199
Teitelbaum, Lee E., 196–197, 209
Terry, Robert, 11
Therapeutic community, 115
Ticket of leave, 307
Token economy, 89
Total institutions, 116

Uniform Crime Reports, 6
United States ex. rel. Bez v. *Connecticut,* 244
United States Supreme Court, 205–206, 211–212, 222–223, 225, 229, 232
United States v. *Coffey,* 221–22
United States v. *Howard,* 213

Ward, David, 133
Walnut Street jail, 41–42
Weber, George H., 161
Wheeler, Stanton, 110
Williams v. *New York,* 222, 224
Wines, Frank, 196
Women's institutions, 126, 132–34
Workhouses. *See* institutionalization

Youth service bureau, 321–322

Zald, Mayer N., 158–160